Ethnographic Methods

D0009914

Karen O'Reilly

Routledge
Taylor & Francis Group

LONDON AND NEW YORK

First published 2005
by Routledge
2 Park Square, Milton Park, Abingdon, Oxon OX14 4RN

Simultaneously published in the USA and Canada
by Routledge
270 Madison Ave, New York, NY 10016

Reprinted 2007 (twice), 2008 (twice)

Routledge is an imprint of the Taylor & Francis Group, an informa business

© 2005 Karen O'Reilly

Typeset in Bembo and Gill by BC Typesetting Ltd, Bristol
Printed and bound in Great Britain by
TJ International Ltd, Padstow, Cornwall

British Library Cataloguing in Publication Data
A catalogue record for this book is available from the British Library

Library of Congress Cataloging in Publication Data
O'Reilly, Karen.
    Ethnographic methods/Karen O'Reilly.
        p.   cm.
    Includes bibliographical references and index.
    ISBN 0–415–32155–7 (hardback) – ISBN 0–415–32156–5 (softcover)
    1. Ethnology–Philosophy. 2. Ethnology–Comparative method.
    I. Title.
    GN345.072 2004
    305.8′001–dc22

                                                    2004006454

ISBN10: 0–415–32155–7 (hbk)
ISBN10: 0–415–32156–5 (pbk)

ISBN13: 978–0–415–32155–6 (hbk)
ISBN13: 978–0–415–32156–3 (pbk)

Contents

Acknowledgements

This book has been written for students and is written with thanks especially to the postgraduate students in Aberdeen, Essex and Lugano who have inspired me over the years with their enthusiasm to learn about ethnographic methods. A special mention is due to Jo Cram, Elizabeth Dinnie, Lydia Lewis, Nicola Marzouka and Gavin Smith. However, I would not have coped without the emotional and intellectual support of several colleagues, especially David Inglis and Rhoda Wilkie. Roger Goodman and Richard Wilson taught me ethnographic methods as a student at Essex University, and I am sure they will note their influence throughout the pages of this book. Of course, the blunders are entirely my own. My partner, Trevor, suffered my insecurities and doubts with nothing but good humour and unfailing belief in my abilities. The ethical debate in chapter 3 was his idea.

1 Introduction to ethnographic methods

What is ethnography? A critical minimum definition

I am very enthusiastic about ethnographic research. It involves the application of the full range of methods available to any researcher in a way that is obvious to common sense, is close to the way we all make sense of the world around us in our daily lives, and yet can be scientifically rigorous and systematic at the same time. It cannot *but* be the best way to learn about phenomena ranging from what older people mean by the term quality of life, to why it might be that young people end up homeless. However, ethnography is difficult to define because it is used in different ways in different disciplines with different traditions. Let's explore how it is described by other authors.

Exemplifying the breadth of ethnography within the social sciences, Stephanie Taylor (2002) brings together a collection of ethnographic studies, including Valerie Hey's (1997) work on schoolgirls' friendships and Lesley Griffiths' (1998) study of how humour is used as a strategy by health care workers to mediate instructions from powerful professionals. The studies range methodologically from what Taylor calls a conventional ethnography, 'for which the ethnographer makes the enormous personal investment of moving into a community for an extended period', to a team project drawing on several discrete methods of formal data collection. However, for Taylor, ethnography essentially involves empirical work, especially observation, with the aim of producing a full, nuanced, non-reductive text, in the ethnographic tradition, however that is defined or interpreted by each author. Hammersley and Atkinson resist drawing firm boundaries around ethnography because, to some extent, we all learn about the social world using these same techniques and thus the distinction between ethnography and other methods is not clear. They define the term loosely, without worrying too much about what does or does not count as instances of it, while suggesting that in its most characteristic form ethnography 'involves the ethnographer participating . . . in people's daily lives for an extended period of time, watching what happens, listening to what is said, asking questions – in fact, collecting whatever data are available to throw light on the issues that are the focus of the research' (Hammersley and Atkinson 1995: 1). In the *British Medical Journal*, Jan Savage also stresses that there is no standard definition of ethnography, but argues that the defining feature is often participant observation entailing prolonged fieldwork, and that: 'Most ethnographers today would agree that the term ethnography can be applied to any small scale research that is carried out in everyday settings; uses several methods; evolves in design through the study; and focuses on the meaning of individuals' actions and explanations rather than their quantification' Savage (2000: 1400). For Willis and Trondman (2000) ethnography is a family of methods involving direct and sustained social contact with agents, and richly writing up the encounter, respecting (at least partly in its own terms) the irreducibility of human experience. Crucial elements are: the understanding and representation of experience; presenting and explaining the culture in which this experience is located, but also acknowledging that experience is entrained in the flow of history. Human beings are therefore part subjects, part objects. For Willis and Trondman, ethnography should be theoretically informed with a critical focus and relevance for cultural politics.

Ethnography then is a methodology – a theory, or set of ideas – about research that rests on a number of fundamental criteria, or critical minimum markers (Oommen 1997), as outlined below. Hopefully the reasons for each element of this minimal definition will become clear throughout this book. Displaying the key themes from the definitions above, ethnography at least (in its minimal definition) is iterative-inductive research (that evolves in design through the study), drawing on a family of methods, involving direct and sustained contact with human agents, within the context of their daily lives (and cultures), watching what happens, listening to what is said, asking questions, and producing a richly written account that respects the irreducibility of human experience, that acknowledges the role of theory, as well as the researcher's own role, and that views humans as part object/part subject. Ethnography can be more than this; Willis' and Trondman's (2000) definition, for example, is more maximally defined. Each ethnographer will choose whether or to what extent he or she wishes to consider historical and/or macro factors, the extent to which to be critical or to engage in cultural politics, and the range of methods employed beyond direct and sustained contact, watching, listening and enquiring. Similarly, ethnography tends to be small scale and tends not to include much in the way of quantification, but these are not crucial to the critical minimum definition.

Ethnography: a critical minimum definition

Minimally ethnography is

- iterative-inductive research (that evolves in design through the study), drawing on
- a family of methods,
- involving direct and sustained contact with human agents
- within the context of their daily lives (and cultures);
- watching what happens, listening to what is said, asking questions, and
- producing a richly written account
- that respects the irreducibility of human experience,
- that acknowledges the role of theory
- as well as the researcher's own role,
- and that views humans as part object/part subject.

This is not a recipe book. I do not pretend to teach you how to do ethnographic research through a step-by-step guide to techniques and procedures. This book aims to sensitise you to the issues involved when making decisions about specific methods. Because, as many ethnographers and qualitative researchers have implied, qualitative research is as often art as science, it is not easy to set out what should be done and how in a given set of circumstances. Every decision is a matter of weighing up a multitude of factors so that I cannot tell you what to do but only what choices there are and how others have resolved various problems, describing the array of methods available in order to encourage you in what Plummer (2001a: 118) calls 'a self-consciousness about method' and what Brewer (2000) refers to as analytical reflexivity. However, you can only give free reign to the ethnographic imagination (Willis 2000) if you are aware of techniques and procedures as well as the shared methodology of ethnography. I recommend reading published ethnographies as a route to understanding what it is and how it is done, what kinds of uses it is put to, what sorts of findings it generates, and the broad range of styles used and methods employed. Throughout the rest of this book I will refer at times to published work that you can search out for yourself but will also use examples of students' work to demonstrate methodological dilemmas and resolutions (published work rarely explicates the myriad decisions, turn-arounds, heartaches and enlightened moments that constitute the ethnographer's daily fare). However, if you are eager for a taster now you could explore the journal *Ethnography* or get hold of Taylor's (2002) reader, mentioned above.

The chapters

I do not think it is essential to read this book in order. It should be treated as a handbook that can be taken into the field with you and consulted at various stages of your journey through ethnography. I firmly believe that the best way to learn about ethnography is to do it, but that this book should raise awareness and a critical reflexivity in you, helping you make informed and considered decisions at various junctures. This first chapter will discuss the origins of the methods of ethnographic fieldwork within social anthropology and sociology. This is because my own work crosses the boundaries between the two disciplines and so this is where my interests and knowledge lie. We will, especially, examine the work of Bronislaw Malinowski, who is considered by many to be the founder of contemporary ethnographic fieldwork methods. I will go on to introduce the range of contemporary uses of ethnographic methods in social science, especially in health and illness.

Chapter 2 explores more practical issues about how one might approach a piece of ethnographic research. It will include defining an intellectual puzzle, reviewing the literature, starting out and selecting cases. The chapter will then take an in-depth look at the role of the philosophy of social science in ethnography.

Chapter 3 explores the myriad ethical considerations raised while conducting ethnographic research, including: the difficult distinction between overt and covert ethnography; gaining consent; disclosure and confidentiality; issues of power and control; and how to balance rights, responsibilities and commitments. This chapter features a transcript of a group discussion about ethics between research students.

The main method of ethnography is known as participant observation, and it is very distinctive as a method. Chapter 4 considers what participant observation actually consists of, then goes on to look at participant observation as a concept and an oxymoron. Key elements of participant observation we will explore here are gaining access, taking time, learning the language, participation and observation, and taking notes.

However, ethnographers conduct interviews as well as participating and observing. Interviews can take the shape of opportunistic chats, questions that arise on the spur of the moment, one to one in-depth interviews and group interviews, and all sorts of ways of asking questions and learning about people that fall in between. It is therefore quite difficult to prescribe how an ethnographer should do an interview. However, there is a quite distinctive difference between an interview that takes place within qualitative research and one that takes place within quantitative research, so chapter 5 deals with that distinction first, before going on to explore the different types of interview available to an ethnographer, including oral history interviews and discussion groups.

Although I prefer not to be too prescriptive about interview styles and techniques, chapter 6 offers some practical guidelines for interviewing, addressing questions such as: how do I get someone to agree to an interview? What is an interview guide? What do I do if they wander off the point? Should I transcribe? How do I test for validity?

There may be any number of things that we would want to collect that would enable us better to understand the group of people we are coming to know. For Malinowski this included collecting and making your own statistical summaries, collecting artefacts, taking photographs, making lists, documenting habits, drawing maps and much more besides. You may want to make use of or collect memos, photographs, advertisements, gossip, diaries, letters. The point of chapter 7 is to make you think about what else might be out there that is worthy of including as 'data'. It begins by thinking about visual data and then briefly considers other forms of data, before exploring two very specific approaches to the analysis of 'texts': content analysis and semiotics.

Chapter 8 moves from writing down to writing up, and examines ethnographic approaches to analysis. This chapter explores the spiral model for ethnographic analysis; using computer software; sorting, classifying and descriptions; and the role of concepts and theories; and finishes by introducing the grounded theory of Anselm Strauss and Juliet Corbin.

Since the reflexive turn of the 1980s the production of ethnographic texts has come under careful scrutiny. Ethnographers must now think critically and reflexively about writing and about the contexts of research and writing. Chapter 9 thus explores modernist (traditional), post-modern and post-post-modern (or subtle realist) writing styles and their attempts to construct, or to think critically about the construction of, authoritative texts. This chapter concludes with an exploration of the subtle realist defence of ethnography and its scientific status post-post-modernism.

Ethnography and anthropology

This section explores the work of Bronislaw Malinowski quite closely as a means of introducing almost all the issues relevant to this book. Malinowski is often considered to be the founder of modern social anthropological methods of fieldwork and participant observation (Macdonald 2001). A Polish man, born in 1884 of aristocratic parents, who studied maths, physics and philosophy at the Jagiellonian University, in Cracow, he was inspired to take up anthropology after reading Fraser's *The Golden Bough*, and in 1910 went to study in England at the London School of Economics and Political Science. He gained the financial support to undertake field research in New Guinea, but war broke out while he was in Australia. However, though legally an 'enemy' in Australia, he was able to move freely about the Pacific islands for the duration of the war as long as he reported his movements to the Australian government. His most famous research was carried out in the Trobriand Islands in Melanesia, off the north-east coast of Australia, where he picked up the Kiriwinian language and was able to dispense with an interpreter within four months (Gerould 1992). Malinowski was not the first person to use fieldwork methods but was the first to systematically record and later to teach his students the canons of the method. His work established the fieldwork principles anthropologists adhere to today (Eriksen 1995, Urry 1984). For social anthropology the theories and theoretical orientation may change but the methodology stays more or less the same. Indeed this is the case to such an extent that many anthropologists seem to believe that the methods of doing ethnography cannot and need not be taught (Johnson 1990). Clearly, I don't agree!

Prior to the early 1900s most ethnographic information had been collected by what Malinowski referred to as 'amateurs' – missionaries, colonial administrators and travellers – and survey work of sorts had been carried out, measuring skulls and charting physical traits for example. Nineteenth-century researchers delighted in collecting artefacts and descriptions of the exotic and supposedly backward peoples they came into contact with and were obsessed with charting and classifying their collections (see Banton 1977), while the anthropologists who analysed the data brought back by such researchers mostly engaged in 'armchair theorising'. By the early 1900s academics had begun to discuss the idea of going out and talking to people and learning about these natives first hand. So Malinowski did not invent fieldwork all alone, but if you look at the first chapter of *Argonauts of the Western Pacific* (Malinowski 1922) you will see that what he did was spell out, fairly polemically, his methods. So what was Malinowski's special methodology?

Malinowski's methodology

Malinowski monographs include an account of the system of ceremonial exchange known as the kula (in which bracelets and necklaces made from shells seemed invested with power and status far beyond their intrinsic worth); a study of Trobriand courtship, marriage and domestic life; a study of gardening and magic, crime, spirits and social control (Malinowski 1922, 1926, 1935, 1960). Above all Malinowski writes polemically about the methods he employed in his research. Malinowski insists that scientific fieldwork has three aims:

- to describe the customs and traditions, the institutions, the structure, the skeleton of the tribe (or what people say they do)
- to give this flesh and blood by describing how daily life is actually carried out, the *imponderabilia* of actual life (how they do it)
- to record typical ways of thinking and feeling associated with the institutions and culture.

At first, a new culture or society seems to an outsider unruly, disordered or chaotic, but when we look closely and carefully we begin to see that everything is carefully structured and organised, controlled by rules and laws, customs and traditions that help to make sense, at least for those taking part, of the activities that at first seemed so strange. In order to understand this we have to spend time watching events and asking people about them, and what they do in certain circumstances. Much of this sort of information, Malinowski suggested, could be obtained through survey work. Survey work can tell us much about the framework of the society we are interested in, it gives us the skeleton, but this lacks flesh and blood. Hence the second aim.

Of course, we must remember, Malinowski and his colleagues at the time were trying to understand 'natives', tribal peoples with cultures and lifestyles (and even appearances) very different from their own. It was very easy to see these as exotic and strange and for the researcher to focus on these aspects. But Malinowski wanted to make sure people understood that was not what proper scientific research is all about. One should not focus on these things only, but should explore closely and carefully the daily habits and customs that might seem boring and routine. These, as much as those things that seem strange to us, can enlighten the observer about the group's way of life. Similarly today, an entire group we thought was familiar can seem strange and exotic when we apply the ethnographic gaze and when we closely explore all the little habits and customs that people take part in. Take a Western Christmas, for example, and the strange compulsion people have to get into all sorts of debt buying gifts no one needs, or the compulsion Shetland Islanders have to engage in a dangerous ball game (The Ba', see chapter 2) that can end in broken legs and arms and can cause rifts between groups of people who normally coexist contentedly.

Finally, we need to understand the native's views of what they do, 'to grasp the native's point of view, his relation to life, *his* vision of *his* world' (1922: 25) (note, the sexist language Malinowski uses is his not mine). This does not involve getting inside the heads of *individuals* but beginning to understand the *group's* views, feelings and sentiments. For example, a 'man who lives in a polyandrous community cannot experience the same feelings of jealousy as a strict monogynist' (1922: 23). In addition to these main aims, there are a few key elements to Malinowski's ethnography. These are that data are collected in context, over a period of time, using participant observation as well as other data collection techniques. I will look at each of these in turn.

Ethnographic data are collected in context

For Malinowski, the ethnographer should not sit in 'his' armchair theorising but should get out there and spend time learning about different peoples from within their own natural surroundings. Nor should we remove people from their natural setting in order to analyse them, observe them, measure and weigh and assess them as objects for research, as was popular at the time. It is unscientific to do this. We cannot trust the reports of others. We, as trained scientists, must use our senses to collect empirical data (sense data) and we must do this within the naturalness (laboratory-like setting) of the surroundings. 'Proper conditions for ethnographic work . . . consist mainly in cutting oneself off from the company of other white men, and remaining in as close contact with the natives as possible, which can really only be achieved by camping right in their villages' (Malinowski 1922: 7).

It is only by being in context, being there to talk with and listen to the people you are researching as they experience things and as they go about their daily lives, that you can get them to tell you about how they feel and think. In this way, Malinowski says, you get so much more from people than you would if they were 'a paid, and often bored, informant'. It is worth noting here that many survey data, interviews, life histories and other sociological data are data collected out of context and should always be analysed as such. What people say they do is not always the same as what they do. What they do varies with circumstance and setting. The other reason for collecting the research in context is so that you can observe the imponderabilia, and can find out how people think and feel as things happen rather than after or before the event. Daily quarrels, jokes, family discussions, all are significant. All give you an insight into the way of life. However, this is not some woolly method involving hanging around and making sweeping generalisations pulled from who knows where. For Malinowski this was a scientific method, which should be approached with due rigour. The context needs to be described, the methods used as well as the setting, the moods and so on. In *Argonauts of the Western Pacific*, Malinowski prescribes that an ethnographer should describe his methods just as a scientist would explain the conditions of an experiment.

> No one would dream of making an experimental contribution to physical or chemical science, without giving a detailed account of all the arrangements of the experiments; an exact description of the apparatus used; of the manner in which the observations were conducted; of their number; of the length of time devoted to them, and of the degree of approximation with which each measurement was made. In less exact sciences, as in biology or geology, this cannot be done as rigorously, but every student will do his best to bring home to the reader all the conditions in which the experiment or the observations were made. In Ethnography, where a candid account of such data is perhaps even more necessary, it has unfortunately in the past not always been supplied with sufficient generosity, and many writers do not ply the searchlight of methodic sincerity, as they move among their facts but produce them before us out of complete obscurity.
>
> (Malinowski 1922: 3)

Malinowski deals with this difficult demand by offering a 'brief outline of an Ethnographer's tribulations' which he hopes will shed more light on the question than an abstract discussion would do. In other words, he describes his methodology, his attitude to his methods, and his reasons for doing what he does and how. He also gives an outline, in a table, of what expeditions took place where, and for how long, and lists some of the events that took place during that time. Unfortunately many contemporary ethnographers seem not to have learned this lesson, and nowadays every ethnographer has to decide for him or herself how much information is necessary for the reader to be able to evaluate the results of the research (see chapter 9).

Time

As Ball and Smith (2001: 307) have noted, 'what distinguished Malinowski's ethnography was the time he devoted to it, and its quality: between one and two years in the field, alongside the obligation to acquire competence in the vernacular'. For Malinowski an ethnographer needs to spend a considerable amount of time actually in the company of the people he or she is studying for the following reasons:

- to become part of the daily routine so as to limit the effects on the research subjects of your presence as an outsider;
- to have time to learn and understand as an insider;
- to have time to add to your questions and to guide your research in alternative directions.

Whenever you begin a new ethnographic study and enter the field for the first time, not only will you feel strange and obtrusive but so will you affect those you are spending time with. Trying to learn about people by spending time living or working alongside them has one obvious problem: they know you are there and this might affect how they behave. How can you know if they are doing the same things in the same way as if you were not there? Well, one way around this is for you to be there long enough for the people to get used to you and to stop feeling strange about you being there. You have to become part of the natural surroundings, to blend in. He says: 'It must be remembered that as the natives saw me constantly every day, they ceased to be interested or alarmed, or made self-conscious by my presence, and I ceased to be a disturbing element in the tribal life which I was to study' (Malinowski 1922: 8). This is one reason why an ethnographer needs time. However, time also allows the researcher to settle in, and to begin to feel part of things and to understand them from the point of view of those being researched. When you begin, everything looks strange and inexplicable. As time goes on and you begin to understand the society better, as Malinowski says, you acquire the 'feeling' for good and bad manners, for how to behave in this new culture, and thus learn it better than if you had merely asked questions about it. The third reason for needing to spend time doing ethnography is that you might not know what you want to explore at the outset. Malinowski's approach was informed by inductive reasoning (see chapter 2), where theory flows from data, but also informs research questions. He explains this better than I can:

> If a man sets out on an expedition, determined to prove certain hypotheses, if he is incapable of changing his views constantly and casting them off ungrudgingly under the pressure of evidence, needless to say his work will be worthless. But the more problems he brings into the field, the more he is in the habit of moulding his theories according to facts, and of seeing facts in their bearing upon theory, the better he is equipped with the work. Preconceived ideas are pernicious in any scientific work, but foreshadowed problems are the main endowment of a scientific thinker, and these problems are first revealed to the observer by his theoretical studies.
>
> (Malinowski 1922: 9)

This kind of development of theory in context takes time. It is not the kind of research where one goes out with a fixed idea of what one wants to study, collects the data and returns to analyse it. The data collection and analysis go hand in hand (this will be discussed more in chapter 8). For Malinowski, it is even likely you would have to return to the field a few times to do more observations once you started to try to write up your research.

Participation

A crucial element of ethnographic research for Malinowski is participation in the lives of the people being studied. As with the importance of spending time with the group (as opposed to simply making brief visits), participation is important for the ethnographer to become part of the natural surroundings or the setting, so that the people being researched cease to be affected by his or her presence.

If you take part in things then everything you want to study becomes within easy reach, rather than you having to renegotiate access over and over again. But more than this, participation helps you experience things as the insiders do and thus understand them better:

> in this type of work, it is good for the ethnographer sometimes to put aside his camera, note book and pencil, and to join in himself in what is going on . . . Out of such plunges into the lives of the natives – and I made them frequently not only for study's sake but because everyone needs human company – I have carried away a distinct feeling that their behaviour, their manner of being, in all sorts of tribal transaction, became more transparent and easily understandable than it had been before.
>
> (Malinowski 1922: 21–2)

As an aside, since the publication of his diary in 1967 Malinowski has been criticised for not really taking part in things at all, and there have been debates within ethnography about how much you can actually experience things as an insider and remain objective. Indeed, the publication of Malinowski's diary placed a mark of interrogation beside any overly confident and consistent ethnographic voice (Clifford 1986). Contemporary ethnography is often described as, or attempts to be, reflexive, that is to say it is conducted in full awareness of the myriad limitations associated with humans studying other human lives (these issues are discussed more fully in subsequent chapters).

Observation

Of course, an ethnographer does not merely participate. Real scientific research, Malinowski insists, is active, purposeful and demanding, with observation providing the more detached and scientific part of the research. It involves an amount of objectivity, of standing back from the culture, group or individual and seeing and noting what is going on. It is better done by a trained scientist than by a casual observer, he says. The ethnographer should observe what is going on in the field, logging the minute detail of every aspect of tribal life. One should not focus purely on the exotic but should observe what he poetically refers to as *the imponderabilia of actual life*: daily routines, the preparing of food, the details of the care of the body, conversations and social life. This also involves making mental and then actual notes of these observations.

Collecting data

For Malinowski, participant observation did not mean merely hanging around or even just being there. It was more active than that. An ethnographer needs to have real scientific aims, and to collect data on as many facets of life as possible. This involved using statistical documentation and building statistical summaries and analyses from concrete evidence. It meant systematically documenting details from daily life. It meant recording speech, habits and customs, as well as magic formulae and myths; making lists, drawing maps, constructing genealogies and taking photographs. Above all one needs to take field notes, recording not only those occurrences and details that are prescribed by tradition, but also the actual actions that are observed as they occur, by the participants as well as the spectators. This insistence on the collection of facts and evidence reflects Malinowski's positivistic approach, but I will discuss this more later.

In summary, Malinowski was insistent that the goals of ethnography were:

- to use concrete statistical documentation to record the organisation of the tribe and the anatomy of its culture
- to use minute, detailed observations to log the actual details of daily life
- to collect ethnographic statements, narratives, utterances as documents of native mentality.

To achieve this one had to spend time with the people one was studying, joining in with their daily lives, observing special events as well as daily rituals, asking questions, collecting information, and also, of course, learning the language.

Malinowski: functionalist and positivist?

Ball and Smith (2001) have argued that Malinowski has become so firmly established as the ancestor of fieldwork methods that those who influenced him have been overlooked. It is at least essential to consider the intellectual context in which Malinowski worked in order to understand his approach. Malinowski worked under two current influences: the need for the study of social life to be seen to be scientific; and current ideas, influenced by Emile Durkheim, about the constitution of social life as external to us, influencing our actions and shaping culture, while culture simultaneously constitutes society, integrating individuals in the harmonious functioning of the 'whole' society. Malinowski was one of the founders of the *functionalist* school of anthropology. He considered it important to look at all aspects of the life of a society, from religion and magic, to sex and family organisation. His was a holistic approach. Malinowski uses the analogy of the body, saying that one needs to get at the flesh and blood as well as the skeleton of a society. This approach sees the society as a whole unit, with all its constituent parts interrelated into a functioning whole, and analyses events and institutions in terms of the functions they serve for the society and the individuals. This is what he says about the response to his work *The Sexual Life of Savages*, of which he says sulkily: 'only sensational bits were picked out and wondered or laughed at':

> I intended to give a concrete example showing that a subject like sex cannot be treated except in its institutional setting, and through its manifestations in other aspects of culture. Love, sexual approaches, eroticism, combined with love-magic and the mythology of love are but a part of customary courtship in the Trobriands. Courtship, again, is a phase, a preparatory phase, of marriage, and marriage but one side of family life. The family itself ramifies into the clan, into the

relations between matrilineal and patriarchal kindred; and all these subjects, so intimately bound up with one another, constitute really one big system of kinship, a system which controls the social relations of the tribesmen with each other, dominates their economics, pervades their magic and mythology, and enters into their religion and even into their artistic productions. So that, starting with the problem of sex, I was led to give a full account of the kinship system, and of its function within the Trobriand culture.

(Malinowski 1932: xx)

Functionalism has now been discredited generally as being ahistoric, static and linked to colonial attitudes and history; Malinowski's holistic approach leading to a tendency to treat societies as if they were isolated islands (Macdonald 2001). Though seductive in its explanatory power, it does not easily allow for processes of change, or for interaction with external structures or external influences. Malinowski's methods, however, have been adopted and adapted to be applied to studies with perspectives such as feminism and Marxism, and to research of specialist institutions, cultures, themes or groups within a society rather than to whole societies which can no longer be seen as isolated discrete units.

Malinowski's approach could arguably be described as positivist. 'Striving after the objective, scientific view of things' (Malinowski 1922: 6) he collected facts and data from the real lives of the people under study in as detached a way as possible. His participation, contradictory to his fieldwork prescriptions, was actually minimal and seemed to mean little more than pitching his tent in the village. He insisted on separating thoughts and opinions from facts and observations and urged that 'the main endeavour must be to let facts speak for themselves' (1922: 20). Early social anthropologists, such as Malinowski, Pitt-Rivers and Haddon, wanted to establish the Natural Science of Society, and thought that for the science of society to have any credibility, to match the achievements of the natural sciences, it would have to mimic its methods. The subject matter had to be conceived as real, factual, out there. Empirical data should be collected using senses, especially direct observation, and preferably by trained scientists (Kuper 1997). The data Malinowski collected were therefore collected as documentary evidence, with the objectivity of the collecting tool (the camera for example, or even the ethnographer) taken for granted. But all this does not constrain contemporary ethnography to being positivistic (see chapter 2); one contemporary approach to 'evidence', for example, is to explore it in terms of the multiplicity of representations being constructed (Wright 1994).

Ethnography and sociology: the Chicago School

Within sociology participant observation and ethnographic field research are often considered to have their roots within the Chicago School of sociology (Wellin and Fine 2001, and see Deegan 2001 for an overview of what she calls the Chicago School of Ethnography). At a time when the city of Chicago was growing in population numbers at a vast rate, with huge influxes of immigrants and the rapid growth of urban areas, social researchers began to see their city as a sort of natural laboratory in which they could do studies. The Chicago School, Deegan suggests, 'towered over the intellectual and professional landscape of sociology from 1892 until 1942', becoming famous for urban sociology and also for innovative empirical research methods, for getting out in the streets and into the city doing field research and participant observation with real people. Robert Park, an ex-newspaper reporter, who held the first Chair in Sociology, famously told his students

> Go and sit in the lounges of the luxury hotels and on the doorsteps of the flophouses; sit on the Gold Coast settees and on the slum shakedowns; sit in the Orchestra Hall and in the Star and Garter Burlesk. In short, gentlemen, go get the seat of your pants dirty in real research.
>
> (Park, cited in Bulmer 1984: 97)

The research the Chicago School produced often included some statistical data but mostly these researchers studied face to face interaction, in everyday settings, and produced descriptive narratives of social worlds. A swathe of ethnographies (though they were not identified as such by name) were produced between 1917 and 1942, often conducted by students of Robert Park and Ernest Burgess and clearly influenced by the ideas of symbolic interactionism and 'social ecology' (Bulmer 1984). The Chicago School heritage includes a number of classical studies, including case studies on geographical areas (such as Zorbaugh's *The Gold Coast and The Slum*, 1929), on organisations and institutions (such as Cressey's *The Taxi-Dance Hall*, 1932), and even on individuals and small groups (such as Anderson's *The Hobo*, 1923, and Shaw's *The Jack Roller*, 1930). The Chicago School also gave birth to the life history and the use of documents such as diaries and letters (Plummer 2001b).

Laud Humphreys' Tea-Room Trade

Despite the predominance of survey research during the 1940s and 1950s there was a resurgence of ethnographic research in the 1960s (Wellin and Fine 2001). I will briefly introduce Laud Humphreys' (1970) study *Tea-Room Trade*, an example of an ethnography of a 'hidden population'. In 1965, Humphreys made a study of behaviour in *'certain men's conveniences in an American city'* (tearooms in American homosexual slang). In other words, he studied anonymous sexual encounters in a men's toilet in a public park in Chicago. Though more often cited in discussions of ethics in social research (see Warwick 1982), the study was a successful attempt to challenge stereotypes and to provide a fuller and more empathic understanding of what was labelled deviant behaviour. So how did he do it?

Humphreys' methodology

This was covert research. Humphreys did not admit that he was a researcher, but pretended to be a participant. Participation involves having an accepted role within the community (as we discuss more in chapter 4), even if that role is the role of anthropologist! Laud Humphreys took on the role of watchqueen, or voyeur lookout. His job was to stand at the doorway of the convenience watching for and warning of the approach of police or minors. For Humphreys this was the ideal role, enabling the observation of sexual acts, which he later was able to describe in graphic detail, as well as the entrance and exit of men to and from the 'tea-rooms'.

Like Malinowski, Humphreys' research involved both elements of participant observation. He used participation in order to become accepted in the homosexual community, taking on a role which enabled observation without raising suspicions and without affecting the behaviour of those researched by his presence. For Humphreys, participation was as a means of access rather than a method in itself (this will be discussed more in chapter 4), and he was able to observe the acts taking place inside the 'tea-rooms' as well as do something he has later been heavily criticised for. He was able to note down the car registration numbers of those using the tea-room, and from these he later used a friend in the police force to gain addresses and do follow up research to discover personal data on the participants. Working on a social health survey, he went to the addresses of the tea-room participants and was able to make enquiries about their daily lives, gathering demographic and personal information as well as information relating to their 'straight' sexual identities. As I have said, this was all done covertly and Humphreys has attracted a lot of criticism over the ethics of his research, but he attempts to justify what appears to some to be unethical but, for others, provides an enlightening analysis 'indicating the thin façade of normality behind which deviant action thrives' (Hobbs 2001: 211). What concerns us for now are his methods.

To continue comparing the themes raised in Malinowski's work, the research took place in its natural setting, and since there was little verbal communication to record Humphreys made what he calls systematic observations, noting down what took place, when, in minute detail and subsequently filling in a Systematic Observation Sheet, in order to ensure consistency and thoroughness in the recording of details, and to enable replication of the study. Humphreys also drew on other forms of data and a variety of methods. He learned from his past experience in the church, in a parish that was known in Chicago as the 'queen's parish', and from three months' clinical training in a psychiatric hospital that 'was well stocked that summer with male homosexual patients' (1970: 23). In order to acquaint himself with homosexual culture, he did participant observation in gay bars, observed pick-up operations in parks and streets, and had dozens of informal interviews with participants in gay society.

Also, like Malinowski, Humphreys was keen to point out that his research was not deductive. The relationship of data to theory for him was that theory should emerge from the data, but not in a simplistic approach to inductivism.

> I have not attempted to test any pre-stated hypotheses. Such an approach tends to limit sociological research to the imagery of the physical sciences . . . Hypotheses should develop *out of* ethnographic work, rather than provide restrictions and distortions from its inception. Where my data have called for a conceptual framework, I have tried to supply it . . . In those cases where data were strong enough to generate new theoretical approaches, I have attempted to be a willing medium.
>
> (Humphreys 1970: 22)

To conclude, we can see a few similarities between Malinowski and Humphreys, that link back to our earlier definition of ethnography. Ethnography involves researching something closely, over time, in its natural setting, drawing on participation and observation, as well as other data collection techniques. There is an emphasis in seeing things from the point of view of the insider (or the native), and an emphasis more on induction than deduction. Whether or not the native's view is sufficient an explanation or whether we look beyond that to other, underlying explanations depends on our philosophical position. The techniques look quite similar in either case.

Contemporary ethnography in social science

Contemporary ethnographies subscribe to the same principles as Malinowski and Humphreys illustrate: the close study, over time, using participation and observation, of a group of people, with the emphasis on obtaining the insider view. Contemporary ethnographies fall into modernist, post-modern and post-positivist traditions; Marxist, feminist, realist and positivist ethnographies are conducted; action and participatory research stand beside commentaries, descriptions and single voices. The journal *Ethnography* will give you an insight into the range of ethnographies being conducted today, as will many journals which report on qualitative studies more generally. Ethnographic methods are now being applied across the social science disciplines, especially within education, sociology, health studies, social geography and psychology. The 'field', which Brewer (2000) defines as a naturally occurring setting, is these days as likely to be a hospital, school playground or street corner as a peasant or rural community. Here is an example of a student's study that clearly fits the critical minimum definition outlined above. We will hear more about Michael's study as we go along.

Michael's study of young people and drug use

Michael wanted to know how young people talked about and justified drug use amongst themselves. He had no set hypothesis to test, simply some ideas about drug use and young people, drawn from his own experience and from what he had read in the academic and other literature. He decided to explore drug use among two groups of young people. He decided to spend some time in each group, going to parties, chilling out in their homes, shopping, going out to bars and clubs, and generally being a member of each group. The research was conducted in its natural setting, with most of the information gathered via participation and observation, but Michael also used the collection of other data. He spent time in the groups and experienced life as a member of each group. He asked questions in his mind and out loud about the drug use and other talk around it. But

continued on facing page

he supplemented what he saw and what he could ask in context with other information. A few more in-depth interviews were conducted with the members of the group by asking them to meet at other times and places. Data on young people and drug use were used as a framework. Michael's own experiences were drawn on in helping him frame questions and direct conversations. Michael's work was iterative-inductive, in that the design and analysis developed as the research progressed.

Ethnography of health and medicine

Ethnographies within the field of health and medicine are still rare, although the method is receiving increased attention, and if we include ethnographies such as Goffman's *Asylums* (1961) as well as the many other studies of health and illness in non-medical settings such as Bloor (1985) and Prout (1986) we see the field is larger than might at first be thought. The *British Medical Journal* has begun to engage with the debates around qualitative research generally and ethnography specifically through its Education and Debate section (see Savage 2000) and has reported findings from ethnographic research (The *et al.* 2000). Of course, in the health field some key problems that we will explore in this book, such as how qualitative data can be generalised and the practical and ethical issues associated with observing research participants, are particularly acute. But the unique advantage of ethnographic research in contributing to the understanding of patients' and clinicians' worlds from their own perspectives (Savage 2000) is worth retaining as we attempt to reconcile these difficulties. For an overview of the ethnography of health and medicine see Michael Bloor's (2001) paper with the same title. You might enjoy reading Sue Estroff's *Making It Crazy* (1981), in which, through participant observation, she encounters and learns from psychiatric outpatient clients: people who have been labelled mentally ill yet are not hospitalised. Or try Dodier and Camus' (1998) ethnography of the ways in which the flow of demands are managed in a hospital emergency service in a French teaching hospital. Several of the examples of research that I use in this book fall into the field of health and medicine because students from health-related disciplines have attended my courses on qualitative and ethnographic methods for many years.

Further reading

For an introduction to ethnography the collection by Ellen (1984) is still my favourite. Buy a copy if you can get hold of one; it has stood the test of time.

The key text for Malinowski's methodology is the first chapter in *Argonauts of the Western Pacific* (1922).

Mary Jo Deegan (2001) has produced a valuable review of what she calls the Chicago School of Ethnography, especially the ethnographies produced between 1917 and 1942. You might also enjoy Martin Bulmer's *The Chicago School of Sociology* (1984).

For contemporary ethnographies explore the journals *Ethnography* and the *Contemporary Journal of Ethnography*, and trawl through journals in your own discipline that will publish qualitative research. Note that ethnographies can crop up in unexpected places, for example in *Society and Animals* (Cassidy 2002).

For a review of medical ethnographies see the chapter on 'The New Wave of Ethnographies in Medical Anthropology' in Kleinman (1997).

2   Where to begin

In the previous chapter I spent a long time talking about the history of ethnographic methods within the fields of social anthropology and sociology, and introduced the range of contemporary uses of ethnographic methods in social science, especially in health and illness. This chapter explores more practical issues about how one might approach a piece of ethnographic research, that is, to repeat the definition established in chapter 1:

- Iterative-inductive research (that evolves in design through the study), drawing on
- a family of methods,
- involving direct and sustained contact with human agents
- within the context of their daily lives (and cultures);
- watching what happens, listening to what is said, asking questions, and
- producing a richly written account
- that respects the irreducibility of human experience,
- that acknowledges the role of theory,
- as well as the researcher's own role,
- and that views humans as part object/part subject.

The chapter takes the reader from thinking about a research interest to designing and planning a piece of ethnographic research. It will include choosing a 'field', the literature search (and bibliographic searches), collecting background information, and writing a qualitative research proposal or plan. The chapter will also think about who we should use as a sample and who we should interview. The chapter will then take an in-depth look at the philosophy of social science in its underlabourer role which informs or guides the methodological decisions and debates covered in this book.

Iterative-inductive research and foreshadowed problems

In chapter 1 I noted how both Malinowski and Humphreys insisted that ethnography should not begin with a rigid hypothesis. In *The Anthropological Lens: Harsh Light/Soft Focus* (1986), James L. Peacock says an anthropologist shines a harsh light on a topic in order to see it clearly, but that this light has a soft focus in order that the boundaries remain fuzzy. This is often described as inductive research, to oppose it to a simplistic deductive approach characteristic of some approaches to scientific research, but I prefer the term iterative-inductive, to indicate a sophisticated inductivism and flexible research design.

A *deductive* approach to research is one where a hypothesis is derived from existing theory and the empirical world is explored, and data are collected, in order to test the truth or falsity of the hypothesis. A key problem with deductivism is that while existing theories can be tested, new theories that challenge existing ones cannot emerge. One wonders where the theories to be tested come from in the first place if it is not from the real world. Many qualitative approaches explicitly reject the deductive approach, or what Berg (2004) calls the *theory-before-research* method, in favour of an inductive approach, where data come before theory.

A simplistically inductive approach to research is one where the researcher begins with as open a mind and as few preconceptions as possible, allowing theory to emerge from the data. However, most ethnographers now accept that it is in fact impossible to start out with no preconceived ideas, no theories about how the world works, and that the best way to be inductive is to be open about one's preconceptions, to read the literature and consider what theories have already been formed on a given topic, then to proceed in a manner which is informed but open to surprises. In this more sophisticated inductivism, theory is precursor, medium and outcome of ethnographic study and writing (Willis and Trondman 2000). As Ezzy argues (2002: 10): 'all data are theory driven. The point is not to pretend they are not, or to force the data into theory. Rather, the researcher should enter into an ongoing simultaneous process of deduction and induction, of theory building, testing and rebuilding.' I refer to this as an *iterative-inductive* approach because, although both words have a wide range of connotations and uses in research informed by a variety of philosophical positions, they are the best way to capture something that moves steadily forward yet forward and back at the same time. Iterative implies both a spiral and a straight line, a loop and a tail (see chapter 8); inductive implies as open a mind as possible, allowing the data to speak for themselves as far as possible.

Ethnography, then, like most qualitative research, is usually necessarily fluid and flexible. But this does not mean ethnography begins with no research design. It simply means that the design has to leave space for fluidity and flexibility. As Hammersley and Atkinson have argued (1995: 24), 'research design should be a reflexive process which operates throughout every stage of a project'. Regardless of how purist a definition of inductive research one is working with, it is in fact impossible to go out and start researching something without some idea of what it is you are interested in. Maybe if you keep looking around you will find something interesting eventually, but you may find lots of interesting things and not know which to focus on. It is far easier to decide what you want to study and aim to do that but allow yourself the freedom to move focus; that is, to be both iterative and inductive. Furthermore, it is very unlikely that your supervisors, your peers, and anyone funding or relying on your research findings, will be happy to let you go out with no plan or design to begin with. Finally, you will not be very happy yourself until you feel more focussed. Because of its iterative nature, then, doing ethnography leads to initial (and sometimes ongoing) feelings of confusion, muddle and lack of purpose, but we can mediate these insecurities at least to some extent by preparation.

All ethnographic research needs some guiding questions or foreshadowed problems: Julia's study of oil workers

Julia, for example, was interested in oil workers and knew of a group of wives of oil workers who met every week, and said she thought it would be interesting to join this group and study it. But she had no research question. She didn't know what she wanted to know about, not even vaguely. She went along to a few meetings but couldn't find anything interesting to ask them about.

A mistake students often make is choosing a setting rather than a question or even a group to begin to understand. Rather late in the day she realised that when she thought it through more carefully she was interested in how these women use the group to help them cope with having the man away so much. She started to ask questions about this specific topic and again shifted focus on to how women talk about their lives in this situation. Not having spent much time thinking about what it was about this group that interested her or what she wanted to understand meant Julia wasted a lot of time. Every piece of research needs some guiding questions, some foreshadowed problems.

In order to get to the point of establishing your intellectual puzzle (Mason 1996) or your foreshadowed problems (Malinowski 1992) it is important to think through the following:

- what it is you think you are interested in
- what it is you think you might find
- what sorts of methods you might use
- what you already 'know' on the subject
- what is already 'known' on the subject
- how it is all relevant in a wider context (in terms of theories and policies).

Let's take these one at a time.

What are you interested in?

Let's break this down into three parts: selecting a topic; summarising it as a short description; unpacking it into a longer description. The first thing we must do is think of a topic, problem or puzzle (Mason 1996) and ask whether it is suitable for ethnographic research. Suitable topics are those which require in-depth understanding that is obtained through detailed examples, rich narratives (if using qualitative interviews), empathy and experience, and which benefit from being studied over a period of time. Topics which are not easily spoken about, or which involve ambiguity or ambivalence on the part of the actor, topics which involve examining processes of change, examining negotiated lived experiences, topics which see culture as constructed and reconstructed through actors' participation are especially suited to participant observation and ethnography. For example, suppose you are wondering how migrants cope in a given setting or how minority ethnic businesses compete with indigenous businesses on a day to day basis, or you want to understand a group that others consider deviant, for example a new political movement or a religious cult. Perhaps you want to discover the insiders' view of life in a psychiatric institution, or life as an outpatient of an institution. Perhaps you have an interest in fiddling or pilfering and wonder how usually lawful people end up getting involved in petty theft. Perhaps you are interested in a group that a survey would not sample and in questions a survey could not ask. Don't worry too much though, Paul Rock (2001: 32) reminds us: '*everything* is engaging, or can be made so. There is no part of the social world that will remain boring after the application of a little curiosity'; a wide range of topics has been researched using ethnographic methods.

The way you describe your research to anyone should work a bit like a tree diagram, starting off brief and to the point and gradually spreading out to a longer and longer description and explanation. It is up to you how far you go with this but you should certainly be able to describe your research quickly, in one or two sentences, should produce a full plan with methods and literature review, and should be able to do something in between the two. Mason says it is often easier for people to write the very short or the very long version but they find something in between a bit of a struggle. She says one needs to be clear about the 'essence of the enquiry', at the heart of which is your intellectual puzzle, or what you want to explain. This may be made up of several questions and sub-questions which you do not so much expect to answer as use to open up avenues of enquiry.

Having selected a topic, make sure you can write it as a single sentence, or just one or two sentences. This short description will only give a brief idea of what you are interested in, not how you might go about studying it, or why it has broader relevance, but it will help you focus. Of course, you are free to change this short description as and when necessary as you do your research. Its function is to help keep you aware of what it is you want to know, not to constrain you. Next try writing your proposed ethnographic study as a slightly longer description that explains it succinctly, just a paragraph or two, but in more detail than the short version. This paragraph or two will explain some of how you might do the research and why it is important. I have given an example below of research that was funded by the UK Economic and Social Research Council (and that can be found on their database). However, it may well be that you cannot write this short paragraph until you have completed steps 2–6 below.

A title and a short paragraph are a good way to begin: McKee and Mauthner's study of the oil and gas industry

Title: Children, family, community and work : an ethnography of the oil and gas industry in Scotland. (McKee and Mauthner at www.regard.ac.uk)

Short description: The last decade has seen dramatic changes in economic and labour market structure, culture and policies, and a now pressing issue concerns the impact of such changes

continued on facing page

on children's everyday lives. Much research has explored inter-relationships between parental employment, workplace policies and family life; yet children's voices have been absent from these debates. This project aims to explore the links between children's lives, parental employment patterns and wider labour market conditions, through an ethnographic case study of children living within families employed in the oil and gas industry in Scotland. Focussing on one industry experiencing and pioneering social and economic change will identify key issues in the relationship between shifting employment patterns and policies, home life and children's lives. Oil companies are at the forefront of changes which are beginning to affect many organisations worldwide (e.g., internationalisation, outsourcing, casualisation). Issues arising from these changes include protracted absences from home, long-distance commuting and job insecurity. The focus of the project will be on children aged 8–12, living within fifty families with a father employed in the oil and gas industry in Grampian Region, and based in three different localities with a relatively high density of such families. The project will take a mixed-methods approach, centring on children's accounts, but also encompassing interviews with other family members and key community and industry figures, to provide a holistic picture of children's lives.

What do you think you might find?

Not all of this will eventually go into a written plan that people will read, but I strongly believe it is important for each researcher to work through, on paper, what their own preconceptions are about what they are researching. Many students tell me they don't know what they will find when I first ask them, and when I insist that they think about it they often say, as one did, 'but isn't that like deciding what you are going to find out before you do the research?' I would argue exactly the opposite: it is only when you face your preconceptions head on that you are able to put them on one side when you actually go out and observe and talk to people. You can only be open to surprises if you know what you expect to find. Gail, for example, who was researching men's friendships (see chapter 4), admitted she expected men not to have strong friendships so she kept looking for this to be confirmed without realising this was what she was doing. Once she admitted it to herself she was open to being proved wrong.

What sorts of methods might you use?

What methods of research will you use? Who will you talk to, when and where? Who will you observe? How? You should think through why you are choosing certain methods and not others; what problems you might encounter and how you might overcome them; and what ethical problems you might face. Think about how the methods you are choosing relate to findings you expect. Think about how long you will need, and how much it will cost, what difficulties you might have, and how you might get over them. This will all be easier to understand once you have read the rest of this book and understand more about the range of methods. Ethnographers often say in a research proposal that they will draw on the range of qualitative methods depending on the circumstances, and do not elaborate much more than that, but it is important for you to think through before you start what you might do and how. Most ethnographers use participant observation, combined with qualitative interviews, and the collection of other forms of data (including perhaps visual images, newspaper cuttings, maps, and even statistics). At this stage you will need to think about who you might talk to or observe and where, even though these will change as you go along. See the section on sampling, below.

What do you already know about the subject?

Linked to the above, it is a good idea to write down somewhere all the things you already know or think you know about the topic you are studying. Then check whether it is merely gossip, or actual information. Where did this knowledge come from? I do a lot of research in Spain with North European migrants, and my first study explored the way of life of British migrants. There had been very little written academically about British migration to Spain but it was important for me to explore in detail all the ways the British in Spain had been portrayed in the media as well as through gossip and informal communications (see O'Reilly 2000a and 2001). For Judith Okely's (1983) research on traveller-gypsies this involved looking at all that was said about gypsies and where such 'knowledge' had come from.

What is already known about the subject?

Here I am referring to the review of everything within your discipline that has been written on your topic. This is covered more fully in the section below titled 'Reviewing the literature'. The literature review does what it says: it reviews the literature on your subject, ensuring that you know what has been done in this area already, so that you can advance knowledge, not repeat work already done, and so that you can fit your study into some wider body of knowledge in this area.

How is it all relevant in a wider context?

It is useful and important to consider why what you are doing might be important. This has three strands: topical, theoretical and policy-related. In terms of your particular topic, your research may well have wider relevance because of what it can tell us about doctors in general, or teachers in general, or whatever. However, it may well be that you are not able to generalise from your small study to any wider population or make any generalisable conclusions. If this is the case, it is likely that you will still want your research to have some relevance beyond merely understanding one particular group at one particular time. This might be achieved at the level of theory, so that though, for example, you can say no more about teachers generally you may be able to contribute to theories in the field of education; or though you might not be able to talk about all white youth, you may be able to contribute to theories of racism more broadly, even if it is only to critique a particular theory (this is discussed more thoroughly in chapter 9). Finally, it may or may not be the case that you want to consider the policy relevance of your research, or what actions might be taken as a result of what you have found, for example in Action Research where expected outcomes are a crucial and explicit element of design. For these reasons your literature review may well review literature on your topic (doctors, white youth), on your theoretical area (racism, education) and on relevant policy areas (race relations, education).

Once you have worked through all the steps 1 to 6 above, you will have a nice neat report to present to someone, explaining what your research is all about and its potential relevance, summarising your intellectual puzzle (Mason 1996), or establishing your foreshadowed problems. It depends on the demands of your supervisors, teachers or funding body how much of this you will actually have to present, but working through it for your own benefit is very useful. The one thing you are likely to be asked to do before a piece of research is to write a literature review.

Reviewing the literature

The literature review is the bit of your dissertation, proposal or write-up that locates the topic within a wider context, demonstrating why the study you propose (or have done) is timely and important. You are usually asked to do it before you start the research, but then usually have to do it again at the end (and all the way through). Why is this? Because ethnographic research is iterative-inductive, you can't go out and study something without having some idea of what you want to study. So you read up on it; as Paul Rock (2001: 33) notes, 'ethnography characteristically begins not in the field at all but in the library'. On the other hand, Nader (1970) reminds us of the dangers of staying in the library too long. The literature review begins to prepare you, but you need to get out there and explore the real world too. As you start to collect data you begin to take an interest in themes that had not occurred to you before, so you read up on these. At the end, as you write up your research, you will redo the literature review so that it makes sense in light of what you studied.

For now we will concentrate on the review of the literature that usually has to be done and written up (depending on demands from external forces) before you start the research. I am often asked how one can do a literature review of a topic that has not been researched before. Also, I am asked how you can locate a study in wider literature until you know what themes you will be interested in (and if you are doing grounded research this comes after you start studying). Well, the answer is that, since you have some foreshadowed problems, you do have some ideas of the sorts of substantive and theoretical areas you are interested in, and those that might be relevant. Maybe you are thinking about ethnicity, or community, or politics, or religion. Maybe crime or deviance has caught your attention. Then, substantively, your topic possibly fits into some wider themes (sport, religion, ageing, migration in Europe). There may have been one or two studies that have been done that are similar to yours.

The literature review is not a compilation of facts and feelings, nor is it a long list of who said what (this is tedious, boring and pointless). Your literature review should be 'a coherent argument that leads to the description of a proposed study' (Rudestam and Newton 1992: 47). The reader should end up convinced that this is exactly the sort of study that now needs to be done to advance knowledge in this particular field. As you prepare the review, be selective with your material and don't be afraid to be critical. In the end you will read far more than ever makes it into the literature review. But you have to read it all in order to become enough of an expert to know which bits aid your argument and which don't (this doesn't mean leave out bits which disagree with you, it means deciding what is relevant). Everything that is included should have a point, so that a reader is not left asking 'and so what?' Also, allow yourself to make an argument that includes other people's useful contributions to the field as well as mentioning the things they neglected or did weakly or poorly.

Long shots, medium shots and close-ups

Joseph Handlon (referred to in Rudestam and Newton 1992) uses the metaphor of camera shots in film-making to draw an analogy between filming and the literature review. Long shots are used for summarising background literature on a particular topic. This literature and the theoretical perspectives need to be acknowledged, but not focussed on in any great detail. A short paragraph or two may be enough, with lots of references in brackets to areas of research. You might produce something along these lines: 'Social class has been researched in a variety of ways: quantitative mobility studies tend to explore (summarise the various approaches, followed by a list of references) and Rosemary Crompton (specific reference) uses what she calls the 'employment' aggregate approach; the qualitative paradigm looks at (summarise the various approaches, followed by a list of references), the life history approach and mobility studies look at (summarise the various approaches, followed by a list of references).' You might even reference some books that review the literature on the topic, saying 'see the following for a good review'. Long shots are your opportunity to introduce a range of topics linked to yours but not directly relevant. The long shot in a photograph gives a broad picture without being able to focus on much detail.

The medium shot is somewhere between the long shot and the close-up and needs a bit more descriptive material. To continue my example above, perhaps I am demonstrating that the research I intend to do falls into the life history approach. I would want to explore literature in this field and studies done on this topic in more depth than the quantitative approaches I had mentioned. What you review will depend a lot on how you have framed your research questions, or your longer and shorter descriptions of your proposed study. These suggest areas of research. For example McKee and Mauthner's study, discussed above, would require long shots on children, family, community and work, and changes in the oil and gas industry as they relate to these. Medium shots would cover where these topics combine. Close-up analysis would be required of literature on the effects of work patterns on children's and family lives.

The close-up is reserved for those studies with direct relevance to the proposed study. It might include former studies on which the present one is based – maybe you are extending an earlier piece of work, applying new methods or looking at a different group – or perhaps you have recognised a gap in the literature or an under-researched area. The reader needs to end up with an awareness of what is known about the subject. For my first piece of research, this meant drawing on media representations and gossip about British migrants in Spain; little had been done academically. It is likely that studies discussed here will be subjected to a close, critical examination of their methods, findings and approach, what they contribute and what they leave out.

Don't be afraid for your literature review to evolve, to draw on literature outside of your own discipline, or to draw on other data than the written word. In the sort of iterative-inductive ethnographic research I have described you may not have a completely clear idea of what areas you are interested in as you start out. You may need to consult new theoretical perspectives to help you sort out interesting ideas that emerge from the research. You may even change direction entirely and start studying something really different. For my research in Spain I had no idea I would be interested in community, tourism and escape attempts, or social geography. So, your literature review may well change. In some situations you may want to look at fiction, as Judith Okely (1983) did in her research on traveller-gypsies. Your literature review might include photographs and other representations. Background material of all sorts can be collected at this stage. As a final point, the literature review does not have to appear at the front of whatever you produce; you can even be flexible about this and thread it through the thesis or report (Wolcott 2001).

Conducting the study

Everything written above makes it sounds as if ethnographic research proceeds in a neat linear fashion from a literature review and research plan, to conducting the study, to writing it up. However, the main argument of this book is that ethnographic research works more like a spiral than a straight line (Berg 2004, see chapter 8). You start somewhere and end somewhere, but in the meantime you can go round in a few circles; in other words, design is continuous (Rubin and Rubin 1995). I have called this iterative-inductive research. I would argue it constitutes the crucial difference between quantitative and qualitative research and is what sometimes can make it so difficult to explain qualitative research to researchers used to quantitative methods. If we were always to mention first that this is the crucial difference between quantitative and qualitative, and that there *is* a difference (without pretending that there isn't, as so many books attempt to do these days) and that the difference is ontological and epistemological, then we might be able to get on with presenting our findings more easily to other audiences.

Starting out: the general gathering stage

There is the chance that as you begin a research project you will know little about the field and will want to get to know what you can, where you can. Suppose, for example, I was doing an ethnography in a summer school. I would probably want to find out something about how the summer school was organised and run, what it was all about. I could do this from promotional literature, web sites and so on before I ever actually spoke to anyone. Paul Thompson (1988) calls this the 'general gathering' stage. It is a bit like putting your toe in the water to test it before plunging in, and it may well make you go back and redesign your whole project. Allow yourself some time for general gathering before you access your group or setting if possible, otherwise it can be too late to change direction easily. Spending a bit of time in a different school or talking to some doctors you are not likely to include in your sample, or to anyone you know about friendships, for examples, may help you to decide who to study, where and when, and may help you frame your research questions.

Sampling

I am often asked by students setting out to do a piece of ethnographic research, 'what should I include in my sample?' Sampling, of course, comes from the language of quantitative research and suggests that there is a population you are interested in of which you can only gain access to a few. The idea is that you choose a sample that can best represent the whole, so that when you have collected your information you can generalise in some way or another to the whole group (with prior knowledge about how your sample relates to the population of interest). Ethnographers rarely worry about sampling for representativeness; this is why they don't talk about case studies. It is not usual that an ethnographer is overtly researching one group or sample as a 'case' that is illustrative of something broader. However, we often do want our research to have wider relevance (which I discuss in chapter 9) and of course we have to choose somehow who to study and where, and when, and what. All ethnographic research, however flexible and free-floating it is made out to be, has to make choices which will affect what is learned. These choices should be theoretically informed where possible, but may have to be made on the basis of practical limitations.

Aspects an ethnographer may sample include settings, people, time and contexts (Hammersley and Atkinson 1995). How do we know who to select for our research? If we are using participant observation, the selection of participants will often be quite clear and will have been part of the research design, and initial puzzle. For example, Claire wanted to know how fishing families in a specific town are coping in the current climate (see chapter 8), so it was obvious where her research would take place. Sometimes the research question itself includes the group or the place, but even here there is the issue of where we draw the boundaries of the group. Do we include migrants, emigrants, networks which extend beyond the group? In other cases, the overall research question is quite general: how do psychiatric out-patients experience their lives (Estroff 1981)? What is the extent and meaning of fiddling or pilfering in a factory (Ditton 1977)? These do not include an actual place or field; this has to be chosen. How do we choose it? These issues are linked to those we discuss later, on representativeness and validity. Do we choose a field, group, place or society which is representative or just accessible? Often the choice is practical. Michael (chapter 1), for example, chose to conduct his study of drug cultures and drug talk amongst his mates initially. Often we have to start somewhere and then change a bit, or at least the boundaries we draw around our setting may change to include other places. Mary (chapter 7) found that she had to include the reception and waiting areas as well as the doctors' rooms in her study of attitudes to asthma. Sometimes a group and a setting are the same thing, but don't be bound by either. You might want to include teachers when you thought you would only look at children, and the streets when you thought the school would be enough. Settings may be chosen because they are representative of other settings, or because they are atypical (and we can therefore learn from their strangeness); they may be chosen because they have been studied previously (e.g., Lewis 1951), or simply because they are accessible (Hicks 1984). Interviewees may well recommend other people you should talk to, which leads to a snowballing of your sample.

Once you have selected your field or setting, you will then need to select situations and people within it to talk to, spend time with, observe. You cannot be everywhere at once and all the time. You may, as Hammersley and Atkinson (1995) suggest, use your own categories to sample; for example, you may have reasons for making sure you access people of different nationalities, or ages. Or you may sample according to the categories of the researched, as ways the group divides itself up become apparent. And you are likely to alter who you sample as you go along, and develop your ideas and your analysis, for example in theoretical sampling. You can even ask the people themselves who and what should be included in the study. People like to be involved in the research that is about them.

You will also have to decide *when* to do the research, and to consider that different times of the day or the year may be relevant. There may be different contexts within the setting that are relevant:

for example, when I conducted a small study of school children of different nationality groups, I discovered that the school staff room was very interesting as it revealed a mix of nationalities of staff, and I began to wonder how their various relationships with the children were experienced. Later on in the study I began to realise that if I wanted to understand how the different national groups mixed I would have to spend time in the streets and the playground as well as the classrooms.

Busy or key participants

One category of research participants worth thinking carefully about is what we might call key participants (or key informants, Burgess 1984). Some people are more difficult to get access to than others. Some people can be chatted to at length over endless cups of coffee; others will maybe allow you one interview, time permitting. These people need much more time in the planning of their interview. If you can only talk to them once, you want to make sure you ask everything you need to know – and you will often not know what you want to ask until later in the project. Two examples of key participants in my research with British migrants in Spain (O'Reilly 2000a) were the British consul, who met and worked with many expatriates, and the chief of police, whose job it was to oversee applications for residence permits. But to return to my example above of an ethnography in a summer school, I might want to talk to the organiser as a key participant, but would be unlikely to be given free and easy access as the organiser would be very busy. Probably I would spend time with other summer school participants, refine my research questions and the direction of my research, and then talk to an organiser when I was better prepared. But my initial research question would not have been 'what is the summer school?' It is more likely to be focussed on a specific group, for example 'what is the extent of interaction between different nationalities during the summer school?' Or 'how is the summer school constructed to appeal to a certain target audience?' The focus of the first of these is more on the participants; the second is on the organiser and the participants. So your choice of 'fields' and informants is always theoretically driven.

Other participants may be key because they are 'encultured informants' (Spradley 1979) who are consciously reflexive about the culture in which they live and are either in a designated position where it is expected they will explain things to outsiders, or are people who simply enjoy sharing local knowledge. Such people are worth nurturing for their insights and efforts to help you, and can often act as gatekeepers, easing access to settings and individuals with whom they are familiar (see chapter 4).

Key events

A key event is where something happens that is likely to be revealing for your research (for example, summer school events that bring everyone together or social events might by key events). Some researchers use a key event to frame all the discussion of one particular argument; Geertz's (1973) study of a Balinese cockfight is a perfect example. A key event can act as a trigger for discussion or can be a time when all those themes you are interested in are played out.

Key events: Sophie's ethnography of the Ba'

Sophie conducted an ethnography of the Ba', a famous Shetland ball game that takes place at Christmas and New Year between two teams whose members represent the entire island. The game can get very dangerous and even bloody, and appears unruly, yet is circumscribed by complex rules that players adhere to rigidly. For Sophie the game itself was clearly to be a key event and her ethnography had to include sampling that. But a further key event for Sophie, who was particularly fascinated as to why people engage in such a dangerous pastime,

continued on facing page

and what meanings it has and functions it fulfils for the participants and the islanders, was a meeting to discuss safety issues for next year's event.

In research in which I explored relationships between children of different nationalities, I discovered after a few periods of participant observation that how children see their futures was relevant. I began to include that as a topic in future group interviews and then heard there was to be a leaving party for those who had finished school and would be moving on. I decided this would be a *key event* that I must explore, a time when the children were looking back on their time at the school and thinking about their futures.

Summary

Ethnographic research is usually iterative-inductive. Rather than beginning with hypotheses to test it is usual to start with some foreshadowed problems or an intellectual puzzle that guides the design and process of the research but remains open and flexible. However, ethnographic research still needs to be carefully planned and designed (and replanned and redesigned as it develops). It is useful to be able to state your intellectual puzzle in terms of a title or short description, a longer description of a paragraph or two, and a full description that includes a review of the literature and what is already known on the subject, consideration of methods and reflections on what you expect to find out (in order that you begin with an open mind). Reviewing the literature is a task often embarked upon before research begins, but in iterative-inductive research it will have to be revised constantly as your ethnography and analyses evolve.

As you begin the study, though you may not have a clear idea who you will eventually include, it is useful to think through issues around sampling and where to go and what to do. This chapter has explored the 'general gathering' phase and the role of key participants and key events. The following section invites you to think about the role of philosophy in social science generally, providing material to inform decisions made before you begin and as you conduct ethnographic research. This section should be used for reference rather than you attempting to absorb it all at once.

The role of philosophy

The difference between approaches and actual methods used by different ethnographers, especially at different periods, can be explained to some extent by the influence of various ideas in the philosophy of social science. In this section, I offer an expanded review of the philosophy of social science in its underlabourer role. You can either read it now, or use it to refer back to. The section, like the underlabourer role of philosophy, is here to help you think about how to do ethnography and make certain decisions, such as how long an interview should last, to what extent your own voice should be heard in the research and so on. According to the underlabourer view of the relationship between philosophy and social science, philosophy cannot provide us with certain or reliable knowledge; for this we need experience and observation – in other words, to get out and study the world using our senses. Clearly, as ethnographers, this is your position too. However, philosophy still has a role for social science because of the many difficult questions we have to address that cannot always be resolved by what is seen or heard, smelt, felt or tasted, questions such as: how can we understand social life? Can we be scientific and objective in our study of human lives? What are the roles of political and moral values in social research? Social scientists are often unsure of their achievements. We don't develop new technologies, or offer cures, or even propose interventions that may suppress negative outcomes as natural scientists do; or if we do we cannot test their success, as it is impossible in human life to control for the effects of external factors. Mainly this is because our subject matter is human lives. As a result there are many ongoing debates about what it is we actually do when we study society. The sense of discomfort about the value of their work is often very acute for researchers working in health fields ands therefore alongside practitioners and scientists who are much more positive about the role of scientific research. As a result, social scientists have become very reflexive about their role and their work. I believe it is important to be reflexive in a systematic and thoughtful way, and philosophy of social science can help with this, so in this next section I will explore the history of the philosophy of social science and will explicate the various positions, from positivism through post-modernism to post-positivism. I introduce the philosophy of social science not so that readers can worry themselves trying to reconcile different positions and determine where they stand but as a tool for thinking reflexively and yet systematically about what we do. As Seale (1999: 25) has noted, 'Philosophical positions can be understood by social researchers as resources for thinking, rather than taken as problems to be resolved before research can proceed.'

Positivism

The nineteenth-century French philosopher Auguste Comte coined the term 'positivism' to label an approach to social science (especially sociology) that would emulate the natural sciences and would be *positive* in its attempts to achieve reliable, concrete knowledge on which we could act to change the social world for the better. Positivism therefore draws from natural science in explaining what social science should be like, and specifically on the *empiricist* view of natural science. It believes that empiricism is superior to any other route to knowledge and, furthermore, that the knowledge gained, just like the knowledge gained by the natural sciences, can be used in practical ways to improve society. In other words positivism is *the application of empiricist natural science to the study of society and the development of policy.*

Positivism is often associated in a simplistic way with quantitative research, and the analysis of large sets of data using statistics, but this is too vague and general. We have already shown that Malinowski was influenced by positivism yet used qualitative methods. This is not to say he was a positivist (he has also been shown to share important features with realism), but, using philosophy in an underlabourer role, the ideas within positivism can help us understand some of what Malinowski was doing when he studied in the Trobriands. Malinowski, like many researchers of his time, wanted the new social sciences to have the authority and respect that was accorded the physical sciences and believed that in order to achieve this he had to demonstrate his understanding of empiricism, his objectivity, his collection of facts, and his respect for evidence.

Empiricism

Positivism then is the application of the empiricist model of natural science to the study of society, but what is meant by the term empiricism? Benton and Craib (to whom this section of this book is heavily indebted) set out seven basic doctrines:

1. The individual human mind starts out as a 'blank sheet'. We acquire our knowledge from our sensory experience of the world and our interaction with it.
2. Any genuine knowledge-claim is testable by experience (observation or experiment).
3. This rules out knowledge-claims about beings or entities which cannot be observed.
4. Scientific laws are statements about general, recurring patterns of experience.
5. To explain a phenomenon scientifically is to show that it is an instance of a scientific law. This is sometimes referred to as the 'covering law' model of scientific explanation.
6. If explaining a phenomenon is a matter of showing that it is an example or 'instance' of a general law, then knowing the law should enable us to predict future occurrences of phenomena of that type. The logic of prediction and explanation is the same. This is sometimes known as the thesis of the 'symmetry of explanation and prediction'.
7. Scientific objectivity rests on a clear separation of (testable) factual statements from (subjective) value judgements.

(Benton and Craib 2001: 14)

Criticisms of positivism

The positivist view of social science, and the empiricist view on which it is based, have been heavily criticised in various ways; indeed, positivism has become something of a term of abuse. Yet it is arguable that little social research has ever been entirely positivistic in its application. Benton (1977) argues that a lot of social science research is actually 'realist' and would benefit from drawing on philosophical understandings of realism (see below). Criticisms of positivism and empiricism can be grouped under two headings: naturalistic and anti-naturalistic. Naturalism is the idea that social science can be studied using the same principles and ideas as natural science. Naturalistic criticisms therefore criticise empiricism as a model of science rather than attacking the positivistic application of natural science models to social science.

Naturalistic criticisms

One key criticism of empiricism is the first doctrine above: the idea that the human mind starts out as a blank sheet. All experience, argue the critics, has to be conceptually ordered; what we see and hear has to be made some sense of and we use our mental capacity for this. The eighteenth-century German philosopher Immanuel Kant, especially, argued that our ability to judge difference, to conceptualise time and space, to think in terms of cause and effect, are all innate, universal capacities. We do not simply receive stimuli through our senses. Similarly, Noam Chomsky identified innate dispositions to learn a language and acquire grammatical competence. Empiricism was insufficient, he argued, to explain this universal ability. Such arguments are about epistemology, or how we can know the world.

Epistemology means theory of knowledge, or how it is we can know anything about the world.

Secondly, empiricist science, drawing on the doctrines outlined above, can actually only describe constant correlations of events (in other words, when one thing happens another seems to happen each time). It cannot demonstrate causes or make predictions; these are only implied and the mind reasons them into existence. The senses don't tell us, for example, that the more white swans we see the higher the chance we will only ever see white swans; we need to use our minds to work that out.

Another key criticism of empiricism is that it is not always clear how we should deal with evidence that appears to go against, or falsify, a hypothesis. For example, we first might consider whether things were maybe measured wrongly or differently in order to produce such evidence, or whether our hypothesis needs refining to account for the new evidence. In the end decisions about how to treat evidence are often based on convention or the prevailing paradigm, as Thomas Kuhn (1970) would have argued, or on theoretical perspectives. Indeed a relativist would say we cannot ever choose between different *theoretical* perspectives, and everything depends on these, not on anything in the real world. It is worth noting here that empiricist views of natural science, and therefore positivism, do not account for the use of theoretical perspectives in enabling us to interpret what we see. Malinowski, therefore, could not be labelled a positivist, even though we can say he shares features with positivism.

A final (for the purposes of this book) problem with empiricism is the second doctrine above, that any knowledge claim is testable by experience (by using our senses). The problem with this is that many entities which cannot be observed are relied on in natural science in terms of explanation. Indeed scientists 'invent' entities that they cannot see yet which explain phenomena they can see; no one has ever seen an electrical current, for example, just its effects, and so the existence of an electrical current is *proposed* by its effects. Realist philosophers of natural science believe in the existence of a real world that exists independently of our ideas about it and draw on these ideas to posit the existence of things that they may or may not need to *prove* exist. Realist science looks for observable phenomena, asks what would explain these, posits the existence of underlying structures or mechanisms, then tests hypotheses based on those. Realist views of science have been drawn on to inform a social science that comes between positivism and interpretivism.

Anti-naturalistic criticisms

Anti-naturalistic criticisms of positivism argue that the social world is so very different from the natural world that scientific methods are inappropriate for studying it. Anti-naturalistic criticisms of positivism then often draw on a different ontology. In other words they say that the sorts of things that exist in the world for social scientists are entirely different from those studied by natural scientists.

Ontology asks what sorts of things there are in the world that we can know. For some, the things social scientists and natural scientists study are so different that completely different methods are required. It is worth noting that different social scientific disciplines and sub-disciplines have different ontologies. In other words the things that are in the world that they want to understand are different from each other.

Interpretivisms

Anti-naturalistic criticisms take the shape of various forms of interpretivism, some with their roots in the work of Max Weber. For interpretivists, it is essential to see humans as actors in the social world rather than as simply *reacting* as objects in the natural world. In order to understand the social world we need to get inside the heads of the individuals or groups we study and understand their meanings about what they are doing. Some interpretivists argue, furthermore, that human behaviour needs to be understood in the context of their particular society or culture. Weber is often described as an ontological or methodological individualist. In other words, at the base of his ideas about social science is the idea that we begin with the individual, or indeed individual actions. For Max Weber, drawing on Kant, there can be no knowledge of the world independently of thought. To have knowledge (his epistemology) is to *interpret* the world in some way. Therefore, what a social scientist should study is meaningful rational action, that is action we take to achieve an end (instrumental action), and which has meaning for the actor, and which is directed towards, or involves, other people. Other types of action (traditional, affective, irrational are not for the sociologist to study). The study of this rational action involved interpretive understanding (or *verstehen*); in other words, in order to make sense of it the social scientist needs to interpret what the action meant for the actor and to understand his or her intentions. For Weber, rather than deduce laws, social science constructs stories, using ideal-type constructions, to explain relations between events. Ideal types are idealised models of those aspects of the social world that interest us, that are unlikely to exist in a pure form in reality, for example capitalism. The ideal type models are tools to enable the researcher to understand complex social reality. The stories have to be plausible and have causal adequacy, but we cannot really identify causes, just contributory factors. In other words, we can identify factors that when absent the phenomenon does not occur, but we cannot say one thing caused another, because the social world is complex and we cannot isolate factors. Note that there is no essential link between interpretivism and qualitative methods; many people use interpretive methods to understand statistical correlations, by trying to understand the shared meanings, cultures, individual motives that led to action.

During the 1960s and 1970s it became popular to describe qualitative research as phenomenological, meaning, in its simplest application, obtaining the actor's point of view. As a philosophy of social science, phenomenology owes a great deal to the work of Alfred Schutz (1972). But beware: the term phenomenology is used in myriad simplistic and more complex ways across the range of social science disciplines. Schutz's contribution is his understanding of how humans make sense of what we receive through our senses, the constant stream of stimuli we see, hear,

smell, feel and taste, by splitting up the world around us into categories and sub-categories and things associated with these. In other
words we identify things through a process of typification. When
we do this to the social world we end up with types of people of
whom we expect types of behaviour, and whom we distinguish
from other types, and this understanding of the social world directs
our own actions towards other people. The ideas have informed
later work by Garfinkel (1967) and ethnomethodology, Giddens'
structuration theory, and social constructionist arguments such as
Berger and Luckmann (1967). Symbolic interactionism is another
interpretive approach to the study of society which shows us how
some of the meanings individuals share are constructed in interaction, with the focus on the individual in society rather than on
the society. Other interpretive approaches focus on culture and
communities rather than individuals, *idealism* for example.

Idealism is a confusing word because it sounds as if it is about
something idealistic, or to be desired, where really it is about the
world of ideas (the ontology of ideas). Idealism is influenced by
the work of Peter Winch (1958), who said different languages
and different ways of viewing the world define different realities;
a group's concepts of the world define their experience of the
world. Understanding a society therefore involves understanding
its language, its culture and its rules. These ideas have had a big
impact on ethnography, with its historical relationship to the
study of culture and its emphasis on studying the human world in
context. But research based on Winch's ideas can take you closer
to philosophy than to social science. What one believes exists is
what exists; they are the same thing. Each culture has its own
form of life, which cannot be translated into an overarching form,
nor can they be judged or compared. The Azande have witchcraft; the British have science. We cannot say which is superior.
The problem is, of course, can a culture be translated into the
ethnographer's culture in order for us to understand it at all?

Winch's ideas can lead to an extreme form of relativism that
argues that all points of view are of equal worth and there is no
way of judging between them. The implications for ethnographic
research are clear: anyone can say anything and no one argument

can be shown to be any better than any other, since any view can only be inderstood within its own context, and that context might be the individual's own life history. But Benton and Craib argue there is no need to take the argument that far. We can say that the Azande are good at some things and the British at others, for example. Alisdair MacIntyre takes Winch's ideas and uses them to criticise modern ways of living. He is therefore using Winch to make value judgements (in Benton and Craib 2001).

Hermeneutics is an attempt to understand groups within cultures but also across cultures; in other words, the interpretation of cultures. Influenced by Gadamer (1989), a hermeneutic approach is hostile to the manipulative and instrumental nature of the natural sciences and to conventional notions of objectivity. It involves not an understanding of individual human action but rather a merging of horizons with the group you are studying, through which you begin to think like them. Knowledge is a historical process of moving between parts and wholes, cultures and individuals, history and texts.

Other criticisms of positivism argue that there is no justification for according science credence as the highest form of knowledge. Feyerabend (1981), for example, argued that 'tacit' knowledge, moral values and so on all have a role in understanding and knowledge. Others attack the idea that the study of social life can be used for social engineering, or for bringing about changes. The complex interactions of social processes mean that interventions may well have unintended consequences, they argue. (In defence, Benton and Craib (2001: 49) note several important advances social science has been able to make.)

For critical theorists, to be rational is to be critical, but the natural science approach precludes this. For some Marxists, and later for Habermas, the task of social science, rather than searching for universal laws or objective truths, is to use reason, through constant dialogue or argument, to free ourselves from oppression or domination. Feminist standpoint epistemology came out of this tradition (Harding 1986). Some feminists have argued that women's unique position in the social division of labour, coupled with their alternative, non-masculine, mode of understanding, gives them a way of understanding the world that is more in tune with an egalitarian, reciprocal and environmentally aware society (Benton and Craib 2001:152). This position takes the argument that all knowledge is contextual to the point of positing a distinctly female form of knowledge, or a feminist epistemology. Some responded with the relativist argument that there is no way of judging what is a superior route to knowledge and therefore all knowledge claims are equal (or what we choose to believe is a matter of preference). Marxist feminists have various ways of dealing with this. Nancy Hartsock, for example, would argue that the ruling groups have a necessarily distorted view of the world, while the dominated, as the actual creators of society, can best understand how the structures of domination are produced and reproduced. One direction in which critical theory has led research is towards Action Research, which 'attempts an iterative cycle between practical struggles, the formulation of research questions and the reporting of research findings in a way that informs further practical struggle' (Seale 1999: 10).

However, the relativist argument dominated a post-modern phase in the philosophy of social science (which is discussed in more detail in chapter 9). Post-modern feminists, for example, have criticised other feminists for presenting one (white, Western, middle-class) view while other categories of women have been subsumed, and in an ensuing celebration of diversity the category 'woman' has itself been deconstructed. For post-modernists such as Michel Foucault truth claims are always linked to power and domination, and for some this implies a radical relativism, where the truth of any claim to knowledge cannot be evaluated so we should abandon the attempt.

To conclude this section, interpretivists aim to understand individual human action either in terms of their daily interactions and common-sense ideas or in the context of the wider culture. But the extent to which we can understand different groups, be objective or value free, identify causal mechanisms or contributory factors and act on society to improve it, remains debatable. However, as Benton and Craib suggest, it is difficult now to imagine a social science that does not take account of meanings, and one way of getting at what people mean is through qualitative methods such as ethnography. But we don't have to stop there; we don't have to be *only* interpretive. Most contemporary ethnography is influenced by interpretivist ideas even where it is not anti-positivist or anti-naturalistic. Until the 1960s various forms of empiricism held sway in natural science with an optimistic view of science as leading us ever more to incontrovertible truths. But the anti-empiricist arguments discussed before began to have an impact. Though, for some time, the choice in social science was simply between a positivist approach, drawing on empiricist science, and an anti-positivist (or actually anti-naturalistic, because it was anti-science of any form) hermeneutic or interpretivist approach, there are non-empiricist accounts of science, generally accepting that scientific practice is socially and historically located, that can inform contemporary ethnography. 'Post-empiricist philosophers, historians and sociologists of science have emphasized the extent to which scientific knowledge-claims are shaped, even constituted by the moral values, prevailing interests or cultural contexts of their production' (Benton and Craib 2001: 73).

Realism in social science

To confuse matters somewhat, some authors talk of naturalism in an entirely different way than I have used it here, to describe research that I would label realist in that it assumes the existence of a real world that exists independently of our ideas about it. Hammersley and Atkinson (1995) equate quantitative methods with positivism and then go on to describe the 'naturalism' of early ethnographies. This naturalism says that the world should be studied in its natural state. It draws on symbolic interactionism, hermeneutics and phenomenology, they say, in an understanding of the social world as constructed and reconstructed on the basis of people's inter-actions and interpretations. The goal for the social researcher (here not necessarily a social scientist) is to learn the culture of the group we are interested in, as the culture is important for under-standing social processes. The way we learn about other cultures, however, is by immersing ourselves in the culture as strangers (Schutz 1971) and it is as strangers that we retain to some extent the objectivity, the ability to stand back and see things as an outsider, that enables us to both understand and interpret. Some of the earlier ethnographers informed by this approach did not go further than describing other cultures, since translation or explanation were not deemed necessary. Hammersley and Atkinson (1995) suggest that this 'naturalism' still appeals to some form of natural science, but, to put this in the language we have been using so far, I would say that this sort of research has always been in some ways realist as well as interpretivist. It sees the world as socially constructed and draws on relativist arguments about the role of culture yet aims to give a realist account (Hammersley and Atkinson 1995). Just as van Maanen (1988) describes some Chicago School studies as realist, Benton (1977) argues that a lot of research practice is implicitly realist and would benefit from drawing on a realist philosophy in an underlabourer role. Later constructivism and relativism have themselves been turned on the realist ethnographer, in the reflexive turn (see chapter 9); the result has been not to abandon realism but to recognise it is problematic where it fails to account for the role of interpretation and interaction between researcher and researched.

Post-positivism/subtle realism

Post-positivist philosophies, as attempts to reconcile the tension between positivism and various forms of relativism, all accept that 'although we always perceive the world from a particular viewpoint, the world acts back on us to constrain the points of view that are possible' (Seale 1999: 26). Seale says there are many examples of pragmatic, subtle realism in research literature. Indeed a researcher who describes him or herself as either constructivist, positivist and realist can often be seen to be influenced by all three traditions simultaneously. Seale even recognises post-positivist tendencies in writers influenced by the linguistic turn, for example Clifford and Marcus (1986) and Atkinson (1992). Ultimately, for Seale, research is pragmatic: a craft skill, which we learn through the experience of doing research and from an appreciation of what is good in other people's research. Seale's pragmatic and fallibilistic approach draws on Popper's falsificationism (1968) and Hammersley's later (1998) subtle realism in regarding 'truths' as provisional until sufficient evidence has been gained to demonstrate otherwise. There is heavy reliance in this position on the existence of a research community as an arbiter of the quality of qualitative research (see chapter 9 for more on Hammersley's subtle realism).

Rob Stones (1996) advocates a past-modernist realism, that comes somewhere between what he calls defeatist post-modernism and sociological modernism. The problems of modernism have been well rehearsed above in terms of the anti-empiricist or anti-positivist arguments. The key problem of post-modernism is that since all stories become as good as each other, social science lacks any critical (or other) role. Past-modernist realism 'is able to make judgements about the status of knowledge claims' and can judge which stories are more fictional than others, which are falsifiable, and which are based on evidence. It achieves this by acknowledging that what we can know about (ontology) is real yet complex, that we can only attempt to know about the social world (epistemology) through the focussed collection of evidence, and yet that anything we think we know is always limited and open to being proved false. Furthermore, all these elements – epistemology, ontology and knowledge claims – require constant reflexive elaboration.

Finally, critical realists combine a version of critical theory with a depth realism which posits the existence of phenomena, in the form of mechanisms and tendencies, beyond the surface of appearances. For critical realists, especially Bhaskar (1997 [1975]), we may want to study what people think they believe, but this may not provide us with all the answers. Social scientific understanding requires both empirical evidence and theoretical argument, and may lead to the description of social structures that differ from or even contradict those described by the actors themselves.

Conclusion

Post-positivist and subtle or critical realist philosophies are in the process of being developed; the ideas are not fixed and are open to constant debate, and we cannot hope to reconcile them for ourselves. That is not the point of philosophy, nor of the methodological debates that occur throughout this book. The role of methodological and philosophical debates is to sensitise us to issues and debates, to enable us to engage in reflexive practice in systematic rather than nebulous ways. One danger we should avoid is that of characterising ethnographic periods (or moments, Denzin and Lincoln 1994) in terms of philosophical perspectives. Traditional ethnographers were no more monolithically positivist than contemporary ethnographies are monolithically post-modern (Atkinson *et al.* 2001). We can see the influences of philosophical debates at different phases of the development of ethnography, but we would be wrong to conclude that philosophy had more than an underlabourer role. Even Malinowski's *Argonauts*, while claiming to be scientific, borrowed from literature such techniques as the presentation of 'intimate touches of native life' (Malinowski 1922: 17, Macdonald 2001), and it is common to find touches of realism in many post-modern texts.

Further reading

Mason's (1996) second chapter on planning and designing is excellent for beginning social researchers.

Some might enjoy Berg's (2004) discussion of the literature review, especially his two-card method for storing references and the up-to-date discussion of the advantages and pitfalls associated with reviewing web sites.

Bibliographic software programs (to help you store and retrieve references) are growing in popularity. Popular ones I have heard of are: EndNote, Library Master, Papyrus, Procite and Reference Manager. I would recommend asking your librarian for help and advice.

Strauss and Corbin (1998) make important use of something they call theoretical sampling, which I have chosen not to cover here. It involves sampling based on emergent concepts and is therefore crucial to Grounded Theory's iterative design (see chapter 8 here for more on grounded theory). Berg (2004) discusses convenience, quota and purposive sampling. Ritchie and Lewis (2003) also cover sampling in qualitative research in far more depth than I have done here, drawing on useful concepts such as purposive, opportunistic and snowball sampling. The same authors have a useful discussion of design in qualitative research.

Blaikie (1993) offers a useful review of applications of inductive and deductive reasoning and discusses a third version, which has been labelled abductive or retroductive reasoning.

For the philosophy of social science I can recommend nothing better than Benton and Craib (2001), but you might want help with understanding the role of philosophy for ethnography more specifically, in which case I can recommend Brewer (2000, chapter 3), Hammersley (1998), Spencer (2001), and of course the final chapter here is relevant and may help make some sense of it all. Chalmers (1999) is a helpful introduction to the philosophy of science.

3 Ethical ethnography

Qualitative research often raises ethical issues which need to be addressed and ethnography is certainly no exception. We are moving into people's daily lives, talking to them, watching them, asking them questions, thinking about what they are saying, writing about what they are saying, analysing what they are doing, and sometimes being critical about all these things. Some would consider this an inherently unethical activity. Luckily, rather than causing us to abandon research because of the ethical problems, the result of ongoing debates has generally led researchers into becoming more thoughtful, more informed, more reflexive, and more critical of their own actions, perspectives and responsibilities. As Ken Plummer (2001a) has argued, qualitative researchers are now much more likely to reflect on their own roles, positions, biases, political affiliations, expectations and justifications, on their friendships both in the field and out, sometimes in a narcissistic way but, more positively, in an awareness of the socially constructed nature of social research. Similarly, most textbooks and courses on methods now include a section or session on ethical considerations (see for example Atkinson *et al.* 2001, Hammersley 1998, Hammersley and Atkinson 1995, Pink 2001, Taylor 2002). Many organisations now have statements of ethical guidelines or principles, and some have ethics committees – researchers who oversee research. Researchers in health fields often have to submit research proposals to ethical review boards before entering the field, and some universities have their own ethical committees. I recommend you familiarise yourself with your own institution's and own discipline's guidelines.

However, some individual academics think even guidelines are an infringement of intellectual freedom, and an unnecessary constraint which only serves to protect the interests of the powerful (Douglas 1976), and so many such codes try not to be overprescriptive or normative. My own position is that we should do our best to protect the rights of all involved in the research process while accepting that at times this can be an extremely difficult balancing act which individuals will resolve in different ways. Guidelines and principles are helpful, especially in sensitising us to issues and in making us aware where consensus has been reached on a point. However, I am particularly nervous about the idea of taking things too far and stunting the development of innovative, exciting and important research because the ethical issues seem too difficult to resolve. Ethical considerations should *not* be a reason *not* to conduct research but should keep us reflexive and critical; and no decision to continue or not to continue should be taken lightly or with little information (either by a committee or by an individual).

The difficult distinction between covert and overt research

Covert research is research that has not gained the full consent, and is not conducted with the full knowledge, of the participants.
Overt research is conducted openly, with the researcher's identity being known to all participants.

Ethical considerations are arguably most likely to be overridden when research is covert: where consent has not even been sought and researchers can be accused of dishonesty and/or deception. Nevertheless, in the past, covert research was common and some very important studies came out of the tradition (Fielding 1981,

Humphreys 1970, Rosenhan 1973). Some of these studies, however, have faced staunch criticism and fears that such a betrayal of trust reflects badly on social science research more widely (Shipman 1988, Warwick 1982). Some criticisms related to harm to participants; Bryman (2001), for example, argues that it is not inconceivable that some of Humphreys' participants (if one can call them that in covert research!) might be identified against their will on publication of findings (see chapter 1). Other criticisms are about deception, dishonesty, invasion of privacy and lack of consent. Later, it was argued that covert research is only acceptable in some extreme circumstances, since it is so difficult, if not impossible, to justify (Bulmer 1982). The ISA Code of Ethics (http://www.ucm.es/info/isa/codeofethics.htm), for example, suggests: Covert research should be avoided in principle, unless it is the only method by which information can be gathered, and/ or when access to the usual sources of information is obstructed by those in power.

However, the distinction between covert and overt research is not straightforward, as is demonstrated in the debate below. If overt means being completely open about what you are researching, what you will do with the material, and who you are and how you think, there may be difficulties. Especially with long-term participant observation, it may be that people forget we are researching them (indeed we often hope they do forget and therefore 'act naturally'), or that we cannot explain fully what we are studying. Martin Hammersley (1998) explains how in one piece of research he did in a school he crossed two boundaries. Because he was not clear himself what he was studying (following an iterative-inductive approach) he was not able to be completely overt in explaining his research to the teachers and students; and because his research took him into the private world of the staff room, he says he was not able completely to respect privacy. However, he balances harm done against what was achieved and was able to conclude that no one was damaged and the findings were useful.

It is very difficult to balance the need to be open and honest with the desire to fit in and become unobtrusive. Even a social constructionist, who wants to include the researcher in her analysis of interaction, is unlikely to want to keep reminding people of her role and updating them as to the development of her 'grounded theory'. As our discussion below demonstrates, some researchers get rather concerned about the extent to which they are being dishonest with research participants when 'you can't tell everyone everything all the time'. But Rubin and Rubin (1995: 98) argue that 'honesty does not require complete revelation . . . You are not lying if you fail to respond to blatant racism, anti-Semitism or sexism', for example. And Punch (1986: 37) concludes that in open, public settings negotiating access from everyone would be impractical and futile, as well as completely undermining the behaviour you wish to observe.

Consent

One of the most difficult issues is that of consent. Most guidelines will suggest that the researcher should gain full, informed and meaningful consent for the research from the participants. You should explain what you are doing and why, and what will happen to any material you collect. There are a few points to raise here. You may not want to explain all about your research as this may affect the way in which the participants act in certain situations. Even when you have explained all about your research, people can still be confused or not really understand what you mean by certain terms. My participants in Spain, for example, did not always understand what was meant when I said I was doing a PhD. Some people generally find understanding more difficult than others, based on their age, life experiences and so on. Children are a special case in that they are likely to view the researcher as a person of authority and feel compelled to participate. If you are going to archive the data for secondary use, which I discuss more fully below, participants might not realise that consent means others can use the data. Even if they do understand this, how can one actually predict how subsequent researchers will use archived data? You may not even be sure yourself at this stage what publications you will produce or how your analyses will turn out. Consent can be especially difficult in long-term research where people forget you are researching them and that they have given prior consent. Finally, people might give consent based on false hopes (that you might do some good for them or for the wider community, for example).

Ultimately, there are no easy answers, but ethics is about trying to ensure that you cause as little pain or harm as possible and try to be aware of your effects on the participants and on your data. Research can give rise to conflicting emotions: participants might enjoy taking part or might feel you have intruded into their lives for no good reason, feeling confused or vulnerable after you have left. Sometimes the best you can do is to reconfirm consent and its limits as you go along, especially at times when participants are sharing intimate or private details with you, and as your research questions change you can reconfirm again where necessary.

Disclosure

Linked to the issue of consent is that of disclosure. If you have explained to participants exactly what the research is about, should you then disclose exactly what you will do with it? That is to say, should they have access to transcripts of interviews, to field notes and to notes around interviews that specifically involve them? Ideally the answer should be yes, but field notes should only be shared if you are sure they are fully anonymised, which can be very difficult. As a feminist, Liz Kelly (1988), researching women's experience of sexual violence, believed it was important to return transcripts to her participants so that joint interpretations of the data could take place. Others believe that research should be a two-way process, with participants having full control over what is produced. Participatory Action Research, for example, invites participants to participate in the research from design through data collection and analysis right through to the practical application of findings. Though it goes by various names, it has been around since the 1960s and has the advantage of dealing with the problem of wondering if we can ever do enough for our research participants in exchange for what they have done for us (Whyte 1993). Partici-patory research is considered particularly important in the field of health, especially because of the gap that often exists, especially in 'majority world' settings, between professional and community conceptions of health and illness (de Koning and Martin 1996).

But this brings me to a further point concerning the balance of commitments. It may be that you want to produce an article, paper or argument that your research participants do not agree with. If your epistemological position is that people involved in the culture are not always the best people to tell you about it, for example in some critical realist research, then sharing data with them is problematic. Who has the rights in this kind of situation, the researcher or the participant? In the end I cannot think of a good reason for keeping the results from participants if they ask to see them, but do not believe you always have to offer. They don't have to agree with you and their response might be very interesting to you and your research. The only reason for not disclosing things is if you are worried about breaking confidences or risking anonymity. Some people would go so far as to say you should always give something back.

Who is in control?

Some feminist authors have argued that the balance of power in research is always tipped in favour of the researcher (McRobbie 1982, Ribbens 1989, Stanley and Wise 1983) but Cotterill and Letherby (1993) respond that it does not have to be that way and attempt to address the problem through reflexivity and auto-biography. You are in a position of being able to exploit people: by making them feel they should respond; by taking from them and giving nothing in return; by extracting painful admissions they might rather not give; by causing upset and then not helping them deal with it; by refusing to explain or being deceitful about what you are doing; or by doing whatever you want with the findings. Generally, we should try to ensure that we are not exploiting people for our own ends. We can do this by asking how the research benefits the participants. But sometimes the benefits of our research will be for another group altogether. (Indeed, we may learn about exploitation from our participants!) Here we are balancing the needs of research against the private needs of participants, and may have to accept that their own needs may not be served, although this is not to say we can condone personal harm.

Confidentiality

Most guidelines insist that we offer confidentiality and anonymity, and that we respect the privacy of those we are researching. This is not always simple. Ensuring confidentiality by changing names, places or other hints at identity can get quite complicated. What about your field notes; how secure are they? How can they be anonymised, and will you do this as you go along or at the end? If you do it as you go along it can get quite confusing for you to remember who and what you are talking about. Also, you should think about your responsibility to others, like office cleaners or members of your family, who might find sensitive material on your desk! These issues are, of course, particularly acute in auto/biographical work (Harrison and Lyon 1993).

The distinction between confidentiality and anonymity in most ethical discussions is unclear. An anonymous study is one in which nobody, not even the researcher, can identify who provided the data. Clearly this is impossible in ethnographic research, but it may be that the ethnographer wishes to retain anonymity for her participants in the writing and archiving of data. Confidentiality means ensuring that what you hear goes no further (or is not attributed to anyone who can be identified). Respecting participants' confidentiality and right to privacy may mean anonymity, but sometimes we have to juggle that against some participants' desire to be recognised. Indeed some participants have been unhappy not to be mentioned in ethnographies (Grinyer 2002). Generally, we should consider what people tell us is confidential, in other words between the participant and the researcher and anyone else who was present, and should be careful not to attribute words or actions to the speaker/actor unless we are clear they are happy to have them attributed.

There is an increasing interest, for UK and US researchers, in the potential of archived qualitative data for secondary analysis. Such storage and reuse of ethnographic data raise myriad ethical, practical and philosophical issues (Heaton 1998, Mauthner, Parry and Backett-Milburn 1998, Parry and Mauthner 2004). If data are to be archived, how can you ensure they will remain confidential? Think about the uses people might make of films and photographs you might collect. The UK qualitative data archive (at www.esds.ac.uk) asks that you gain written consent where possible for interviews at least, and they have downloadable forms you can use for this purpose, but asking people to sign a consent form can stilt a conversation and make people feel wary. They are reminded that they are respondents rather than participants. And, as Rubin and Rubin (1995) point out, you may even be endangering them: how can they later deny that they ever spoke to you, should they need to?

Balancing rights and commitments

Much of the debate around ethics is about balancing the rights of one group against those of another, including yourself! You may have to balance commitments – to write a PhD, to produce a report for those who are funding you – with respecting the privacy of informants, for example. We then have to ask in whose interest it is that we say what we say. What effect might it have? It is not always a simple matter of discovering the truth. What we find will depend on how and where we look, and on who ultimately we think the research is for. Frederick was researching the experiences of men who stayed home to care for their children while their partners went out to work. His feminist perspective was that enabling men to experience the caring role in a positive way is important. But as time went along he started to notice some negative effects of male primary care giving. This caused a dilemma for Frederick. On the one hand, he did not want to report negative effects in case this was interpreted to mean that men should not do the caring, yet he wanted to portray a balanced viewpoint. He had to write his report with these demands to be faithful to his findings as well as his perspective carefully balanced.

You may study small powerless groups, or you may be studying large organisations or powerful experts. Do you afford them equal courtesy, or is it your job to expose exploitation or injustice? If so, where does this leave your responsibility to your participants who have been so kind as to help you? Where do we *respect privacy* and where do we decide it is in the interest of others that we do not? Where does showing such respect mean we give up on our work? It is deemed important to respect people's privacy, but what if the group or person is hurting another? This leads us to ask questions like: how important is our research? Who is it for? Some of these issues are resolved through the route of philosophy and when thinking about our epistemological position (see chapter 2); most, however, have to be resolved on a case by case basis involving constant awareness and reflexivity (Punch 1986). Below I will discuss some particular responsibilities you have and how these have to be balanced against those of others.

Responsibility to participants. Of course our first responsibility is to our research participants. Most of the discussion above is about honesty towards, and avoiding harm for, participants; about gaining their informed consent for the research; and about their rights within the research process. Overall, our first concern should be that what we do is justified, and should cause no harm. The UK Economic and Social Research Council when giving funds for research insists that the research should not 'give rise to distress or annoyance to individuals', and asks researchers to ensure honesty, confidentiality, independence and impartiality (www.esrc.ac.uk). I am not sure we could ever know for certain what effects our research had on participants, but we must attempt to avoid known harm.

Policy research. Willis and Trondman (2000) argue that ethnography should be critical. Should our work be directed towards policy issues? Should academic work be linked with wider projects and outcomes? Should our research participants be encouraged to become agents in their own politics? Should we at least try to circulate knowledge about different forms of life? There are diverse positions on this; you may want to work out your own.

Risky situations. The point to make here is that harm cuts both ways. In other words, it is not only the research participants who may need protection from harm. You should avoid risky situations for yourself as researcher and others you are working with. When Miles and Huberman (1994: 292) wrote a report that seemed to be threatening someone's key interest they were threatened with litigation and with threats to intervene with their funding agency. But they cite an even more dramatic story of a *New York Times* reporter who asked a drug dealer if he felt comfortable talking frankly. To which the dealer responded, 'Sure. If I don't like what you write, I'll kill you.' Perhaps this is a little extreme, but there are all sorts of ways we can become involved in risky situations. One student researching attitudes to, and fear of, crime on a housing estate in north-east Scotland was told about various criminal activities and then subsequently became afraid of how such information might compromise her future safety.

Responsibilities to and for assistants and key informants. If you hire or use a research participant to help you gather information, you have the responsibility to ensure that this does not put that person in an awkward position in relation to other participants. On the other hand, you must ask whether you can trust what you are told, and whether you are thus abusing the privilege (are you gaining information about people who have not given you access?). If you hire research assistants, think about their own careers, and their future research. You should ensure they are sufficiently trained and you do not put them in awkward, dangerous or upsetting situations.

Responsibilities to funders, sponsors, gatekeepers who have given access. You do have responsibility to funders, sponsors, gatekeepers who have given access, but it can be difficult balancing their rights against others, especially if your research has a wide focus and you want to research things not in your original design, or if you have findings that do not suit those who have enabled access directly or indirectly. Maybe these people think what you are doing is irrelevant, or worse, they may simply disagree with your findings. If you are funded by a government agency or a private company they may well have their own agenda. However, as a rule of thumb, it is not a good idea to accept constraints on your research, publication or dissemination where it will hinder honest research or where your integrity is threatened.

Responsibilities to colleagues and future research. You have responsibility to other researchers in your field and other ethnographers. Colleagues may have to research somewhere after you, so think about how you might have closed the field off for other researchers if you upset anyone or abuse a participant's willingness to help. People can be swamped with researchers, become bored or wary of consequences, and stop being helpful. You need to think about your behaviour in the field as well as how what you publish might impede future research in the area. Finally, you have the responsibility not to publish untruths or misrepresentations. You have the responsibility not to pretend to be able to do a piece of research for which you are not qualified, or to present results you cannot support.

Other issues

There are other issues that do not fit under the headings above. Sometimes what you research is simply seen as unethical, as in the case of Sarah Pink (2001), whose study of women bullfighters was seen by some colleagues as unethical simply because they considered bullfighting itself unethical and her unethical for seeming to support it by going to bullfights (and even enjoying them!). Rubin and Rubin (1995) note that ethical considerations are especially difficult with an iterative research design. Review boards often ask you to specify what you will ask of whom and why, but in iterative research you cannot always predict the answers to these questions. In the end, if the review board will allow it, the best a researcher can do is keep ethical considerations in mind throughout the research instead of treating them as something that can be resolved before you begin.

An ethics group discussion

Because ethical issues are a matter for debate and constant argument, I decided the best and most interesting way to explore some of the issues would be to conduct a debate and present some of the themes from it. The following discussion is transcribed (not verbatim) from a debate I had with some of the postgraduate students in my department. We did not resolve the dilemmas we discussed, but did conclude that ethical issues are complex and can only be resolved on a case by case basis, and individual interpretation of basic guidelines. We began with a discussion about whether I was exploiting their position as students in using them to help me with my book (and I think we concluded that they did not feel exploited) and a discussion about whether or not they should be anonymous. They felt they could talk more freely and openly if they were anonymous, so the names I have used are not the real names of the students and some details of their projects have been withheld. At the time of the discussion, Jane was in the middle of a feminist study in an organisation, John was doing participant observation exploring workplace interaction in an organisation, and Emma was planning ethnographic research within a religious community. Having told the students to feel free to raise issues themselves as and when they wanted to, I began with a question.

K: Can being covert ever be justified?
E: Yes. Well first of all I don't think there's a clear cut between covert and overt. I don't think you can neatly box them off like that. And, I think you have to consider issues like access. I think covert access is probably more difficult to justify than covert participant observation but I would argue that nearly all participant observation is covert to a greater or lesser extent, in my own experience.
Jo: Is that because you don't embellish, fully, to the participants, what you are doing?
E: Yes, and because you are in a situation where, if you are in a group with thirty or forty people, unless it's some kind of meet-

ing where somebody can stand up and say at the beginning, well this person is doing some research, you can't tell all those people what you are doing. And anyway, you don't tell everybody everything all the time in normal life, you are always hiding things about yourself, about your relationships, so, while you're not being completely honest . . .

K: So being overt would involve telling everybody about yourself?

E: Yeah, well, I think I see it as a matter of honesty rather than overt/covert.

J: I think the way that you present your project is always important, especially if it has specifically political dimensions, so for example if it is a feminist project you might present it as having something to do with gender, so, you know, you're never going to tell everybody everything about, well it wouldn't be possible anyway.

Jo: Why would you tell everybody everything anyway? Why would a research participant want to know everything? If you keep reminding the participant all the time of your identity then your presence is always there. You are reminding them that you are a researcher and you are probably going to get some sort of reactivity to that.

K: Should we draw some bottom line then, where we say, obviously in a public place we can't tell everybody, but where we do meet people and talk to them and ask them questions we should tell them on some level what we are doing?

Jo: I think so, even just for pragmatic reasons. I mean if you are covert then taking notes is such a problem. I mean, someone like Jason Ditton, when he did his study in the bakery, I mean he had to keep taking toilet breaks and eventually his act got blown and had to reveal his identity. So I think the covert is very difficult to pull off over a long period of time – not to mention draining.

E: Yes.

Jo: It's more stress on the researcher as well.

K: But even in a situation where taking notes is easy would you still want to tell people what you are doing?

J: Yes, because then it's an issue about misleading people. I mean it's one thing just not telling everyone everything and another thing explicitly misleading people. I mean, I hope common sense would help you. Mind you, *I* think you can be quite explicit about what you are doing, and I think there is an argument for doing that. If you are doing a feminist project, for example, I mean going out and telling people it is a feminist project and not trying to disguise it in some way that would make it more acceptable.

K: I guess this is partly an issue of not deceiving people and partly about not affecting the outcome. I mean too much of you saying, 'well I believe this and I believe that' might have an effect.

Jo: Yes, I mean people do say things to make you happy to a certain extent, you know, what you want to hear.

K: Or they might hide embarrassing opinions or things they are not sure how you will react to.

J: I think I would argue for a social constructionist stance. I mean the whole argument that you are always going to be having an effect anyway, you're always going to be coming from some political, or some perspective anyway, so the only thing you can do is be up front about that and try to sort of engage with it reflexively, and think about how who you are affects your setting. Rather than trying to pretend you are value-neutral.

E: The trouble is loads of issues overlap here don't they? We are talking about being covert or overt, about deception and honesty.

K: But every time we talk about ethics this happens doesn't it? Everything gets all tangled up together. I mean, my next question was 'can you ever really be overt in participant observation?' But we already answered that didn't we?

J: Well, I had some experience of that. I decided to be overt and I wished I hadn't, because it made it just, really stressful, it was quite unnecessary. I don't think I'll be using my notes from these sessions I went to that much anyway. It more acted as background and sort of contextual information, and it just made me stand out like a sore thumb and I don't think it would have been particularly unethical just to have said, I mean not to have done what I did and stand up at the beginning of every meeting I went to and say 'I'm doing this project and this is what it's about and I may be using what people say' and so on and 'has anybody got any objections?', because it became quite ridiculous after about three meetings. I don't think it was necessary. I could have just said I was a researcher.

E: I have terribly difficult decisions about whether I should tell the organisation I am studying or whether I should just go in as a member of the public. I'm struggling with this at the moment. I mean I could be overt when it comes to access but then covert when it comes to daily routines.

K: Yes, that means telling those in charge but not the general public I suppose.

Jo: It depends on the type of research you are doing, whether you are doing investigative research or more empathetic style research. I mean, I think if you are doing investigative research then being overt is very difficult. I suppose I'm making a journalistic distinction between trying to uncover something, like structures of power, and going in and studying vulnerable groups like children and trying to understand their point of view. So, it has something to do with your role, I think. Covert is usually linked to investigative journalism type of research that's trying to expose something that's hidden or is deviant, whereas I think empathy is used for a group that is more powerless, or has stigma attached to it.

J: I think it has something to do with your research population and their level of empowerment. Maybe you feel better justifying covert research of a powerful group than you would going in and exploiting the disempowered.

Jo: Jack Douglas argues that, in his sort of anything-goes mentality, that at the far end of the spectrum powerful groups have got loads of ways of protecting that power so you have to go in as a covert investigative journalist so as to expose them. Because otherwise you have to go through all these channels of access and they've obviously got all sort of ways of denying entry.

Whereas powerless groups have got less means to protect them-selves.

K: I think you can stand back as well as empathise though, don't you?

J: Yes, but there's ethical issues there as well, this whole idea of faking empathy. The participant could come out of an interview thinking 'oh well, they agreed with everything I said, and left me completely unchallenged' and then you write something else.

K: Yes, but I don't think you have to agree with everything some-one says in order to empathise. I think you can very often disagree with someone in a way that still allows them their voice. I mean, you can say, 'I'm not sure if that is where I am coming from but right now what I am trying to understand is your point of view.' I mean, what you are doing, John, is obviously quite critical at times. How do you be both overt and critical?

Jo: You see, this is where I am getting the role tension Jane is speak-ing about really. I mean on the one hand I am going in and studying individuals whose job it is to watch people. Watching people has always to some extent been a powerful thing to do, I mean, powerful groups have always watched over the weaker groups. So, in a sense I am going in there to critically observe how the watchers use technology, whether they use it fairly, who is watched and why. But at the same time these people are quite constrained in that they work long hours, and get paid very little and they are in a very small room, and their job is to watch so many things at once. So, on one hand I can see why there might be some informal dynamics in the room, such as playing with the technology and games and time wasting and such, but on the other hand, it is a pretty powerful technol-ogy and it is sort of abusing a system, or money, that could be used elsewhere.

K: Do you tell them that you see what they are doing as some sort of abuse of power?

Jo: No, and that's one of the problems. I sort of play the game as it were. I mean, I am not playing myself, I am not being myself, I am trying to be one of them.

J: But you can't always go around, in daily life, disagreeing with people or challenging them, so really what you are doing is no different to normal life in some ways. I guess colluding with a viewpoint that you don't really agree with is problematic but,

Jo: Studies of football hooliganism and other deviant sub-groups are notorious aren't they for participant observers having to decide whether to take part in deviant acts. For example, if people are being racist or doing something criminal do you join in, or what? I mean if you are covert you have to take part really don't you? But if you are overt how will it go down if you say 'look I just don't agree with this, this is just not on'?

J: Well I suppose in that kind of situation people would say the means justify the ends, kind of thing.

E: You often have to make your mind up on the ground don't you?

K: Yes, I guess this is why many ethical guidelines say things like 'to an extent' or 'within limits', so that they are not putting down hard and fast rules but asking us to think about things.

Jo: But that is so blurred, isn't it?

K: But I think most professional ethical guidelines will draw the line and say they draw the limit at where you have to break the law, for example.

J: I think with many of these studies the problems are resolved when you see what the end product is.

K: So you could break the law, or thump someone?

E: No, you see I couldn't do that, not even for research. I'm not sure I could even keep quiet if I saw someone hitting someone for example.

J: But I don't think you should engage in research that might put you in that kind of situation, unless the end product is going to be something that's really going to justify it. So it would have to be something pretty amazing. You do read of some research, where you wonder what was gained from it and how they can justify it.

K: Would you say, then, that unless something very novel or different or ground-breaking might come from it, that you would always rather be as overt as possible and as legal as possible, and as moral as possible?

J: Yes, but it's not just about being new and novel, it's about the research having some benefit for the group I think.

K: So, could we justify Laud Humphreys' research then?

Jo: I think you could justify it. It challenged stereotypes.

J: But some people would say that you shouldn't do research unless it actually benefited the actual group you are studying, and I am thinking more and more along those lines.

K: Personally I think I can say there are certain things I would not do and cannot imagine justifying, for example taking drugs, breaking the law, hitting someone. I cannot think of research projects where me doing these things could be necessary, and I would not do it. Similarly, while participant observation in a public place like a hospital means you can't go around telling everyone who comes and goes what you are doing exactly, on the other hand I cannot imagine working alongside a group in a shop, for example, getting to know people, getting them to confide in me, befriending them, and not telling them what I was doing. So, to me there are lines I would want to draw, and I think the ethical guidelines of most groups draw lines similar to this. Let's move onto another question. How do we ensure consent?

E: You can't (laughs).

Jo: Oh dear, this is very difficult, what precisely constitutes informed consent?

E: I don't think absolutely, but you can do the best you can.

J: I think you should always explain the study as much as you can and then how their contribution will contribute, and then, where you can, get them to sign a form.

E: See, I think if you go through all this you would never do any research. You would be so busy filling in forms, and filing and pen pushing, you wouldn't do anything.

K: Mmm. It doesn't actually take that long, but the problem for me is more one of changing the dynamic of the relationship. It seems so formal to ask people to sign forms, when you have spent time asking people to chat about their lives and being informal, and putting them at their ease and then you say 'can you just sign this to agree to the research'.

J: I did it with my interviews.

E: Do people always understand what they are signing?

K: Well people often don't understand about the world of research at all, so if you say 'this might be archived so that future researchers can use the data', they won't really know what that means in practice.

J: For mine it has served a function in that it has been an opportunity to explain my research more and the contribution they will make.

Jo: I personally don't think, in interviewing, consent in that sense is that necessary. I've seen too many researchers bogged down with administrative details, with moral dilemmas, transcribing everything, and so on. I think the interview is better seen as a chat, as a conversation, where you gather data and it doesn't have to be transcribed, just important things taken from it.

J: Do you offer back transcripts to your participants?

K: Yes, I offer anything: tapes, transcripts, to see what I have written, and so on, but no one has said they want to. Well, they like to see the report or the book, or whatever, but I can't remember anyone asking to see the transcripts. They say things like, 'no don't worry about it, that's fine' and are happy to chat.

J: That's interesting. I've had a completely different experience. I have had a lot of people ask to see transcripts and want to follow up on it.

E: But I think that is the nature of your research topic Jane, and the people you are researching and how you've gone about it. You rely more on interviews than participant observation and your interviews are quite formal in some ways.

K: It does seem to vary with the actual topic you are studying.

J: Well, interestingly, giving back transcripts raises other ethical issues. Some people feel obligated to ask for their transcript back and things like that, when they really don't want to. I did feel that some people felt they ought to take an interest and read through and comment and stuff, and the other thing is retraumatising people. When you are doing really sensitive stuff and raising sensitive, traumatising issues in an interview, then there you are going back and saying 'would you like to go over that all over again'! I mean, one woman I asked if she wanted to look at the transcript said she'd rather not because it just opens old wounds all over again.

K: Isn't it rather unethical to be interviewing people on such sensitive topics that you open up old wounds in the first place, though?

Jo: Well, that is causing psychological harm to participants isn't it? And that is something you should try to avoid.

K: Yes, I mean if you start asking people questions about their lives that they had never asked themselves before.

Jo: Yes, how does that leave them? Although some people say it's quite therapeutic to talk to someone, like to a researcher.

J: I've had a few people say that to me, that they found it very beneficial actually, so there is a flip side to that. But.

Jo: Yeah, and if we didn't study people like that we would have, well it limits rich social knowledge of the social world.

J: No, that's right. And the alternative stance is quite paternalistic, you know, that's more problematic isn't it?

K: I don't know. It goes back to consent doesn't it? I mean, when you say you are going to interview people and ask their consent do they know you are going to raise issues that might disturb them? I mean, is that what they are agreeing to?

J: Yes, well one thing I wish I had done is show people the topic guide before hand, so that they know what sorts of topics will come up.

Jo: It is interesting that, actually, we are focussing on qualitative research aren't we? But there are problems with quantitative research too, aren't there? I mean, I won't go into them but, its not just qualitative research that raises ethical issues.

K: That's true.

J: One key thing seems to be, we are asking can research be ethical, and there are all sorts of problems involved, and maybe all you can really do is minimise harm as much as possible.

Jo: That's true, but how can you predict harm? I mean you can't know how your findings will be used can you, or to what ends.

E: No, but you can take measures to make sure that it is not used in harmful ways.

K: I think harm is a good way to think about it, to ask yourself whether you are hurting anyone.

J: Yes, but others would say it is only justified if you are benefiting someone.

Jo: One thing I worry about is when you get consent from a gate-keeper but not from the actual participants. I mean, you can go to the chief police officer for example, and ask 'can I study in this place', and they can say 'yes', and off you go. But you haven't really asked the participants as well.

J: No, but you can ask them as well.

Jo: But why should one bother? Once they've been accepted formally, why should one inform everyone else?

E: Well, one could try to balance the different options. On the one hand you ask 'why *should* I tell them?' Well because it's in the interest of informed consent, because I'm being open about what I'm doing. And on the other hand you might ask, 'why *shouldn't* I tell them?' Well because it will affect their behaviour too much, because I won't get the information I need, and so on.

K: Yes, but you might say I don't need to tell everyone what I'm doing, because I'm only doing what I do in everyday life, but what about when you start to build a friendship with someone? That can feel pretty uncomfortable.

J: Um, I had something a bit like that and I ended up trying to avoid personal encounters.

E: Why is it a problem? Do you feel you are exploiting them?

K: It makes you feel uncomfortable and I'm not sure why. Maybe you feel it's alright to write about someone you don't know very well.

J: Maybe it's to do with trust. You are hoping people will grow to trust you, but if you make a friend of them you are maybe getting them to open up more than they might. The boundaries get so blurred don't they?

E: There was that case in Finch and Mason, where one of them interviewed clergymen's wives. Apparently she was a clergyman's wife, and she interviewed other clergymen's wives and because she was in the same, occupied the same social world that they did, she found they opened up more to her, so she crossed that boundary and had to deal with that. And then, is that personal information just for you as a friend or is it for you as a researcher?

J: There's no clear boundary is there?

K: Let's have another question. How do we deal with people seeing us as an authority figure?

Jo: Ha! I think that depends on who you are and how you present yourself. I can't see people seeing me like that. But maybe for someone middle aged and better dressed, that could be a problem, but I tend to go in there as, you know, very informal, and I'm young.

E: I don't think anyone has ever seen me as an authority figure!

K: I can say from experience that it becomes more of a problem as you go through your career. Now people know that I am ten years from my PhD, and it's kind of awe-inspiring to some people, and even though I think personally I am quite informal, people have sometimes decided 'that's a person who has a PhD' and I guess, that kind of power can be exploitative.

Jo: Yes, I can see that.

J: I had this in two ways. If you are researching political activism you often get people telling you their opinions and then they started to ask what I think, and my opinion and such. But there is also a problem if people see you as being high status and therefore expect a lot of you in terms of acting on what they tell you. You know, they think you can change things.

K: That's interesting. It raises the question of our responsibility to actually do something with our research. Because you are getting all these people to agree to you researching them, or you're not in some cases, and surely we have some responsibility to do something with the findings.

J: Yes, and sometimes when you set out you try to be convincing that your research is worthwhile and then you find the most you can do is publish it, if that!

E: You do take a lot of liberties, don't you? And maybe people who don't do research don't feel it's so important as we do. I think we sometimes end up talking ourselves into thinking our research is ethical if we want to do it, though.

J and Jo: Yes, yeah.

E: But, I do think people like being researched mostly.

Jo: Oh, yes, I think people like talking to you.

E: But if someone asked me I don't think I would agree (laughs).

K: What do we all think of ethical committees?

Jo: Well I have to say it would be much better if there were some committee that you could go to and talk things over with and discuss these dilemmas. Cos these ethical guidelines are so flimsy, and everything is a matter of debate isn't it? You can't always sort it out on your own.

E: But some committees act as gatekeepers and end up protecting the powerful groups' interests and making sure what they think is important gets researched and other stuff doesn't. They are too powerful.

Jo: Yes but I'm not talking about these committees being gate-keepers and making decisions for you. I think something like a panel would work better, some group of peers you could, as I say, discuss the dilemmas with. To me that's what an ethics committee should be.

K: Well, that's a good point to end on. Thank you ever so much. Are there any other issues that I have left out that you want to raise?

Jo: No, I think we covered most things, didn't we?

E: Yes, access was the big dilemma for me; whether to be covert or overt at the point of access, but I still don't know.

Jo: Yes, we haven't really resolved my dilemma about being critical of the participants, but that's the trouble with ethics discussions isn't it?

K: Yes, unless they are specifically addressing a single issue, it's very difficult to draw firm conclusions.

Summary

This chapter has explored the myriad ethical considerations raised while conducting ethnographic research. Ongoing ethical debates have led to researchers being increasingly reflexive and critical but also informed about their ethical practices. The extent to which we are, or can be, open and honest about our research, gain fully informed consent from participants, disclose what we are studying and producing, respect confidentiality and avoid exploitation raises dilemmas for every ethnographer. In the end we have to attempt to balance competing rights and responsibilities for different groups and individuals, including ourselves. This chapter concludes with a debate demonstrating that while we may be able to establish ethical guidelines for ethnography the interpretation of these for each case will always be complicated.

Further reading

Virginia Morrow and Martin Richards (1996) provide a much-needed overview of ethical issues related to social research with children, concluding with some practical and methodological considerations.

The role of a research ethics committee is explored on the web site of the UK qualitative data archive (at www.esds.ac.uk). This same site has a discussion of ethical issues in relation to children, helps with legal issues associated with research, and has references to lots of further reading.

Codes or Statements of Ethical Practice. The International Sociological Association Code of Ethics can be found at http://www.ucm.es/info/isa/codeofethics.htm. The British Sociological Association Statement of Ethical Practice can be found at http://www.britsoc.org.uk/about/ethic.htm (first published in 1992). The Ethical Statements of the American Sociological Association and American Anthropological Association can be found, with several further resources cited, on their web sites at www.asanet.org and www.aaanet.org.

Bryman (2001) introduces various ethical stances: Bulmer's (1982) and Eriksen's (1967) universalist approach that argues that ethical principles are universal and determinate; Punch's (1986 and 1994) situational ethics, that says ethical considerations need to be decided on a case by case basis; and Douglas' (1976) 'anything goes' approach that is able to justify investigative, covert research.

Laud Humphreys' (1970) research on homosexual behaviour in men's public toilets and Warwick's (1982) response provide material for an interesting discussion of ethics in context. Adler (1985) also provides material for an interesting discussion, especially about covert research and risky situations; and Estroff (1981) has interesting material for a debate about how far one should take the participant role.

A discussion about archiving and secondary analysis of qualitative data is an interesting way to frame ethical discussions, especially around confidentiality. Some are covered in Corti, Foster and Thompson (1995) but also see Parry and Mauthner (2004).

4 Participating and observing

Ethnographic research is a special methodology that suggests we learn about people's lives (or aspects of their lives) from their own perspective and from within the context of their own lived experience. This involves not only talking to them and asking questions (as we do in surveys and interviews) but also learning from them by observing them, participating in their lives, and asking questions that relate to the daily life experience as we have seen and experienced it. It involves doing this over time, taking mental and actual notes as we go along, and collecting other relevant data through interviews (or talk) and the collection of artefacts, statistics and whatever else may be relevant. The main method of ethnography is known as participant observation, and it is very distinctive as a method. This chapter considers what participant observation actually consists of, then goes on to look at participant observation as a concept and an oxymoron.

Key elements of participant observation we will explore here are gaining access, taking time, learning the language, participation and observation, and taking notes. Of course, talking to people, in groups and individually, and collecting other forms of data are also crucial elements of participant observation, and these will be covered fully in chapters 5, 6 and 7.

Access

First of all, in order to do participant observation, you have to gain access to a group. It may be that you already have access, that you are already part of the group you wish to study. When Michael wanted to study young people's drug cultures (chapter 1) he was already a member of a group of young people who regularly smoked cannabis, and used this as a starting point. Similarly, Gail, who researched men's friendships, decided to do participant observation within her own friendship circle. At the other extreme, others will often set off to distant places to do ethnographic research amongst people who are completely unknown to them. It can be daunting to ask a group, 'Can I come along to your meetings, spend time in your school, live alongside you?' You can both feel and appear very strange, the early stages especially 'filled with the mixture of elation, depression, missteps, and drudgery that any anthropologist will recognize' (Scott 1985: xviii). People generally do not understand the concept of participant observation; it sounds awfully like spying and can feel like cold calling (Rock 2001). However, if we do not ask for permission and do covert research, we are open to all sorts of criticism, as discussed in chapter 3. Of course, not everyone is granted access to the group they want to join, and if the answer is no you may have to accept that. Often, however, you can explain what you want to do and why, and if you have a good reason for doing the study people are usually happy to participate. But issues of access are not only a matter of getting people to agree or not. In fact, generally, I, my students and colleagues have found it surprisingly easy to gain access in terms of someone agreeing to your presence. People often do not mind you hanging around with them and asking them questions. Most people are flattered by your interest in them. There are other reasons why access can be difficult.

Access can be difficult because of some of your own personal attributes. I have had students ask how to get access to some very difficult groups: one Nigerian man wanted to research a white youth gang. He was interested in youth sub-cultures and wanted to compare a white and a black gang. Access to the black gang would be difficult enough, but access to the white gang was not simply a matter of asking if he could join them. Joining in, participating, becoming part of a group in a way that they get used to you and forget you are there is not so easy when the one thing that sets the group apart from other groups is skin colour. The student eventually gave up. When Stephen Moore (2000) decided to undertake ethnographic research with youths who 'hang around' street corners, he did not think he would have much luck accessing rural youths himself and so employed younger, 'cool' researchers to do the fieldwork. There will always be some places you just cannot access because of your own attributes; your age, sex, colour or even social class may be such a bar that access is impossible. It would be very difficult for me as a middle-aged woman, for example, to do ethnographic research of teenagers' lifestyles in Spain, although I have often thought it would be interesting. On the other hand, difference can of course be used to your own advantage when you are trying to see things from the perspective of the stranger (see below).

It may be that what you want to know about and what you want to research is too uncomfortable for your respondents to face, or your own prejudices or biases may come across too clearly for the respondents to feel they can trust you. Another student wanted access to social services teams to find out about prejudice in allocation of resources. He was finding it difficult to get access, and when I spoke to him at length about it I could tell that he had already decided that there was racial prejudice in the allocation of resources, and his prior opinions were probably coming out when he asked for access.

Those things mentioned above are about the researcher, but there may be things about the setting itself that make access difficult or impossible. Carol wanted to participate and observe in doctor/patient consultations but was not granted access to such private meetings (the extent to which she would participate would of course be minimal, which we will discuss more below).

One decision that has to be made is the extent to which you will be covert about what you are doing (see chapter 3). Overt research means openly explaining your research to your participants, its purpose, who it is for, and what will happen to the findings. It means being open. Covert research is undercover, conducted without the participants' knowledge or without full awareness of your intentions. Patricia Adler's (1985) research in a drug dealing community involved juggling covert and overt roles; a balancing act that was both difficult and dangerous. Chapter 3 argued that no one should do covert research without very good reason, for ethical reasons. However, it was also noted that participant observation can be like spying and there are always ethical problems. In my own research I have usually allowed people to forget I was researching them. Once we realise that the purpose of participant observation is to live amongst the group in their natural setting we also realise we want to upset that setting as little as possible, and in order to do this we hope they will forget about us being there and act naturally. So, gaining access will usually involve explaining about our research overtly and then settling into a semi-overt role, where participants know what we are doing but do not always have it in the forefront of their minds.

Access can be overt or covert, or a combination of both: Jason Ditton's (1977) ethnography of part-time crime

Jason Ditton (1977) did research amongst staff working in a bakery. He was interested in fiddling and pilferage and how ordinary people could find themselves taking part in petty theft. He began covertly, watching people and taking notes in a setting to which he had already gained access, but eventually he became overt, explaining to the management and the bakery staff what he was doing. Being overt actually got him better access than being covert as he was able to ask people more questions and ask to work with different groups of people.

Access is not something you do once, and then you are in. It has to be negotiated all along to different groups, different people, different topics

My research for the past ten years has been on various aspects of life of British and other Northern European migrants in Spain. When I conducted research in Spain the first time, I spent over a year there living and working alongside British people. My children went to Spanish school and my partner worked in the British community doing manual labour. Access had to be negotiated as we went along, with different groups. For example, I wanted to access a group of women whose husbands were all in prison. I knew they met in a bar, and so I kept going along to the same bar every week until they got used to me being there, felt comfortable to say more and more in front of me, and then finally they let me join them. They knew I was doing research, but couldn't trust me immediately. Time often allows people to accept you. Later I wanted to spend time with a group of people who play bowls regularly, as I had not yet done participant observation within a club and it seemed club life was very important for these migrants. Here access was gained using a gatekeeper (see below). As the year went on I noticed that access was something I also gained by becoming a member of the group in subtle ways such as dress and behaviour. I learned to wear gold sandals and smarter (non-student) clothes. I also had to accept that I was too old to access some settings and too young to access others (O'Reilly 2000a).

You may have to think carefully, prior to accessing the group, what your role will be within the group or setting. This choice can affect how people see you and therefore how they act towards you, and it may also affect who you subsequently gain access to. When doing research in a school, for example, you could ask if you can be a supply or support teacher for a while, but remember that once you have done this you have cast yourself in the role of teacher and access to student groups informally may be very difficult later on. Sometimes your role will be chosen for you, and we can learn from this experience about the group we are studying. Before I did research in Spain for the first time I tried to decide what my role in the community would be, but I knew too little about the way of life to decide. I thought perhaps I might work in a school as a teaching assistant for some of the time. As it turned out, however, my role was that of woman doing research in the community, and wife and mother. People knew what I was doing but they found it easier to relate to me as the mother of my children and the wife of my partner. I learnt that in this group there were women of my age not working, who could do voluntary work, go into bars for coffee during the day and join social clubs without arousing any suspicion or uncomfortable feelings. This is a retirement community to a large extent, so although I was relatively young I could join in those things the retired people were doing without much difficulty. Jason Ditton (1977), discussed above, changed his role during his research in order to improve access. He became a salesman in order to ask more questions and delve more deeply. Sue Estroff (1981) did research among psychiatric clinic out-patients. She wanted to understand their way of life and began by spending time in the clinical setting, where access was granted by the clinic staff not the patients. Then she gained access to the patients as they lived their lives out of the clinic. Access for her involved trying to fit in and not stand out as an obvious outsider. She learned to dress more casually, sit more sloppily, look more dishevelled.

There are other issues about how to present yourself, politically or in terms of your position/thoughts on different issues. This leads to worries about deception and so on. How much do you be yourself? These are discussed in the previous chapter. It is good to be naïve as well as knowledgeable, as discussed more fully in chapter 5. When Lorna did ethnographic research with farmers, for example, it was useful to her that she had grown up on a farm and was therefore comfortable around animals and knew some of the terminology farmers used around her. However, she had not been involved in farming for several years, and this too proved to be an advantage as she was able to innocently ask questions about veterinary practices and about feelings towards farm animals that the farmers felt able to answer in depth. Knowing too much can foreclose in-depth conversations; knowing too little can appear rude and uninterested.

As discussed briefly above, however, there are some places you will never access. I never managed to access one particular school and could not find out why. I was merely fobbed off at every turn. Much later, I heard that the head teacher at the school had retired and then people felt happier to tell me he was simply obstructive by nature. If you are determined to access difficult places, be sure whose interest it is in. Ask yourself why you need access to this specific situation. I have seen people push and push for access to a group or meeting when they really could have found another group or setting to use. Do not insist on getting access as if it is your inalienable right. Consider why anyone should participate and use that to persuade them. Check that you are not being biased in your approach. Show due respect. Be fascinated with the person. Be open-minded and show that you want to learn about the group from their perspective. They are telling and showing you about their lives.

Access is not separate from the research itself. You learn from it about how people view things, what they want you to see and what they do not. You may find that something you thought very private will be spoken about easily whereas something you thought you would easily be allowed to observe is taboo. I was obstructed from a meeting of representatives of social clubs at a council foreign residents' department. I could not make out why, until I realised that there is a lot of mutual respect between the foreigners' department and the clubs, and the foreigners' department did not see themselves as being in a position to grant access. I had misunderstood the power structure.

If you are really lucky, someone will emerge 'like a fairy godmother to help the forlorn ethnographer' (Rock 2001: 34), with getting to know people and to understand how things work. William Foote Whyte's (1981) friend Doc is a perfect example of this kind of key person. For my first period of fieldwork in Spain my fairy godmother was Ann Symonds, who knew so much about the community and so many people she was invaluable to me; and best of all she enjoyed showing me around, telling me things and introducing me. Such gatekeepers or key informants may be crucial to your gaining access. There are often people who are key to the group because without their approbation you will not gain access, or because what they know about the group is wide ranging and deep. Sometimes they are people who are high status; sometimes they are simply the people who always like to know what is going on and make it their business to find out; sometimes they are merely well connected and well known. Getting access to or through these individuals may aid your general access to other people and to information you might not otherwise have gained. A final aspect of access you might have to consider of course, is official permissions: visas for travel to other countries, or permission of people in authority in a school, university or health service for example (Hicks 1984).

Gatekeepers are key research participants who ease access to a group or setting

In order for Nigel Fielding (1981) to gain access to a National Front group he befriended National Front members at head-quarters. This meant others felt they could trust him. The National Front organisation represents the political extreme right in Britain; it is an activist organisation. It was a group Fielding could not like or feel any sympathies for and he felt it would be a good test of methods for producing insider understandings: an unlovable group whose ideology was completely alien. Fielding had to pretend to sympathise with his participants because they are very distrustful of outsiders, so though he was overt in telling them he was a researcher, he was covert with respect to this thoughts. He did begin to understand their actions from their perspective.

Time

Participant observation takes time. Time gives you the chance to settle in and start to see things more clearly. First of all you have the newcomer's view, which is good. You see things that after a while in the setting you stop seeing. It is important to note these things down quickly while they are new to you. But it takes time for you to notice the smaller details, the little things that happen, and find the time to ask questions about these things (to yourself as you develop your analysis and to the research participants as you want to know more). Once you have settled in and started to notice things you did not see at first, you also start to forget things you noticed in the first place. You stop feeling strange and start to fit in, but it has been this process of moving from the strange to the familiar that has taught you so much about the group and the setting, about how to behave, about the rules and norms and customs of the group. Or as Malinowski put it, 'certain subtle peculiarities, which make an impression as long as they are novel, cease to be noticed as soon as they become familiar. Others again can only be perceived with a better knowledge of the local conditions' (1922: 21).

Time enables the strange to become familiar and the familiar strange

The first time you enter a classroom you notice the way the desks are set out, what the teacher looks like to some extent (though no small details – I know this is true because I get mixed up with other teachers that I look nothing like!), and you choose a seat. As a newcomer to a setting you see things that after a while you take for granted. You notice the tables are small and the chairs are cramped. You see the spotty boy sitting opposite you and the nice-looking girl who smiles at you. Later, when you have got to know the boy you have stopped seeing his

continued on facing page

spots. You stop noticing the size of the chairs and the cramped room, but now you see that there are books on a shelf on the wall, that there is a picture next to the window, that the teacher has a strange squint as she pushes her glasses up her nose when she talks! You have become part of the group, but without realising it you have also learnt a lot about the group, about where to sit and how to behave. In some classes it is okay to chew gum and drink water, in others this is not acceptable, for example. If, while doing all this, you had been doing participant observation you would have been taking notes as you went along so that those things you stopped seeing when you had become familiar with them would nevertheless be in your notes, and those things which revealed themselves to you as you became more familiar with the setting would lead you to begin understanding the group more and more.

You also need time for others to get used to you and to stop seeing you as a disturbing element in their lives. People can alter their behaviour when someone new enters the scene, but they can only keep this up for a short time. When you have hung around long enough you become part of the setting, part of the background that others are taking for granted.

Time also enables you to observe changes as they happen, so that instead of a focus on static elements of people's lives your focus is on processes and 'how' questions – how one thing leads to another, what are the separate elements of a sequence of events – rather than trying to ascertain why people act in certain ways. Time also enables you to observe events that happen at different times of the day, week, month or year. Anthropologists often advocate spending at least a year among the group, because this is for many groups seen as a natural cycle during which most rituals and events will be observed no matter how a culture divides up its time (Hicks 1984). Obviously, spending a year is not an option nor even necessary for all research using participant observation, but how a culture divides up its time is important. British migrants in Spain divide the year up into hot and cooler months, and events such as Christmas and Easter. Finally, as I said in chapter 2, you need to think about what times you want to sample, be it times of the day or times of the year, or whatever.

Time enables you to build relationships

Time was very important for me when I was doing research with women in Spain. People generally told me that they love their lives in Spain, that they would never go home, and that no one wants to go home. However, over time I got to know people more intimately, and they came to trust me more and to realise that I was not a journalist looking for quick answers to a few questions but an ethnographer seeking a deep understanding of their lives. Eventually women started to confide in me that they do occasionally feel lonely, that they would go home if anything happened to their partners and that they do get bored from time to time. Without spending time amongst the group I would not have understood this aspect of the migration experience (O'Reilly 2000b).

Note, however, that a short period of participant observation can make an important contribution to any study. Fieldwork is not always necessarily long term, and certainly not always over a year. Patricia Paperman (2003), for example, did just three months' fieldwork accompanying underground railway police teams as they worked and was able to take no ongoing notes and transcribe no conversations at the time. All was written after she left the presence of the police, yet she has produced an important study of how metro police resolve problems related to the hidden nature of the deviance they 'hunt' while being so conspicuously visible themselves. Rebecca Cassidy (2002), on the other hand, spent six years looking at the world of horse racing, working in stables, learning to ride and generally immersing herself in the lifestyle. Of course, all depends on the problem, the situation and what you hope to achieve; some would think it arrogant or deceitful to write authoritatively about a group or topic on the basis of a short period of participant observation, but value its contribution to a project using a combination of methods (Hicks 1984).

Learning the language

I noted in chapter 1 that an aspect of doing participant observation is learning the language. This seems an obvious necessity for people researching groups who speak a different language, but is more complex than is first apparent. It may be a matter not simply of learning to communicate in another language but of identifying subtle differences in dialect, understanding colloquialisms, acquiring slang terminology, and learning when and how to use a polite or a casual tone. These things can be difficult and can take time. Some ethnographers can feel quite embarrassed about their lack of language skills, yet are reluctant to admit it or to employ an interpreter (Tonkin 1984). What is recommended is an awareness about language and how it is used to convey meaning as well as distinction and status. On the one hand we have to be aware that our level of understanding of a group or culture may be affected by our language skills, and not be afraid to use an interpreter on occasions where this would help considerably. On the other hand, we can perhaps accept that imperfect language skills do not mean we have completely misunderstood. However, there is even more to this than mere linguistics. Even if you are not studying a group who speak a different language from you, in modern ethnography, if you want to learn about the way of life of a certain subculture or institution, you will need to learn certain ways and words that are expected and accepted. There are often sets of behaviour and vocabulary which are used to mark outsiders from insiders, for example. As you immerse yourself in the group you will learn the cultural language as well as the spoken language, and learning this language enables you to begin to understand the group more fully.

Participating and observing

Of course the key elements of participant observation are participating and observing. Once you have gained access to your group, what do you do? Well, remember Malinowski said the point of participating is so that we can learn things from the natives' point of view and so that they will get used to us. In your own ethnographic research you should participate to the extent that people get used to your presence and start to act naturally around you, but also so that you can then learn from the experience and empathise. This is not always easy, as will become clear. You have to kind of pretend you know nothing, but also know enough to fit in. At first you can feel very strange, insecure and lacking in confidence. You may have your own ideas about what you are doing but your research participants may have other ideas and expectations (Hicks 1984). The problems of living with or spending a great deal of time participating in the lives of a group while retaining the sense of being an observer and outsider are immediately apparent. You are Schutz's stranger (1971), either literally living in a strange land or trying to distance yourself from your own culture in order to make it strange. In order to be accepted and talked to and have people share their experiences and their ideas with you, you have to gain trust and establish friendships, while all the time you are never completely *in*. Many ethnographers tell stories of mistakes they made, how they got things wrong and how stupid they felt. But we can learn from such mistakes about the culture of the group, its rules and norms, and as long as we retain a sense of humility we are usually forgiven (Goward 1984).

We can learn from the times when we make mistakes

A group within which I was doing participant observation used to run informal coffee mornings. Anyone was welcome to come along. Coffee, tea and cakes were for sale, there were second-

continued on facing page

hand clothes stalls, and a book stall, and occasionally a visiting speaker would talk on a topic of interest to the community. I volunteered to help at these coffee mornings and was given the task of making the coffees for the other volunteers before the doors were opened to the public. One morning was particularly busy and I stayed on after the doors were opened to help out serving to the customers. I stayed an extra two hours and was quite pleased with myself for having worked so hard and been so helpful. However, the supervisor came to me later in the week and asked me if, at the next coffee morning, could I please simply serve coffees to the staff and then leave. It turned out I had almost caused a strike amongst the other volunteers whose positions were hard-won and jealously guarded. I felt embarrassed, lonely and stupid, and went home determined never to go back. I did go back, however, and gradually learned more about the important role of voluntary work in the lives of retired women (see O'Reilly 2000a: 130).

Arguably, the objective part of participant observation is the observation part. If you are simply being there, hanging around, taking part, you are no more than a participant (as we all are in our daily lives), but as a participant observer you are someone who is observing as well as taking part. You want to learn from the group so you have to mentally stand back and notice things, and note them down. You will be asking questions and actively seeking access to certain groups and certain situations that another participant might not access. There is a tension between the subjective and the objective which Malinowski fails to tackle, and which is discussed below. However, a participant observer needs to observe details in different settings, at different times. It may be that you have to be at every gathering and every event, and be the last to leave and the first to arrive, to be unobtrusive and yet ask questions, to join in and yet remain an outsider.

Note-taking

Taking notes in the field, during participant observation, is not something that can be taught to people easily. The point is eventually to have written down all information that you think may or may not be relevant to your research. It is not easy to decide what is or is not relevant, especially in the earlier stages, and textbooks often advise that you write down everything that might be important (Becker 1998). My first day of participant observation I spent a few hours walking around the streets familiarising myself with the neighbourhood and the British bars that are evident in the Costa del Sol. I went home and wrote up my field notes from my memory and, trying 'not to preclude or censor anything that might be germane' (Rock 2001: 35), I spent three hours writing! I soon realised that if you try to write everything down you will not actually have time to do any research. So, you have to make choices. As I discuss in chapter 2, you should have begun with some ideas about what you are interested in and should start there. However, ethnographic research is iterative-inductive, moving back and forth between foreshadowed problems and theory grounded in data, and does not usually decide exactly what the focus of research is until near the end. Without being precise about what you are exploring you somehow have to write down what you think might be relevant. As a result field notes are unruly and messy (Marcus 1994).

Your notes should be written daily; it is easy to forget what you noticed, thought or heard. Usually you will have a small notebook that you can keep in your pocket where you note down things that trigger your memory, or short quotes, details such as dates and names, and anything else that you find useful. Some people use a dictaphone instead of, or as well as, a notebook and talk into this when they get a private moment. One resourceful student recently told me he was keeping short notes on his mobile phone, texting them to himself. This was easier than writing in a notebook for his research in clubs and discotheques, as his research participants merely thought he was texting a friend. Mental notes should be written up more fully into jotted notes and then full notes

(Emerson, Fretz and Shaw 2001) as soon possible and certainly each day. The longer you leave it the more details you will forget. At this stage work with the maxim: 'If in doubt, write it down.' Make sure you add details such as who said what and when, where necessary, and add some background information to aid your memory of events later on.

Field notes begin broad and become more specific as you go along and your research becomes more directed and focussed. You become more reflexive and more active as time goes on, with your research questions becoming clearer, and so you may be writing much more at the beginning and much less later on, but what you write later on may be more relevant to your final analyses. Your note-taking may also become increasingly overt and you may start to supplement your data with video and taking photos, and asking for specific details.

Note that as you take notes you impose a structure on events. You are shaping what you see and hear because it is impossible to record everything. Field notes are a way of reducing events, and are inevitably selective (Emerson, Fretz and Shaw 2001), and of course however full they are they will never be able to explain fully the intellectual work that went into you determining what to do and write, when and how (Jackson 1990).

Diaries and memoranda

As well as noting down what you observe and what people say to you, you will also be thinking about what you hear and see and its implications for your overall research puzzle. It is important to keep memos of such analytical ideas, what Whyte (1951) calls those flashes of insight that come to you when you were not even consciously thinking of a research problem, and their progress. This helps you retain the viewpoint of the stranger; it enables you to stand back, avoid overinvolvement or 'going native'. This is also where the analysis begins. I keep such notes in a separate file that I call my intellectual diary. It is where I log thoughts and reflections on what I am collecting and it is where I start to begin pulling ideas together ready for analysis. Some people keep these sorts of reflections with their field notes, and indeed it is sometimes difficult to separate the two. Indeed some would go so far as to say the distinction between field notes and diary notes is artificial since all notes are a record of one's reactions and an attempt to sort and to analyse (Jackson 1990). Schatzman and Strauss (1973) urge ethnographers to distinguish theoretical notes from observational notes, while Lofland and Lofland (1995) suggest that those analytical ideas that come at you as you write your field notes should be jotted down but distinguished somehow. Emerson *et al.* (2001) go even further, distinguishing 'asides' from commentaries and 'in-process memos', all of which chart the development of the ongoing analysis. Whatever techniques we use, Malinowski would have told us we must keep them apart, and I think it is possible to distinguish what we see, hear and so on from what we think about it, although they might be actually recorded in the same place.

A further thing you might wish to keep is a personal diary as you do participant observation. This enables the natural history approach in which over time the odd becomes familiar, the strange usual, and in which reactions and the directions of the research can be traced to the experience of settling in and getting to know the rules. You may even find you write up in this way, remaining faithful to your emergent methodology. The diary does not have to be treated as something entirely separate from the research itself. It enables you to keep in touch with feelings and emotions that participants in the field may well share (Lofland and Lofland 1995), as well as acting as a guard against prejudices and biases you may develop unwittingly (Emerson *et al.* 2001). But a diary can have an analytical role as well; as Malinowski wrote in his own diary, it can serve 'to integrate one's thinking, to avoid fragmenting themes' (1967: 175). Malinowski's diary was published by his wife after his death and has been most often cited to demonstrate his antipathy towards the natives, but it best of all expresses what many ethnographers since have expressed:

The feeling of confinement, the obsessional longing to be back even if for the briefest while in one's own cultural surroundings, the dejection and doubts about the validity of what one is doing, the desire to escape to a fantasy world of novels or daydreams, the moral compulsion to drag oneself back to the task of field observation.

(Firth's Introduction in Malinowski 1967: xv)

The participant observation oxymoron

Participant observation is a problematic term for a method for two reasons. First, it is not really a method on its own: it involves making notes, asking questions, doing interviews, collecting data, drawing up lists, constructing databases, being active in research. It is never simply a matter of participating and observing. The more active parts of ethnographic research are discussed in subsequent chapters as if they are separate from participating and observing, but in fact they are inextricably linked, and I would like to argue that many people who do research using interviews would benefit from actually permitting themselves to realise that as well as learning from the data they are collecting as people speak to them, they are also learning through participating and observing, and could learn more if they allowed themselves to do this more freely. They could also learn through collections of other data, such as those discussed in chapter 7. So, this book is not only about how to do ethnographic research but a call for it to be used more widely.

Second, and this is the topic to be discussed in the section that follows, participant observation is a problematic term, which is interpreted in different ways by different researchers, and with an inherent tension. As J. Middleton (1970: 9) noted, the central problem of participant observation is trying to 'live as a human being among other human beings yet also having to act as an objective observer'. Participant observation then is an example of an oxymoron: a contradiction in terms. This tension is nowhere more neatly captured than in Schutz's 'The Stranger' (1971). Though he was describing not so much a methodology as a phenomenological sociology (Maso 2001), Schutz superbly illustrates the way the participant observer has to balance attempts to make the familiar strange and the strange familiar. The tension is in the fact that you can only really understand a group when you act within it without thinking, but the very act of trying to do that prevents you from ever truly being a member: 'to *participate* involves getting involved, joining in, being subjective, immersing yourself; to *observe* involves being objective, keeping your emotional and perhaps physical distance, being scientific, clear-eyed, unbiased, critical. This tension does not have to be resolved: it is what gives participant observation its strength, but the roles of participation and observation within ethnography have not always been equal.

Emphasis on observation

I said in chapter 1 that anthropology developed within a specific context, in which the goal was to be scientific, and within a theoretical framework of structural functionalism, therefore the object of study was a society or group and its component structures, and how these interrelate and become interconnected as part of a functioning whole. Typical feelings and opinions were important, not individual ones, that is, the culture of the group. Anthropology at the time to some extent emulated the natural sciences, which implied observation as the crucial component of participant observation. The way in which phenomena which were believed to exist in the world were available to anthropologists to learn about and explain was through observation (rather than trusting the description of others, even the participants). Observation provided sense data, available through sense experience. The next step, following this thread of ideas, was to advocate that anthropologists, as scientific professionals, should collect their own data rather than rely on non-professionals. This led to the advocating of fieldwork, as we know it today. Always the approach was to be scientific. We have seen how early anthropologists advocated participation to some degree along with observation, but observation was the main method of data collection. Observation was deemed to be detached, scientific, able to capture what was really going on despite what people might say. Participation was often minimal. Malinowski actually spent less time interacting with his natives than his methodological writings suggest (as is evidenced in his diary, 1967). In early anthropology (as is the case in many contemporary uses of participant observation), participation had often not been considered as a means of gathering data. If we are attempting to be scientific, objective, detached, then participation does not really have a place. It violates the separation of observer and observed. You will affect the conditions of the situation. This is why Malinowski (and others) insisted on spending long periods of time – so that you can stop affecting the behaviours of people around you and attain the ideal scientific situation. But if you accept that this is an impossible task, and that some subjectivity is inevitable, some *interpretation* of events is always necessary, then you can use participation in order to learn through experience, and also as a means of access and as a way to observe without upsetting the setting.

Emphasis on participation

Within philosophies of social science there has been a clear move away from the theory of social facts as things to the theory of social things as constructions. Closely linked to this, there has been a move away from using observation as the primary method of data gathering. According to this paradigm, which we can label *interpretivism*, the social world is not simply an objective thing existing independently of our ideas but is based on interaction, reflection, meaning, action, interpretation, reflection, further action and so on. In other words, the social world is constructed and re-constructed through its members' interactions. Ethnomethodology, phenomenology and symbolic interactionism are all part of this tradition in social science (Blumer 1969, Cicourel 1964, Garfinkel 1967, Lassman 1974). Participation thus enables the researcher to be involved in the construction of the social world and thereby to begin to understand the actions of others as the actors themselves understand them – through interaction and interpretation.

> A logical corollary of the theory of social world as constructed through its members' interactions and as intrinsically mean-ingful is thus a theory of its cognitive availability through participation in the construction of its meaning, which implies a research procedure in which the notion of participation in the subjects' activities replaces the notion of their simple observa-tion as the main data yielding technique. It is a research pro-cedure in which the researcher does not participate in the lives of the subjects in order to observe them, but rather observes while participating fully in their lives.
>
> (Holy 1984: 174)

Contemporary aims of participation

So what exactly is the role of participation in ethnographies today? In contemporary use participation ranges from spending some time in the community being studied in order to obtain access, to full immersion in the culture of the group, with much participant observation taking place between these two extremes. Such immer-sion as Estroff's (discussed below), whether it is to be recommended or not, is never easy to undertake. Even the extent of immersion that Malinowski was advocating, that the ethnographer should 'put aside camera, notebook and pencil, and join in himself in what is going on' (1922: 21), was demonstrated in his diaries to be more than a matter of simply joining in. Ethnographers have to cope with being a long way from home, in a strange place, among people they do not immediately understand, yet still to be an ethnographer, an outsider, an academic, one of us but not one of us. As Geertz (1988: 77) rather poetically puts it: 'It is a question of living a multiplex live: sailing at once in several seas.'

Participant observation can be used as a means of access and at the design stage of a project, or at the other extreme, can take the form of complete immersion within the group's culture

Trudy wanted to explore female sex workers' views of their work and designed a study which compared female sex workers in London and New York. She decided her research would use in-depth interviews, but before she could obtain access to sex workers for interview she spent some time doing participant observation in clubs and coffee bars and on street corners in London, and later in New York. Her participant observation was used merely as a means of access, and though it also helped her to understand the group and to decide what sorts of questions she might ask of whom, she did not write up any of her findings in her final report. Indeed it was as if the participant observation had never taken place. The research findings were based on the interview material only.

Sue Estroff (1981), who conducted an ethnography of psychiatric out-patient clients in an American community, immersed herself so completely in the field that even after just six weeks, when she left the field to spend a few days with her father, she felt strange and distant: 'I was shaken and resentful that we spent $30 for one meal when I had been living with people trying to eat on $4 for a whole day. The money we spent for cabs, tips and drinks seemed so indulgent and wasteful. I had already forgotten that some people talked easily and consistently with each other when together. It seemed odd that no one had pressing, paralysing problems to contend with just to get through the day' (1981: 4). For Estroff such immersion was essential to understanding, and so she lived, shared daily life and even shared her home with clients, and as a result she says: 'I have acutely experienced the urge and propensity to flee to psychic disorganisation and disability – have felt the lure of craziness in ways that further sensitised me to the world of my friends.'

The aims of participation actually vary from case to case. The point is to ask yourself why you might participate. Participation is often linked to the ethnographer's personal commitment to the group being studied, as exploited, oppressed or discriminated against. Some research on minority groups and on deviance, and some feminist research, falls into this category. Researchers are often already working as aid or relief workers in the area and this has led to their interest in the topic. Or are you using participation to enable observation, and to enable the collection of data through film, photograph, informal interviews and so on? Participation can be used to enable access to different groups of people at different times. You can then do opportunistic interviews, or ask questions as they occur to you. You can observe things happening as they happen rather than ask about them afterwards. You can really see what goes on rather than rely on an informant to tell you after the event, or to tell you what usually happens. You can learn about events, feelings, rules, norms in context rather than asking about them. You can learn about the context and add to your research questions rather than rely on what you thought you knew beforehand. Participation thus has many and varied uses. Or are you participating because you want to live alongside people and feel as they feel, empathise with them, become one with them in some way?

The classic text often quoted on the subject of the participant observation oxymoron is the one in which Gold (1958) describes the four positions of complete participant, participant as observer, observer as participant and complete observer. The first is covert and runs the risk of 'going native' and therefore losing any sense of objectivity, and the last is overt, with the ethnographer not participating at all. I will not elaborate because I do not find the distinction particularly useful. To me, no observation in ethnography is non-participant. We do not use one-way mirrors or pretend not be there, and, as Mason (1996) points out, even trying to act as if we are not there would have effects. On the other hand, a complete participant is not an ethnographer. He or she is a participant. If she decides to research the group or culture in which she participates she becomes a participant observer. The distinction between the middle two positions is far more interesting and is more of an attempt to disentangle the various ways an ethnographer approaches the extent to which he or she participates and observes. However, these typologies (see also Junker 1960) confound several discrete themes, as follows:

- overt/covert
- participant roles
- the aims of participation
- practical considerations.

Overt/covert. As discussed above at length, and in chapter 3, an ethnographer needs to think about the extent to which he or she is overt or covert. This is not a simple dichotomy, since many participant observers hope the research participants will forget they are there and act 'naturally', while overt access may have been obtained from gatekeepers but not the general public. Clearly a covert ethnographer will have to adopt a participant role, but he or she may not then learn about the group through empathy and experience. Indeed the role of participation might still be seen to be a means of access. Some people do under-cover research and try to portray their findings as if they were never there. Admittedly this happens in journalism more than in anthropological or socio-logically informed research, but it occurs in degrees. Alternatively, an overt researcher, who has explained her research fully to partici-pants, might nevertheless adopt a participant role and use participa-tion in order to learn through experience. These elements, then, need to be distinguished.

Participant roles. The role or roles adopted within the community may be more or less participant or observer. Gail's research on men's friendships (discussed in chapter 2) was undertaken within her own friendship circle, so she was a participant in the group before she began. When Frederick decided to explore men who work as full-time carers of children (chapter 8), however, there was no role within the households he could adopt and so his role was as observer. He participated fully in the lives of the family, making breakfast, washing up, going on outings and even baby sitting, but he did not adopt a participant role. However, the roles adopted within one ethnographic study may not necessarily remain static. When I researched British migrants in Spain for the first time I immersed myself in the culture to the extent that I moved with my family to Spain, my children went to a local school, my partner worked with other migrants, I joined clubs and made friends, and generally speaking the whole family became expatriates in Spain (although we always were aware that one day we would be going home). But not all of the activities in which I took part involved full participation to the extent of 'being one of them'. At times I was a mother, partner, friend. At other times I was a researcher, investigator, the person who designed that study, the woman who was writing a thesis.

The aims of participation. Ethnographers disagree about the extent to which we can learn through participation. For some the role of participation, as discussed above, is to get close enough to be able to collect data in an objective, detached way, through observation, interviews, collecting statistical data, taking photographic evidence and so on. For others, as with Estroff (1981), the role of participation is to sensitise yourself to the world of others through experience and through the construction of that world. When Anna researched what quality of life means for older people (chapter 8) she included some participant observation in people's homes as they returned from hospital, and in the hospital setting. However, she was not attempting to understand the hospital culture or the daily life of the participants in general but was focussing on what quality of life means for a specific group in the context of a specific set of events. She did not therefore immerse herself in the group or setting.

Practical considerations. Finally, the extent to which an ethnographer adopts a participant role, is overt or covert, or manages to immerse herself in the culture of the group may not always be her own choice. Carol, studying doctor/patient consultations, would not be able to participate much, whatever her beliefs about learning through participation. Sometimes one is called on to participate in ways one might not have anticipated. Raymond

Firth, for example, in his ethnographic study among the Tikopia, found himself rushed to a neighbouring hut to the call of: 'Come quick! Ata . . . is killing his wife!' The scuffle stopped when he entered the hut, but he did not quite know what to do next: 'each blamed the other'. He says: 'I therefore took the line that eminent persons in Tikopia take – that any disturbance in their neighbourhood is an affront to their dignity – gave them some counsel about the advisability of husband and wife agreeing, and an intimation that if I heard any further noise I should have to come in again' (Firth 1957: 134). He then carefully left, not at all sure what would happen if he had to come in again and hoping the warning would suffice. During Lorna's ethnography on farms she was asked to muck in, and help feeding sheep, milking cows and even, once, herding. Other times you might hope to participate but not be permitted, as has happened to me on more than one occasion.

Trying to resolve the participant observation oxymoron is like trying to resolve the difference between subjectivity and objectivity, or the need to be scientific while acknowledging that humans create their world. The reasons for participating will affect the extent to which you participate rather than observe. Practical considerations will also affect how much you participate. You should not insist on having to participate if it is not working for you. The important thing is to ask yourself why you want to use participation, to what ends. In my own research sometimes I participate more and sometimes less. Participation may even be less than useful. It may be easier to take on the role of researcher and to be seen to be collecting information in an acceptable way, such as a question-naire. In your own milieu (i.e. not in some exotic outpost) it is sometimes possible to adopt the role of researcher since this is a recognised role, and it is sometimes quite difficult to go further (although some participation is still inevitable). For some, for example Schutz (1971) and Maso (2001), the tension is exactly the point. We need both to empathise and to sympathise, to balance destrangement and estrangement. Participating enables the strange to become familiar; observing enables the familiar to appear strange.

Summary

Participant observation involves participating in people's daily lives over a period of time, observing, asking questions, taking notes and collecting other forms of data. The specific aspects covered in this chapter are: gaining access, the issue of time, learning the language, participating and observing, and taking notes. Access to the group or setting is not something done once, but is negotiated and renegotiated to various people, times and places and with you taking on a variety of roles and personae and sometimes having to acknowledge you cannot get access at all. If you are lucky you will have a gatekeeper or key informant who will enable access for you, but not everyone has such a 'fairy godmother'. Participant observation takes time and is rarely done fleetingly. Time enables the strange to become familiar and the familiar strange. Time enables you to observe processes and change. There may be certain times of the year, month or day that have special relevance for your research. Time also enables the learning of the cultural and linguistic language of the group, the process of which is a learning experience in itself. Of course, we must not forget the role of writing in ethnography. Writing begins with mental then jotted notes and ends with the writing up, but there are many varieties of things an ethnographer might write in between, including analytical thoughts and personal diaries.

Participating and observing are key elements of participant observation but the term is something of an oxymoron. The roles and aims of participation and observation can vary with an ethnographer's philosophical position, relationship to the group, routes of access and roles adopted, and as a result of practical considerations.

Further reading

If you would enjoy reading more about a particular key informant and his role in an ethnographic study go to Appendix A of Whyte's (1981 and 1993) *Street Corner Society* to hear more about Doc.

For an extended discussion of field notes in ethnography see Emerson, Fretz and Shaw (1995 and 2001).

As discussed above, Gold (1958) and Junker (1960) are classic texts on participant observation roles. However, I find Holy's (1984) discussion more sensitive and valuable.

On the topic of balancing participation and observation, you might enjoy the debates raised within Jackson's edited volume, *Anthropology at Home* (1987), and Messerschmidt's *Anthropologists at Home in North America* (1981). Most qualitative methods textbooks include a discussion of similar issues around participating and observing (e.g., Berg 2004, May 2001).

The best way to learn about ethnographic practice is from ethnographers themselves, where they reflect on practice, and of course to go and do it for yourself. Schutz's 'The stranger' (1971) is still relevant to discussions around the participant observation oxymoron and is a useful piece around which to base a discussion.

5 Interviews: asking questions of individuals and groups

While the main method of ethnography is participant observation, ethnographers conduct interviews as well. These can take the shape of opportunistic chats, questions that arise on the spur of the moment, one to one in-depth interviews and group interviews, and all sorts of ways of asking questions and learning about people that fall in between. It is therefore quite difficult to prescribe how an ethnographer should do an interview. However, there is a quite distinctive difference between an interview that takes place within qualitative research and one that takes place within quantitative research, so this chapter will deal with this distinction first. We will then explore the different types of interview available to an ethnographer to use, including group interviews and what have become known as focus groups (and which I will call group discussions).

Qualitative interviews: quality versus quantity

As well as being about ethnographic methods, this book could be seen to be about qualitative research more broadly. But what is the difference between quantity and quality? Is it something to do with techniques and procedures or does it reflect more philosophical decisions, the difference between those who believe that society can be studied using methods similar to those of the natural sciences and those who do not? For Alan Bryman (1988) quantitative research often exhibits all the hallmarks of a natural science approach. Let's explore this idea a little further. If you were doing a large, quantitative survey of a number of people via interviews you would probably be aiming to gather hard data, facts (or at least *unambiguous data*), on a number of issues which could be generalised for a whole population. You would be looking for those patterns and regularities which occur (and not at random) within society, and later would be looking to find explanations for those. This is the logic of social research according to Rose and Sullivan (1996). But why interview in the first place if these are the kinds of data you want to obtain? Well, quantitative researchers may interview rather than sending out questionnaires for a variety of reasons. If the research includes questions on opinions and feelings which are not suited to mail or telephone questionnaire research, or if the topic is sensitive, face to face interviews in a private setting in which the interviewee feels comfortable and at ease may be appropriate. Some quantitative surveys are conducted via interview because they take a long time and are complicated to complete, so the presence of an interviewer eases the process. Nevertheless, the aim is still to obtain hard data which can be generalised.

Quantitative researchers are often concerned with interviewing a *large* enough number of people in order to be able to make claims of *representativeness*. Possibly more than one interviewer would be used to conduct the survey, and in this case they would want to ensure *standardisation*. The questions themselves, the order in which they are asked and even the way they are asked, and the approach of the interviewer, would all need to be standardised in order that comparisons can later be made between one set of results and another, and in order to turn the resulting data into general rules or laws of behaviour. One would also be concerned to avoid *interviewer bias*. It is accepted that an interviewer's attitude, facial expressions, responses, even gender, may affect the outcome of the interview and especially the replies given by the respondent. To protect against this the survey organiser might train interviewers in correct procedures, and teach them to be wary of getting too involved, of affecting the outcome (May 2001). This brings quantitative research close to the positivist tradition that we discussed in chapter 2. I am not saying that all quantitative research is conducted in the positivist tradition, but generally the quantitative researcher is hoping to collect quantifiable data, facts, truths – tangible data which can be collected, logged, sorted, compared, generalised and analysed. That is, *numerical data.* In order to collect such data it is important to ensure standardisation of techniques, to control for interviewer bias, and to have a large, representative sample.

This is not the sort of interview I will be talking about in this chapter. What I will be talking about is interviews which are more qualitative in approach and which are influenced, very broadly, by interpretivism in the social sciences. In the interpretive tradition it is accepted that human societies cannot be studied in the same way as the natural sciences. Humans are able to make choices, to be reflexive, to have a certain amount of free will, thought and calculation. They act rather than react. Interpretive, qualitative sociologists stress the importance of the *quality* of the data they collect over the quantity, and so they move away from pseudo-scientific interviewing techniques. Qualitative interviews are an opportunity to delve and explore precisely those subjective meanings that positivists seek to strip away in their search for standardisation (O'Connell Davidson and Layder 1994). In the interpretive tradition, it is those subjectivities, those subtle changes of mind, ambiguities of feelings, those ambivalences, confusions and strongly held beliefs, which are most interesting to the researcher. An interpretive sociologist hopes to capture and to interpret these from the interviewee's perspective. This is often much more interesting and insightful than spending an hour and a half trying to get 'the truth' out of someone or some firm data which are necessary in order to complete the list of interview questions prescribed for the interview.

A qualitative interview also often goes beyond just questions and answers. Even subtle differences between one interview and another, such as where the interviewee chooses to sit and how, or what time they agreed to be interviewed, can be analysed by the ethnographer who is less concerned with standardisation of technique. This means that a qualitative researcher places less importance on how many people he or she interviews and is more concerned with the quality of the interview itself. The approach may well not be standardised in terms of approach or questioning, but this is not worrying because we understand that different techniques and different approaches will elicit different responses. What we would like to understand is what the different responses tell us about the group we are studying and about the social world more widely.

The ethnographic interview

For ethnographers, interviewing, and listening go on all the time. There may not be a clear distinction between doing participant observation and conducting an interview. A good ethnographer will take any opportunity to listen and to ask questions of individuals and groups whilst participating and observing. Discussions go on all the time and in a variety of contexts. However, it could also be that the ethnographer finds it useful or necessary to take people aside and try to talk to them in a more predetermined way, when place and time have been prearranged and when there may be fewer interruptions from other people and from unfolding events. It may be that you are taking a *factist* approach (Alasuutari 1995) which sees interview data as yielding the one truth, that can only be obtained by sitting and talking to people in depth, getting at what they really think. Indeed, to put this another way around, it may be that the main data gathering technique is interviewing, in which case ethnographic fieldwork provides a context for building relationships with people that can improve and inform qualitative interviews. Several classic studies from the Chicago School, for example, are considered ethnographic in methodology and content yet were based to a great extent on interview data (Hobbs 2001). Or perhaps yours is an *interactionist* perspective which depends on a combination of methods and which sees confessional type statements as one type of discourse among many, and which doubts if there is really one true way/thing that a person really thinks.

Whatever the reason for asking someone a question or a series of questions, it is more likely that an ethnographer will use a qualitative rather than a quantitative style. It is fairly safe to say that ethnographers will normally be using an unstructured interview style, with open-ended questions, on topics raised from within the research setting, in places and at times to suit the participant, and they are usually fairly informal. But there is no normal within ethnography. There is a range of interviewing styles that can be drawn upon by the ethnographer, and the key is to be flexible, and to be aware and reflexive at every stage about why you are using what approach. However, your choice may well be determined for you by the topic you are interested in and/or by the participants themselves and the contexts in which you find yourself. The following paragraphs explore styles of interview and the criteria along which interviews vary, in order that readers can begin to make intelligent, informed, thoughtful decisions and be able to justify these in terms of what they want to know and how.

Structure

Methods textbooks often distinguish between structured, unstructured and semi-structured interview styles (May 2001).

- A *structured* interview falls into the survey style I have discussed above. Questions are predetermined, and there is no room for extra questions to be added as you go along. The interviewee is asked those questions and only those, in the stated format and order, in order to preserve standardisation.
- An unstructured interview is more free-flowing. The interviewer may have a guide or plan, or simply a topic to address, and the interviewee is given the opportunity to respond in a leisurely way. This is more like a conversation than an interview.
- A semi-structured interview will contain elements of both styles, in order to explore ideas with the participants but also to get fixed responses for some criteria.

Ethnography tends to rely on unstructured discussions in order to encourage reflexivity, to give people time to delve into their thoughts, to express their contradictory opinions, their doubts, their fears, their hopes and so on. They may start with an outline, a guide or a plan (see chapter 6), but are usually pleased to let the interviewee wander off the point if this happens. This is because an ethnographer is usually attempting to learn about people from their own perspective, to get an insider's view, and this cannot be done by imposing one's own line of questioning on people.

Interviewing and participant observation are complementary methods: Judith's study of older people's friendships

Judith wanted to understand how older people make and maintain friendships when they are living in an old persons' home. Do they rely on past friendships? Do they forge new ones? Does friendship mean the same as it did when they were younger and more independent? In order to find some answers she did ethnographic research in an old persons' home in her town. She was able to ask people about friendship as they ate dinner, as they watched television, as they joined in activities, and as they sat alone. In this way, interviewing went on all the time, as Judith sought to learn more about what friendship means to older people. Of course, she was able to observe people making and maintaining friendships of all varieties and was even able to build some friendships herself. This led her to direct her investigations in ever new directions and to ask questions that were more and more relevant to the experiences of the partici-pants. However, she also wanted to know what the older people felt about friendship and how they reflected on it privately. For this, Judith arranged qualitative, unstructured, informal interviews with people in their rooms or in private spaces (for example in a quiet part of the garden). Here people were able to explore for themselves what friendship means now and what it meant in

continued on next page

the past. They were able to talk freely and openly, to change their minds as they went along, as they reconsidered things they had said in the light of new memories, and to add subjects to Judith's research that she had not considered. For example, it emerged that for many people their partner was seen as their best friend and the loss of a partner was a crucial phase in attitudes to friendship.

Whether or not an interview is structured will depend on what you want to find out, or on the purpose of your interview (which is not necessarily the same thing). Some will simply have a topic, an event, or a vague area of interest they wish to discuss with the interviewee, such as the Spanish Civil War (Fraser 1979) or an area of one's life, for example work experiences or friendship. Usually one will want to bring the interviewee back to the topic under discussion if he or she wanders too far from it, but a sensitive interviewer will do this gently and slowly and with an awareness that new yet relevant topics may emerge from allowing the interviewee to wander a bit (as with Judith, above). William Foote Whyte (1981: 35) argued that 'the whole point of not fixing an interview structure with pre-determined questions is that it permits freedom to introduce materials and questions previously unanticipated'.

However, although the discussion above may have made it sound as if qualitative interviews are in direct contrast to quantitative, ethnographers do use some structured interviewing. In survey research, questionnaires or interview schedules are standardised in order that comparisons can be made and general conclusions drawn. It may well be that an ethnographer wants or needs some more general data from the participants. These may be quantitative data as part of a larger study, such as data on age, numbers of children, ownership of cattle and so on. Some data may need to be collected from all participants, such as age, date of birth, or even 'do you own a watch?' Lorna's ethnographic study on working farms (introduced in chapter 4), for example, included data from each farmer and family on how long they had done the work, their nationality, age, social class background and other interests. In order to obtain these kinds of data an ethnographer may have a standardised element in his or her interview plan or schedule, or a few questions she asks of everyone in order to get the more general, standardised information. An interview may therefore have some more structured parts, or a researcher may conduct a series of structured interviews as part of a larger research project that otherwise relies on fieldwork and participant observation. However, the main emphasis in ethnographic research is likely to be on the unstructured elements, for reasons discussed above.

An ethnographer will sometimes collect systematic data from all participants: Michael's research on drug use

Michael's research (introduced in chapter 1) on young people and drug use did not rely on individual interviewing very much at all. It did not make sense for him to ask people questions about how they felt taking certain drugs. He spent much more time having opportunistic discussions with people in groups, and thus learned more about how people construct their ideas about drug use through interaction. However, as he reached the end of the research he realised he wanted to know more precise details about the individuals in the groups he had spent time with. He was interested in the ages of the participants, their work experiences, their family background (especially parents' social class), and what drugs they had ever experimented with. He had learned a lot of this during participant observation but wanted to be sure that he had collected the data systematically, as he believed it had implications for certain general conclusions he wanted to draw. He therefore constructed a very short questionnaire and asked his participants either to fill it in or to give him the answers to the questions as he filled it in himself. His approach was still fairly informal, as he had built relationships with these people

continued on next page

and he did not now want to alienate them by appearing to be formal and distant. He explained why he needed these kinds of data and got positive responses, even to the extent that some participants suggested questions he might add to the questionnaire. As an aside, he was able to do this because of the iterative nature of his research and, because he had built such strong relationships, he was able to approach his participants several times while trying to obtain this more systematic data.

Questions

Interview questions can be open-ended, allowing a range of responses and allowing the participant to interpret each question in a variety of ways, for example 'what is going on here?' or 'how do you feel about friends?' Or questions can be closed, implying the possible range of responses within the question, for example, 'what time did you go to bed last night, was it before nine or after?' In qualitative research, questions are likely to be open-ended for various reasons. A closed question gives stilted answers. With closed questioning the participant is not able to respond freely; the researcher will not obtain a range of responses, thoughts or reflections on the issue. Closed questions tend to impose a researcher's own framework of ideas on the participant and restrict the possible range of answers. If your task is to understand the other person's world-view then you will need open questioning techniques in an unstructured interview. However, the actual questions an ethnographer asks vary from pointed, closed questions like 'how many friends do you have here?' to open-ended questions such as 'how did that make you feel?' depending on what you want to know. But, it is not so much what questions are asked as *how* they are asked and the range of responses permitted that matters. An ethnographer who sits with a list of closed questions asking each in turn, clearly recording responses briefly, perhaps even ticking boxes on a questionnaire, will receive a certain style of response that may be useful, as in Michael's case above, but will not elicit warm, considered, ambiguous, depth responses. On the other hand it is possible to ask a question like 'how many friends have you got here?' in such a way that your respondent realises she can actually talk about what friendship means to her in response to that question.

The type of response you want to a question is demonstrated in how the question is worded but also in your body language and the interaction between you and the participant

I asked British migrants in Spain 'how many friends do you have in this area?' I asked some of them this question as part of a survey, using a questionnaire, and if people responded that they didn't really know, what do you mean by friends, then I prompted for a number, as this was what the questionnaire demanded. When I asked the same question in in-depth interviews, the responses were more full, considered and discursive. I allowed this by having the tape recorder on, so I could sit back and listen and not take many notes, by not having a questionnaire on my lap indicating that I wanted responses that could be written down, and by allowing people to talk and determining my next questions based on their response. Here is one quote in response. Note that I wanted to know how Jackie felt and talked about friends rather than exactly how many she had. Once you are clear what sorts of things you want to know it is easier to determine how to ask, how to listen and how to prompt.

KAREN: *How many friends would you say you have here?*
JACKIE: Ooh, that's a difficult one. What do you want, a number?
KAREN: *Whatever you think.*

continued on next page

> JACKIE: Well, that's, phew, I don't know, everyone will say some-
> thing different won't they and it won't mean anything to you.
> I mean, what do you mean by a friend? I mean, it takes time to
> establish real friendships and we haven't been here long enough
> for that, not to really get to know people. But you meet people
> all the time and they become your friends and that. I mean
> we've got lots of people we go out with and chat to and that.
> I would say a few, yes, a few.

In ethnographic research using interviews, you are likely to have a list of areas to cover and maybe a few questions already pre-determined, but otherwise you will want to be free to introduce ideas as they occur to you or as the interviewee introduces them. Even the overall topic you want to cover in the interview may be flexible, ranging from particular areas of research interest to topics arising on the spur of the moment.

The topic on which the interview focusses may need to be flexible: Shelley's study with general practitioners

Shelley was researching general practitioners' attitudes to domestic violence, using interviews and ethnographic methods of participant observation in waiting rooms and the collection of other forms of data. During interviews she began by talking about domestic violence but found it difficult to keep doctors to this subject. At first she thought this a problem and told me, 'they kept wandering off the point. I felt like they didn't want to talk about it.' However, after some consideration of the transcripts she had collected, we realised that the doctors saw domestic violence not as a topic aside from everything else in their practice but as one element among others. Shelley's line of questioning which centred on one topic alone was not working, so she broadened the topic for interviews and talked to the doctors about a variety of patient–doctor interactions, and then later in the interview got on to the topic of domestic violence in particular.

Fixing the time and place

The time and place an interview occurs in ethnographic research can range from arranging a set time and place with your participant to opportunistically turning a situation into an interview. We therefore have to distinguish between opportunistic interviewing, and arranged interviews. Conversation and talk go on all around and an ethnographer or participant observer using interviews needs to be able to listen, hear, ask questions, and glean information in many circumstances (Kemp and Ellen 1984), taking the opportunity to ask questions casually and spontaneously, without being too demanding. But there often comes a time when you want to fix a time and place with someone (as discussed above) in order that the participant has time to sit and talk without unnecessary interruptions. Generally it is better to save such interviews until your questions have become less naïve than they will be at first and you are clearer what you want to ask.

In-depth or focussed interviews often take place after a period of participant observation has sensitised the ethnographer to the setting

Jack and Francis run a car hire firm in Spain. It is the sort of business where customers are coming in and out all the time but also where Jack and Francis might well spend a lot of time alone in the office with no customers. I spent a fair amount of time in the office doing participant observation and asking questions of them about life in Spain, about running a business, dealing with bureaucracy and learning Spanish, and about their friendships. I learned a lot from this couple and from the people coming in and out chatting with us about life in Spain. However, there came a point when I wanted to speak to Jack and Francis individually and in more depth. I had learned a lot about how they talk about certain aspects of their lives and how they shared these

continued on next page

> with others, but I had little perspective on their private thoughts
> and feelings, and their own individual expectations, desires,
> wishes and experiences. To obtain these I had to arrange inter-
> views, requesting that we meet outside of the office or when
> the office was closed to avoid interruptions. Both Jack and Francis
> told me they enjoyed the opportunity to talk to me in more depth
> and to reflect on their move to Spain individually.

Finally, interviews may be one-off or several return visits may be
made. For life history interviews the researcher will probably
become well acquainted with the interviewee over a number of
visits and meetings; other projects will involve interviewing a few
participants once.

Informality

The formality of an interview varies along a continuum from very
informal, almost casual questioning or conversation, to a more
directed approach where the researcher is more obviously in control. An interview within ethnographic research is usually informal.
If it is opportunistic it is very informal, a matter of directing questions towards somebody on the spur of the moment that they may
or may not answer in ways you had expected. I once asked a woman
in a café if I could talk to her about living in Spain and she sat down
immediately at a table and waited for my questions. I explained that
it takes some time and she said 'that's ok, I'm free all day'. If it is
arranged, then still you would normally be fairly informal in your
approach, attempting to make the participant feel at ease, and not
forcing yourself on them, not exploiting their willingness to help
someone who may appear rather powerful (see chapter 3). However
sometimes a more formal interview is necessary for the research.
This is more often the case when the person you are interviewing
is considered higher status, and you are interviewing that person
in their status role, rather than as a private individual. In these

situations the respondent is likely to work hard to preserve front (Rubin and Rubin 1995) and this is easier when a formal interview style is employed. For example, those interviewing police officers, council officials, doctors, lawyers, bank managers or politicians may find a more formal approach works better and is more appropriate.

A more formal approach may be necessary in some situations: Peter's ethnography of power sharing

Peter was interviewing politicians as part of his ethnographic study of power sharing in politicians' offices. He tried the informal approach advocated in qualitative methods textbooks but found that the participants were not taking him seriously. They found excuses for not having time to be interviewed in depth and for not talking in depth while being interviewed. Yet Peter wanted depth rather than off-the-cuff unconsidered responses. He switched to a more formal approach, first requesting time for an interview by letter and then confirming the time and place by telephone. He took the opportunity to portray himself as a serious researcher associated with a respected university. He further gave the impression of formality using formal dress code and body language at the time of the interview, and gave the appearance of being in control of the interview by arriving with a clear interview schedule. Interestingly, this enabled the respondents to begin by giving the responses they would give in their role of politicians but then as the interview progressed they were able to relax more and spend some time reflecting on things they had discussed and adding more thoughts of their own. Peter had allowed the space for these participants to respond in their role, to show their public face, before engaging with the topic on a more personal level.

Other reasons why one might use a more formal interview style are that the participant expects it, and is unnerved by the idea of very informal interviewing styles. When Judith was interviewing older people they were unsettled by her informal style to begin with and so she used a few more formal interviews, where she was less informal and chatty and showed respect for her respondents' ages and generation, to let them get used to her. They then relaxed because their interview was over, feeling they could talk to her more informally as well, in full awareness that they were still participants. A more formal approach can also enable access to a group. Once a few members have been interviewed by you in a style they recognise as an interview they can often feel they have established a reciprocal relationship with you and will introduce you to others in their group and will talk to you at other times during participant observation. And a more formal interview can be used as flattery or recognition that someone is important enough to include in the study. One woman I had spoken to on numerous occasions during fieldwork was upset that, as she put it, she was not interesting enough for me to interview. I had 'interviewed' her many times, in a very informal style and she was aware that she was a research participant, but until I interviewed her more formally she felt she had not been given full opportunity to tell her story.

Summary

In conclusion, different people and different situations require different techniques, varying along continua of structured to unstructured, formal to casual, predetermined to open-ended, and free-floating to fixed topic. However, if you are wanting to learn about feelings and thoughts and opinions, or if, in the language of the definition of ethnography in chapter 1, you are aiming to produce a richly written account that respects the irreducibility of human experience, then questions will mostly be unstructured and the approach informal.

A few points about interviews within participant observation

In fieldwork a passive approach to interviewing is usually best to start with. Leave detailed probing until you have been accepted, especially if you want to mingle and reduce your effect on your surroundings; interviewing reminds people that you are there as a researcher and can alter participant observation relationships. However, as discussed above, if handled sensitively interviewing can also complement participating and observing in positive ways.

For some groups, an attempt at direct questioning may be completely futile. You may have to glean information in various ways. Nigel Barley (1983) found he had to be very imaginative in dealing with Africans in Ghana, who will not answer any question directly, and even think it is rude to ask. This is an extreme example, but some people do make it very difficult for you to ask them things and you may have to be very sensitive.

Interviews combined with participant observation can result in you being told different things at different times. Interviews often yield superficial answers or the formal line, or what people *say* they do or say they *should* do in certain circumstances rather than what they actually do. This is not problematic if your epistemological position is that society's rules and individual actions do not always coincide. You are thus learning about the society's structure – the rules, institutions, formal organisation, norms, customs and myths people live by – and, through participant observation, how these rules and norms are interpreted in practice. On the other hand, in-depth interviews will lead to more ambiguous data, and to the private realm of ideas, thoughts, opinions and feelings, to what people actual do/did in given circumstances and how they feel about it.

Do not forget that interviews can simply take the shape of informal, opportunistic questioning, and do not be surprised if others chip in (to offer their little bit of information). Try to think of fieldwork as one long conversation with someone you are fascinated with (Rubin and Rubin 1995).

Specific interview styles

The individual life history and oral histories

There are some special types of qualitative interview worthy of a mention as you may want to employ the techniques in your own research. Life histories, for example, where a person is interviewed on a specific topic in the context of their whole life story, have a heritage that runs from the Chicago School and includes such classics as Nels Anderson's *The Hobo* (1961 [1923]) and of course *The Polish Peasant in Europe and America* (Thomas and Znaniecki 1927). There are various reasons why you might want to do life history interviews: maybe the person is famous, or has led an interesting life, or perhaps has lived a life that is typical of a certain era or culture, or maybe the person is completely insignificant and is interesting for that reason alone. For life history research people are usually visited many times, while the researcher and participant build a relationship. They will be encouraged to talk about their lives, perhaps within a given context, perhaps within their chosen context. They may be permitted to ramble a lot, wandering on to what might seem to the researcher to be irrelevant topics. Life histories fit well with the ethnographic tradition because of the emphasis on the meanings the participant/interviewee places on his or her own life story and events, and because a life history interview often builds up a rapport between interviewer and interviewee that shorter interviews might not achieve (Heyl 2001, Spradley 1979). See Rosie (1993) for an interesting combination of life story with other techniques in the construction of a narrative account, and Humphrey (1993) for a series of life stories conducted within a single community.

Others use oral histories, which are less focussed on a whole life and more focussed on a topic or part of a life. As well as contributing rich material to historical data previously collected, this method can be used to give voice to minority groups, to pay close attention to the minds of great individuals or to permit inclusion of usually silenced groups in a population, and has even been used as a form of therapy. Oral history methods have wide support in many disciplines as well as outside of academia. Oral history groups are being formed in many small towns and villages, in which locals explore their own histories. Life histories and oral histories can yield rich data alone, with no other method, and can be considered ethnographic in their own right. I will take Paul Thompson's advice:

> In a discussion of the achievement of Oral History it is right to end with Theodore Rosengarten's 'All God's Dangers', the autobiography of an illiterate Alabama sharecropper born in the 1880s, based on 120 hours of recorded conversations: one of the most moving and certainly the fullest life story of an insignificant person yet to come from Oral History. By fruits such as these one would gladly see the method judged.
>
> (Thompson 1988: 99–100)

Group discussions

In ethnographic research talk goes on all around. You are hearing, listening, joining in conversations and taking the opportunity to slot in questions of your own. The language of interviews and focus groups makes little sense in this sort of context. What we are doing is making sense of the world around us as we do normally in our daily lives and yet in a more directed, reflexive way than is normal, and we are writing about and thinking about what we see and hear. This is what makes ethnography different from simply being there. Sometimes we manage to ask something of someone on their own, many times we are within groups and our questions are directed to people in group settings, and the conversations we take part in are group conversations. On the other hand, as discussed, ethnographers do make use of individual interviewing techniques and approaches and may well take people aside to ask them some questions in a more directed way away from the rest of the group. Implicitly the idea of an interview is that you are asking the *individual* to report, reflect, and share with you. But within ethnography (as in the case with any research using interviews) you cannot always control who will be there when you do an interview. You should not be surprised to turn up and find someone there with their partner, or a friend, or even a whole group of people who have gathered around. If this happens you may be able to ask to speak to the person alone, if that is important to you and your research questions at this time, but it may inappropriate to ask. If you are interviewing a woman and her husband has decided he will be present, or an employee and the boss turns up, it may not be the case that you can ask them to leave. You may be able to take advantage of such a situation, by watching the dynamics of the group (or couple) and how they share ideas, or how thoughts are shaped in interaction. Similarly groups can be creative, bouncing ideas off each other and thus raising issues and going off in tangents you had not even considered. It is, however, usually more difficult to get people to go in-depth into a subject when they are in company. Furthermore, if one of the participants is considered or feels subordinate he or she may measure the responses more carefully, in consideration of what the other person thinks.

People will also relate to you in different ways in groups and individual interviews. Research participants tend to draw on what they are familiar with in the real world to know how to interact with you, and in an individual interview situation they may be drawing on the model of job interview or journalistic interview, or even on the model of therapeutic or confessional sessions, or as a confidential discussion with a close friend. In a group discussion the model is different. It is no longer a confessional or a job interview, but something people experience in their everyday lives at work, at home, down the pub, a normal discussion or conversation in a group with all the rules and norms that attach to those (Alasuutari 1995). In a group discussion, therefore, your own presence may become immaterial as you gradually lose control completely. Of course new ideas can emerge, but then so can the discussion wander off on to a subject that is completely irrelevant. In one group discussion I conducted spontaneously (having planned to interview just one person) the conversation turned to decorating and paint colours, painting techniques and where to buy paint-brushes. I couldn't bring it back because all the participants were enjoying their new discussion too much. However, all material is potentially interesting; it depends what you make of it, and unexpected events can turn out to be surprisingly revealing. Nigel

Gilbert (1993), for example, tells a story of a very successful group interview among abused women. The women alone, he found, would say certain things about their experiences, but in a group of people who had shared similar experiences they became more frank and open, talking freely about experiences they would not easily share in another setting.

An ethnographer may thus take advantage of naturally occurring groups and may turn the discussion around to suit their research purposes, or may turn an individual interview into a group discussion because others turn up. I call this an Opportunistic Discussion Group – 'discussion group' rather than 'group discussion' because to some extent the researcher is controlling or manipulating events.

An Opportunistic Discussion Group

One Discussion Group I conducted was entirely unplanned. I had arranged to interview one woman and when I arrived at her house there were four there. The interviewee herself was down the road knocking on a neighbour's door, trying to add to the group even then. Eventually five women sat around the small living room, some on the floor and me on a high dining chair (I asked to move to the floor but they insisted I sat there) and I proceeded to attempt to conduct individual interviews with each. I knew nothing about any of them so I had to start with questions like, 'do you live here?' 'when did you come?' and 'how many family members are here with you?' I felt embarrassed to be asking this sort of question in front of other people but the participants assured me they didn't mind, they all knew each other well. Having gleaned some information about them as individuals I couldn't proceed in this manner. I had to open it out to a group discussion so that some didn't wander off bored while I spoke to others, and so that some were not made to feel uncomfortable while all eyes were on them and their story.

continued on next page

I then asked questions like 'I see you all know each other well, how did you get to know each other?' and I developed issues that had been raised when I had spoken to each one individually, such as 'what sorts of things about home do you miss?' One thing that surprised me was that the women challenged each other, arguing and debating, and encouraging each other to admit things they had not stated at the outset. For example, one woman asked another, 'you are very unhappy here aren't you?' In my research I have often noted the problem of people saying different things in different situations and how we might deal with this (O'Reilly 2000b). One possibility is to try to note under which conditions what is said and how. Discussion groups offer another way of exploring people's stories and how they tell them and how they frame them.

Focus groups and 'Planned Discussion Groups'

There is a distinct style of research being developed in various disciplines that goes under the name of *focus groups*. The actual format a focus group takes varies with disciplines and approaches but many key characteristics are shared: a group of between four and twelve people, often strangers to each other, are selected and brought together to share a discussion around a specific topic. The aim is to generate a range of experiences, views and/or responses (Gibbs 1997, Morgan 1988). The use of focus groups has its roots in market research, where it is used to test reactions to new products. Focus groups are also increasingly used by government agencies to test reactions to new policies and ideas. The main advantage in these situations is that, since focus groups are a good way to get people to think broadly about something, a range of attitudes and responses is generated on a subject more quickly and cheaply than a survey would have provided. They can also generate responses a survey might not have included and may be better at obtaining the interviewee's perspective. Krueger (1994: 7) links the development of focus groups to the move in social research in the late 1930s (influenced by the work of the Chicago School) towards more non-directive research that aimed to understand the reality of the interviewee from his or her own perspective. Focus groups are also becoming more widely used in social research, somewhat triggered by their use in media and cultural studies to research audience interpretations of cultural and media texts. Here the notion of *how* people react to something *in interaction* is emphasised; how meaning is created in groups. In this way focus groups are faithful to the idea that people's feelings, perceptions and attitudes are formed not in isolation but in interaction with others.

The advantages of focus groups are that they generate conflicting ideas, making people change their mind and think again; they are therefore very *creative*. In some ways they are more creative and less directive than an individual interview. Ideas emerge and are introduced that the interviewer might not have considered. They can be more naturalistic than individual interviews, reflecting the idea that people make sense of their world in interaction, not as individuals, and taking on a life of their own even to the extent that participants can forget the researcher is there. The data gathered on interaction can be interesting itself of course, and (used with interviews and participant observation as other data-yielding techniques) it can be a really interesting way of looking at the gap between what people say they do, what they say they should do and what they do. Of course all of this is also true of ethnographic group discussions and discussion groups.

The problems are many. Keeping control of the situation can be very difficult, with people easily wandering off the point, and maybe even getting angry or upset with each other. They can be difficult to arrange. How do you encourage people to participate? You have to make decisions such as whether you will pay them for coming. Some focus group textbooks discuss sampling, but deciding who to include and who to exclude can be problematic. You also have to think about how to manage group effects. If you encourage quiet or reticent people to speak up, how naturalistic is the discussion? Sometimes people end up agreeing for peace and quiet. Can we say that the way ideas emerged in this setting is how they would emerge in others? Finally, recording a focus group and transcribing it can be very difficult. Before you rush to use the technique (which is becoming increasingly popular in some fields) ask why it might be beneficial. Will it generate ideas, attitudes, feelings, opinions that you wouldn't otherwise get? If so, why? Would you get the same data through natural observation? Focus groups can often artificially produce a reaction in a group more quickly than hanging around waiting for a natural situation to occur. Would you ever be able to observe such a situation? Power relations or access problems might inhibit that kind of access. Are you particularly interested in the uses of language or the generation and maintenance of culture? Or do you have a focus on conflict or consensus, and how it is achieved?

Since the technique is being increasingly used in social research more broadly, some authors have tried to distinguish between focus groups and group interviews. Gibbs (1997), for example, says a group interview involves interviewing a number of people together but the interaction is between the researcher and the participants as individuals, rather than between the participants themselves. I personally cannot imagine the kind of setting where several individuals would be interviewed at once, in a group, without any interaction as a group. For this reason I am trying here to move beyond the language of group interviews.

Planned Discussion Groups

Focus groups are dynamic and creative; they can be superficial in their treatment of a topic, giving breadth rather than depth, but also yield important information on interaction and on consensus and how it is achieved. But in order to learn about the culture or group we are interested in, it may not be necessary to organise something so formal. We can learn from the discussions that go on all around us. Spontaneous group discussions give us the opportunity as ethnographers to compare private and public discourses, and the effects of interaction on ideas and beliefs. Spontaneous group discussions then are very beneficial to our research, and we may be able to turn them around to discussion groups (discussing our own topic). However, we may not always have that opportunity and may want to arrange something that looks closer to what some people call a focus group, yet is more appropriate for ethnography, a planned discussion group (PDG).

Focus groups and PDGs have some things in common and a few key differences. Focus groups typically involve four to twelve participants (Gibbs 1997, Krueger 1994, Morgan 1988). A PDG can include any number, depending on the situation, but may be kept small in order to be more manageable. The participants in a focus group are selected because of their relation to the topic, whereas the participants in a PDG are likely to be a naturally occurring group, who have a relation to the topic because they are already part of the context of your ethnographic research. In a focus group participants are usually strangers, whereas in a PDG they are unlikely to be. The level of control of the researcher in a focus group will depend on the purpose, where in a PDG the researcher will probably learn from spontaneous interaction. Focus groups are often conducted in a series, whereas a PDG can be one-off or one of several. Focus groups are seen to be more natural than an interview because people make up their minds in groups, whereas an ethnographer using a PDG will consider the advantages and disadvantages of the various methods employed. A PDG is usually conducted in settings with which participants are familiar, or in the field, whereas a focus group is likely to be organised within an institutional setting.

A Planned Discussion Group

I was conducting participant observation in a school and wanted to talk to children about what it is like to live in Spain and their experiences of integration. I decided to ask the sociology class for their advice, and was given permission by the teacher to use one class session to ask them their views on my study and how I might go about it. One of the first things I learned in this

continued on next page

Discussion Group was that the word 'integration' does not mean much to 14 year olds. I had to operationalise my terms better and broaden the scope. We ended up talking about things that had much more meaning for them: their friends, who they hang out with after school, how they relate to people from other countries, and a whole new area emerged as relevant – where they might live in the future. The group enjoyed the discussion and decided that the best way to talk to young people about these topics was in groups rather than as individuals. That way I would generate a lot of responses at once and people would bounce ideas off each other. Organising small, homogeneous, groups was not feasible within the school day and it was no good me waiting for such groups to emerge naturally, so I decided to conduct planned discussions groups with different age groups in the classroom setting. The size and make-up of each group was therefore predetermined. They were not strangers and were homogeneous in some ways (age, some experiences) and hetero-geneous in others (nationality, gender, social class, other experi-ences). The advantage of a PDG was that it is faithful to how ideas are formed and shared in interaction. As a result I began to wonder about racism and the forms it takes and what it means in people's lives.

Discussion groups can be useful in the early or exploratory stages of ethnographic research for generating topics and responses to topics so that future research can be directed in line with participants' views of their world, rather than the researcher's. A planned dis-cussion group can be used to gain larger amounts of information over a shorter period of time than in participant observation (Gibbs 1997), and may give you the opportunity to talk to people who normally are overpowered. Madriz (2000) makes the point that focus groups (and other group discussions) can be a useful tool in feminist ethnography. Women can sometimes feel physically and emotionally safer talking in a group than on an individual basis, she has found. But we have to be sensitive to the fact that some groups of people are simply not used to discussing things in groups.

Discussions will not work for some groups

Mary was doing voluntary work in Peru and decided to use the opportunity to do some ethnographic fieldwork. The community she was working with had recently gained a community hall but did not seem to be using it very much, especially the children, who were expected to benefit most from it. She decided to try putting together some group discussions with children to see if the result would be the generation of ideas for uses of the hall, but it didn't work at all because the kids were not used to talking about their feelings or opinions on the one hand, and were not used to talking to adults at all. Mary's attempts to run a discussion were met with stony silence, giggles and stilted answers. She had an idea to let children run their own discussion groups, but still they were not able to relate to the idea of discussing ideas as a group.

Summary

This chapter began by comparing ethnographic interviewing with interviews conducted within quantitative research. Ethnographic interviewing goes on all the time and can take the form of spontaneous interviews, informal chats and questions asked on the spur of the moment during participant observation. However, there often comes a time when an ethnographer wants to take someone aside and ask some things in a quiet, comfortable setting, and some ethnographies are even based around this method as much as participant observation. Because ethnography aims to produce a richly written account that respects the complex nature of the social world, ethnographic interviews are usually unstructured and informal. However, this chapter has explored cases where you might find a more formal, structured approach and even closed questioning appropriate.

Some specific styles of interview were introduced. Oral and life history interviews have a tradition that dates back to the classical Chicago School ethnographies. Focus groups are becoming popular in many disciplines, so this chapter has explored the role of what I call discussion groups and group discussion in ethnography.

Further reading

Specialist texts on qualitative interviewing that are worth exploring are Spradley (1979) and Rubin and Rubin (1995). See Heyl (2001) for a review of ethnographic interviewing, including feminist interviewing, and Skeggs (2001) for more on feminist ethnography.

Thompson (1988) is the classic text on life histories and oral history. For a review of essays and volumes on life history and its role in ethnography see Reed-Danahay (2001), and see Plummer (2001b) on the same topic.

Gibbs (1997) and Morgan (1988) are useful texts on focus groups. Ritchie and Lewis (2003) have a fair bit on focus groups and interviewing, but not necessarily ethnographic.

6 Practical issues in interviewing

Conducting the interview

Having said in the previous chapter that I refuse to be too prescriptive about interview styles and techniques, there are a few practical guidelines I can give that relate to interviews that are pre-arranged, where you ask someone to agree to an interview, arrange a time and date with them and turn up specifically for the purpose of asking them some questions. These cover the stages of an interview, from arranging an appointment to deciding whether to record or transcribe the interview, and in most cases apply to discussion groups as well as individual interviews.

Setting up an appointment

Whilst you are doing participant observation all sorts of opportunities might arise for you to have a more in-depth conversation with someone. You find yourself listening to people, joining in conversations, slotting in a few questions of your own, directing discussions towards topics related to your research, and even initiating conversations. When you want to explore some issues or ideas in a little more depth you may be able very casually to ask someone to join you for a coffee, or to sit somewhere quieter and more private. Or you can ask someone to meet you later for more of a chat. However, it is likely that at some stage you will want to arrange an interview with someone a little more formally and concretely than that. How do you go about it? Well, first of all I should say that in my experience people enjoy being interviewed and are happy to agree as long as they are not nervous about what you might ask, and can fit it in to any busy schedule they may have. So, it is important that you give the participant some information about what you are doing and why and that you fit in with them in terms of place and time of the interview. Of course, the actual approach depends on the person you are interviewing and the topic. Some people require a letter or phone call or both. Others don't need to be approached so formally. Some will want to know about your research in great detail, others will be happy to have a vague idea of your interests. Generally, you can consider the standard approach in ethnographic research to be informal, an approach that puts people at their ease, is not exploitative or demanding, and gives them power and control where possible. You should begin by telling participants what the research is all about, and giving them the chance to ask questions. Do this via a letter, a phone call, or (better) face to face. You should explain what you mean by an interview, how long it might take, what sorts of questions you will ask, and what will happen to the data. You should reassure the participant that they do not have to say anything they don't want to, that the research is confidential, that if they think you are asking the wrong questions they can tell you, and that they can change their minds at any time. I find a fairly humble approach works best, that demonstrates fascination and empathy with the person, making them feel that their contribution is crucial to the project. However, this approach must be combined with professionalism and a sense of earnest. If you are flippant, or too casual, and do not appear to be taking what you are doing seriously then why should anyone respond? Furthermore, being too casual might not work for some people. You might need to be more formal and more in control of the situation for some groups and some individuals.

Access can go through several stages and styles of approach

John undertook ethnographic research in a school. His access to the school and to interviews went through several stages.

He had a friend who was a teacher in the school, and she told the headmistress informally about John's research.

John then wrote a letter to the headmistress explaining more fully and asking to meet her. At this meeting he described his proposed project in full and presented the headmistress with a written summary of it that she could read more closely later. He used headed notepaper from his university, and included the name and telephone number of his supervisor, in case the headmistress wanted to verify anything. The school was told in an assembly about John's research and a short summary of his project was pinned on a notice board for all to see.

John then began visiting the school regularly, sitting in lessons, walking around the playground, chatting to people in classrooms and as they played outside during breaks, and talking with the staff during their breaks. He wanted to talk with a few members of staff in more depth so during their coffee breaks arranged a time and place when they might be able to concentrate more and be undisturbed.

He also wanted to interview the headmistress of the school but, although she had agreed to be interviewed, each time he approached her she had an excuse for not fixing a time or place. He was approaching her too informally and when she was busy thinking about other things. In the end John wrote the headmistress a short note saying that he was pleased she had agreed to talk to him, and that as time was getting short he hoped it would be okay for him to come by her office at 4 p.m. (a time he knew things were a little calmer) and arrange the interview with her. He turned up at her office at 4 p.m. with his diary and pen in his hand, and a big smile on his face, and asked 'is this a good time to try to fix an appointment with you for the interview?' It was.

Whether your approach is less or more formal, setting up an appointment is usually easier if the person has seen you face to face, or if they know someone who has met you before and can vouch for you on a personal level. Some people use a letter or phone call as the first step and in that ask to meet the person to explain about the research and ask for an interview. You might consider using another word than 'interview', asking people to meet you to talk about something, or to have a chat, for example. You can still demonstrate that it is the other person's point of view you are interested in, not your own, but the word interview is already infused with meanings from other areas of social life – job interviews, for example. If you believe what you are doing is important and you put that across it is usually possible to persuade someone to agree to an interview. Here are a few points to bear in mind:

- Ask the person face to face for time to share a conversation or, if that is difficult, use a phone call or letter to explain something about your research and to ask for an interview.
- Consider using a letter to ask to meet the person to explain more about your research before they agree to an interview.
- When setting up the appointment give the participant the opportunity to ask about the research and the interview. Prepare a short paragraph or two on the project that you can leave with them to read later if they want to.
- Try using other words than 'interview', e.g. can we meet to chat, discuss, talk, have a conversation.
- Combine professionalism with empathy and interest, but avoid sounding patronising.
- Explain about your research and what will happen to the data.
- Give participants a good reason to contribute to the research.
- Reassure participants that they can stop the interview, change their minds, refuse to answer, add new questions.
- Ask permission if you want to record and transcribe (and maybe archive) the interview.

Time

People often ask me how many interviews can be conducted in a day. If we focus merely on in-depth interviews rather than on the myriad conversations that can go on during participant observation, then I would have to say do not try to do too many interviews in one day. It is exhausting. You are listening attentively, empathising and drawing on your own emotional reserves, while also thinking about the implications of what the person is saying for your overall research interests, and for what you might ask next. You may be taking notes, you may be keeping one eye on your tape recorder and the other on the time, yet both on the participant. You may be listening to harrowing details of a person's personal experiences on the one hand, or on the other hand, as they are telling you a long-winded story about how their cat was brought down from the neighbour's tree you might be thinking how to bring the subject back to your topic or determining whether this might after all be relevant. Interviewing is completely engrossing. I doubt anyone could manage more than two in-depth interviews in one day, and even less than that if the interview is very long or intense.

It is worth remembering that interviewing can also be tiring for the other person, so even if you are feeling fresh and relaxed watch out for signs of tiredness from your research participants. Most in-depth interviews last between forty-five minutes and two hours. This is because less than forty-five minutes is not long enough to begin to talk in-depth about a subject, and after two hours people are generally getting tired. However, this is not to say that longer or shorter interviews are of no value. People have been known to tell me some very intimate things as a result of a great deal of reflexive thought in just fifteen minutes (usually because we have spoken before) and others have talked freely and happily for three hours without showing any signs of tiredness (usually because we have stopped for coffee, changed the subject several times, and the interview has not been intense).

Try to find some time to sit quietly directly after the interview to think about the themes that arose, to listen to your tape (if you used one) and make sure it worked, to check your notes and add anything to them that you didn't have time to note during the interview. You may want to note down a few things about the setting, about body language, atmosphere, facial expressions. You should also spend some time merely reflecting on the interview and letting what was said work through your brain. You should never go straight from one interview to the next. If you do, there is a danger you will get the two participants confused, think you have asked something when you haven't or ask the same thing twice. You will not be able to give the participant due concentration, effort and interest.

As an interviewer you have to be fairly flexible with regards to time: you are subject to other people's whims and fancies, fears and frustrations. You might suggest the participant allows an hour and a half but they might have other ideas. Some interviews take much longer than you had expected. I went to interview one couple and they had invited five of their friends round for tea within an hour of the start of the interview. They hoped I would stay and meet them all and talk to them as well. I was there for five hours. Others are cut short for various reasons, and some just do not happen at all. A couple I went to interview had forgotten I was coming and were on their way out. They said, 'that's okay, come with us and interview us on the way'. So I did. It might be an idea to take some sort of snack in your bag in case of emergencies.

Remember there is more to interviewing than interviewing. Interviewing involves thinking, planning, writing, discussing with friends and colleagues, sorting through for themes, reading notes and transcripts and thinking again before the next interview. This is all part of the work. If you can avoid it, don't try to do several interviews in a row as if you are picking flowers. The flowers metaphor only works if you stop to look at the flowers and try to arrange them as you go along. A few points:

- Interviews usually last between forty-five minutes and two hours (as a rough guide).
- Allow time after the interview to reflect on it intellectually and to check tape recording and notes.

- Try to do no more than two interviews a day.
- Have a flexible schedule so that you can deal with the unexpected.

Role

It is important in interviewing as well as participant observation to think about how you present yourself, what role you adopt, and how this might affect the interview. People react based on who they think you are, so think carefully what sorts of responses you are looking for. Perhaps you will take on a role similar to a therapist or an activist, a reporter or a historian. Some of my interviewees in Spain were anti-academic and anti-professional; it worked for me to be more like an interested friend and an empathetic observer (useful being a participant) or a type of therapist – not an academic. Of course, you are not a therapist and should not try to be one. What I am suggesting is that as part of the reflexive approach to interviewing you consider the nature of the interrelationship between you and the other person or people. The questions you ask will also affect how people see you. I got cast as tax inspector for a while because I had been asking about money. When Frederick interviewed men who took on the mothering role (chapter 8) he took on the role of empathetic bloke who was fascinated by the idea of men taking on the caring role but was not sure he could do it himself. This meant the participants could feel comfortable talking to him about their successes as well as their difficulties. However, this should be more a matter of emphasis than pretending to be someone you are not. Don't put yourselves at the risk of destroying an interview by being caught out pretending to be someone else; apart from being unethical this would be quite dysfunctional. Rubin and Rubin (1995) insist you need to be warm and responsive in order to make a relationship. It is okay to smile, grimace, and even look shocked, as long as it is *with* someone and not *at* them. They suggest that a good role is to think of yourself as developing a friendship, where you are the one doing the listening.

Place

Where should an in-depth ethnographic interview take place? If possible, choose a small, comfortable setting with few distractions. I find it useful to let the other person choose the place and time, to an extent, as long as you give them an idea that what you want is the opportunity to talk freely and comfortably. You can learn a lot about the person from allowing them these decisions, and it also makes them feel the interview is theirs as well as yours. A conversational-style interview will work better in a comfortable, small and private or intimate setting. Frederick asked his participants for some time when the children would be in bed or out for his in-depth interviews, explaining that the participant would be able to relax and enjoy it more that way. Too much background noise will affect your taping, if you do it, and certain settings may make intimate discussions difficult. However, I have conducted long interviews about people's personal lives and backgrounds in a busy Spanish bar with the television on and it has worked quite well.

Conduct

Try to think of the interview as a conversation with a difference: the difference is you are in control! Try to think of it as a conversation where you are focussing on the other person, guiding them, asking for explanation or depth. Try not to interrupt long renditions, but if you have to, guide the participant gently back to your topic. Encourage depth by asking for more details, for specifics or thoughts, when given brief answers. But always be polite and respectful. I have treated you as intelligent researchers and not included prescriptions such as don't ask questions like 'how often do you beat your wife?' (that is, very pointed or sensitive questions). or 'what do you think about friendship?' or 'how was it to be a male mother?' (that is, very general and vague questions). Avoid questions which are confusing, full of negatives, obviously expecting a certain answer, too closed (unless you want closed answers) or too nebulous (unless you want nebulous answers). But it is difficult to be prescriptive about such things. I tend to ask myself questions such as, was the participant able to argue with me if he or she wanted to, could they expand or interject where necessary, did I allow them to ask questions and to think things through and change their minds? If you are sure of the quality or type of response you are hoping for it will enable you to check that you are making space for this to emerge.

The ethnographic interview

The best kind of in-depth interview takes place in a comfortable setting and consists of an hour or two of meaningful conversation between two people, who chat freely and undisturbed. One is doing more of the listening and the other more of the talking but both feel relaxed and are enjoying the experience.

Some rules can be broken – people can chip in, the room can be large and noisy, the approach can be fairly formal to begin with, that is all okay, as long as the participants feel comfortable and unpressured, and are able to talk to you freely and happily. If either of you feels pressured, if either can't concentrate (for example, because children are running around), if the conversation is not flowing well, or if it is hurried, the quality of what you hear will be affected and it is probably better to leave it and try again another time.

Beginning

Hopefully you have had time to discuss the interview and confidentiality previously, but reiterate it here, especially where there is concern shown. However, don't insist on it if things are flowing nicely; you can remind them at the end. Typically, begin with an informal chat, with phrases like: 'it's nice here isn't it?' Don't be afraid to make a joke or two to put the person, and yourself, at ease. Then get on to the topic you want to focus on gradually, starting from its edges. This early chat allows you to show empathy. In Frederick's research on male full-time carers, for example, he could start by talking about the children, the flat or house, being at home and not working, and so on – topics related to the one under research. Eventually he would need some more directed questions that begin to get to the topic, such as 'so, when were the children born?' and 'were you working at the time?' But *not* 'how did it feel to be a male mother?' or other such sweeping questions early on. Gently encourage openness and frankness. Demonstrate that you really are listening by repeating what's been said and asking relevant follow-up questions. Generally, you will have to wait until you have shown whose side you are on before asking very sensitive questions, but sometimes you will have to continue talk around the subject rather than being too direct.

Don't be afraid to be in control of the interview, but allow the participant some control. Show you have some understanding of the subject by talking about your own related experiences or reading you have done, or people you have talked to, but be careful not to influence the response too much, and remain naïve in as much as you admit the interviewee can teach you a lot. Showing that you are sort of in charge (that is, not overpowering but that you know what you are doing) is more likely to put participants at ease than if you are fumbling and mumbling, but showing that they are the expert on the topic will encourage their responses.

The interview guide or plan

It is very difficult in ethnographic research to prescribe what an interview guide or plan should look like. Sometimes, more directed questions will be used early in the stages of research when learning about a subject, then the information gleaned will be used to guide more informal discussions later, where you are less directed, less formally addressed, and hold interviews that are more like conversations. Other ethnographers will work the other way around, asking all sorts of little informal questions early on then being more directed as the theory and analysis develop. But informality in no way equates with lack of preparation! It is important to know what you want to achieve and then design a guide to suit you. Rubin and Rubin (1995) talk of a conversational guide which has a set of *main questions*, and *probes* which enable these to be explored in depth if the participant gives brief answers, then *follow up questions* to take you into more depth. Rubin and Rubin insist any interview guide needs some kind of structure yet flexibility to enable you to respond to the interview situation. Personally, I have a topic or two that is the focus of the interview. This is broken down into a list of questions that I hope to cover, and these are broken down into sub-questions to help me if I am not getting the depth I hoped for. The list never goes over one page as this looks rather daunting to the participant. But I often find that responses to one or two questions will lead to a conversation that covers many of the others. A guide is there to help you if a conversation does not flow, and as a checklist if you need it, but should not restrict free-flowing conversation. Certainly, do not be afraid to ask questions that are not there, and do not feel every question you have listed must be covered. If you don't need a guide don't use one, especially for chats that go on within participant observation. When you have pre-arranged an interview, some participants, however, feel more comfortable when they see you have a list of things to cover.

In preparing for the interview, the degree of naivety which may help you find things out during participant observation may be something of a hindrance. You will usually get nowhere unless you know a little about your subject first (whether that be a topic or a person). 'Busy people will not consent to be interviewed repeatedly by the manifestly inept' (Rock 2001: 34). Even a life story interviewer has usually read a little about the person's life, town, area of interest. It is a sign of respect, giving value to the person. But knowing too much can leave the participant with nothing to tell you. The best advice I can give is to be knowledgeable with regard to background information, but naïve with regard to the precise topic you are wanting the participant to tell you about.

Finishing

Do not try to cover too many topics and do not feel you have to cover everything you planned to. The interview should be enjoyable for both (or all) of you, not overwhelming. You should try to move away from emotional topics as you come to the end of the interview, by steering people off gently on to other topics. Try to end on a cheerful note (incidentally this goes for all types of interview, including quantitative ones). I usually finish by resuming the informal chat I began with, then thank the participant, and ask if I can stay in touch, either for clarification of points or to share findings, or even the transcript. Check points of confidentiality, sharing of notes, etc. Remind them if necessary of what you said at the beginning about confidentiality. If someone was being taped and said some very sensitive things, check that it is okay to use it.

Recording the interview

You might want to video or tape record an interview. Videos are especially good for discussion groups, for example. Or you might take notes, or you might write notes up afterwards. Whether or not you decide to tape record an interview depends on the amount of detail needed and the potential effect on the participants. It depends how much recording equipment might disturb the interview, and on the comfort of the interviewer and interviewee with recording equipment. This means you also have to account for the feelings of the interviewer – you! Judith's (chapter 5) older participants were initially cautious about talking to her and she felt it was inappropriate to ask to record interviews she had insisted were informal and confidential. The British Consul, whom I interviewed about British migrants in Spain, did not mind being recorded but said much more after I had turned the recorder off than when it was on. Interestingly, when I asked if I could use the material that had not been recorded he agreed happily. It also depends on the circumstances of the interview, where you are, how long you have had to prepare, what the reception (sound) would be like. There is also the nature of the material to be taken into account. Some topics are far more sensitive than others and the presence of a tape recorder may make some people feel very uncomfortable. Frederick (chapter 8) had no problem asking those men who were caring for their children full time for taped interviews; Gail, who did ethnographic research amongst her boyfriend's mates, felt very uncomfortable to ask if she could record interviews. Rubin and Rubin (1995) note how incongruous it appears to ask to record an interview when you have simply asked someone for an informal chat; however, since a distinct advantage is that you are then free to listen and think, this is what I explain to participants as my main reason for wanting to record.

Of course if you want to donate your data to an archive so that they can be analysed by subsequent researchers, you will need to tape record as much as possible, and of course you have to think about what to do with the information you gleaned when the tape recorder was off, and what it could not see. The advantages of recording are that you get all of the interview, but you should not forget about what happened before and after the tape was on. You can then keep the tape or transcription for future reference and you don't have to worry about memory. However, do not leave it too long before listening to it, making sure the tape worked, making additional notes, noting the context and body language and adding any other explanatory notes. Recording can also be useful in indicating to the interviewee that you are taking a professional approach, or that you are taking the interview seriously. I began one interview with my recorder off as we were in a busy bar and the interview was somewhat opportunistic, but the man I was interviewing stopped and asked me 'are you going to switch that on, then?' I said I thought it might be better for me to take notes afterwards and he said 'well, I've got a lot to tell you, you'd be better recording it'. I switched the recorder on and the interview flowed much better from that moment. It turned out to be a very good thing that I had turned it on because two other people joined us, and as we spoke some Spanish and some English it would have got very difficult for me to continue remembering what was said. Recording also allows you to concentrate rather than having to keep notes, thus leaving you free to plan follow-up questions. You can relax more and listen better rather than worrying about missing bits. You might, nevertheless, be glad to have a pen and paper handy so that you can jot down thoughts and points you want to follow up. I would conclude by saying that to tape record is the best option if it is possible. It can be made more palatable by offering transcripts of the interview to participants. But, if you cannot record then it is better to do the interview unrecorded than forget it simply because you cannot record it.

One disadvantage is that the interview can take longer. You need longer to get into a conversation if either you or the other person feels at all uncomfortable. Some interviews work better without recording, for example some official interviews work better without a tape recorder, since the presence of such equipment can stilt conversations and encourage guarded behaviour. There is also a tendency for you to think less about the interview and the themes that are emerging from it when you are recording or have recorded because there is the security of knowing you have it all on tape. Yet, taking the time to listen to it all again or to read through the transcript adds to your workload. Thinking during an interview is crucial, if ethnographic research is to be iterative. If you do tape, get the technology right, know your equipment and make sure you have enough batteries or access to power to last! Don't be tempted to do a series of tapes without looking at the material in between. You should check it has recorded properly, and in an iterative research design you need to be thinking about what you will ask the next person in light of what the last one said.

Transcribing

If you have recorded an interview then it makes sense to transcribe fully, and verbatim, if you have got the time and/or money. Verbatim transcripts enable a range of later analyses (and archiving for secondary analysis). Verbatim transcripts are not selective, as your memory and notes would be. You may not yet know what themes are significant for your research and so verbatim transcripts enable the storage of themes you had not considered. But transcribing is very time-consuming and costly if you pay someone to do it. One hour of tape can take six to eight hours to transcribe (and more for discussion groups). Many people get around these problems by transcribing early interviews fully and then taking themes from later ones. You should always do some of the transcribing yourself as the process enables you to start identifying themes and making connections. You become very familiar with the data and know later exactly where to find the bit you were looking for. Keep a note pad handy to write down thoughts as you transcribe.

You must always ask permission from participants before tape recording and mention that you might record, in notes, more than is on the tape. You can offer copies of the transcripts and should alert respondents to sensitive discussions by saying afterwards 'that was very frank – is it okay to use it?' Liz Kelly (1988) makes the point that a transcription of an interview is important since even one word left out can make a huge amount of difference to the meaning, but on the other hand, meaning is also conveyed in tone and gesture, and we need somehow to make sure these are recorded too or accept that someone reading a transcript will never get the full meaning.

Note-taking during interviews

If you decide not to record an interview, you have to take notes. Note-taking requires skill and practice. You need shorthand or quick writing and a good memory. It takes time to write things down, however quick you are, and sometimes the most you can manage is to jot down a few points. Immediately afterwards reread your notes and write them up in full. Add points of context, and pad out your notes to as full a record as you can achieve. This process also enables you to think about what you heard and plan your next set of questions. To help you reconstruct from memory, jot down all the main points as soon as you can and leave space to pad them out as you remember more and more. Some people talk into a dictaphone as soon as they leave the interview. This can work for participant observation too, making comments whenever you have the opportunity and then writing it all up later. Where possible, do *not* wait until after another conversation before writing up your notes (or at least making whatever notes you can) from an interview. If an interview is tiring anyway, doing one and taking notes can be exhausting. During the interview your concentration will be very high, listening, extracting themes, asking for clarification or depth, remembering points to raise later. Note-taking can stilt the conversation, and can be open to accusations about lack of validity, or of putting words in the respondent's mouth because you have no proof. On the other hand, I have found that when I conduct an interview the notes I compile from it afterwards can be almost as full as the length of an interview transcript. With practice, it is amazing how much you can remember. Of course, you will never be sure if you have remembered something as it was said or have slightly altered phraseology or wording. For this reason in a report or write up I find it more honest not to use a direct quote unless I am absolutely sure that's what it is, and to find some way of indicating (for example, by using different font styles) where a quote is from memory or from a transcript.

Interpretation of results

Always remember that people may be answering what you want to hear, or what they think you want to hear, or even what they want you to hear (they may have a political agenda of their own). The person could be deliberately misleading or even lying or being purposely evasive. Validity can be checked by the following means:

- using internal triangulation (eliciting the same data from the same person using different techniques);
- by external triangulation, or comparing reports of various informants;
- by comparing reports with own observations.

You can take note of contradictions between when the tape recorder is off and on (if you use one), watch for facial expressions, and if necessary probe for more information. But, ultimately, the lies people tell, the myths they live by or the contradictions they express are data in themselves. You should ask yourself what you are trying to get at: how people feel or what really happened?

Samuel and Thompson (1990) for example, draw on life history data to show how, in the telling of their stories, people reshape their memories, and recycle their traditions in order to make sense of the past in the context of the present. People tell their stories as fictions, for example as the successful business woman, the coping mother, the second-generation Muslim. The issue is whether what people tell you should be seen as a direct report of their experiences or as 'actively constructed narratives' (Silverman 2000: 32). Rosie (1993) for example, through a case study of how one young boy uses stories to achieve specific aims, suggests a way narratives can be interpreted even if they are clear fantasies. I recently interviewed some children in an international school. They told me stories of racism from Spanish children. I am not sure whether all the stories were true; certainly some sounded exaggerated. I could check using various techniques, but what is important to me is that if these children feel so aware of racism, and are constructing it as a story to talk about their relations with Spanish kids, this may well affect the form relationships actually take in the future. Finding out what is really going on may well be a way of addressing this as a problem.

Summary

This chapter has attempted to outline some prescriptions and guidelines for conducting planned ethnographic interviews. The first step, of course, is arranging an interview, which may require a phone call or letter or, even better, a face-to-face invitation. In encouraging people to participate it is important to think about why it is in their interest and show due respect for their point of view. It is nice to be able to present potential interviewees with some kind of summary of your research that they can read at their leisure (and show to their friends). The chapter suggested guidelines for the conduct of an interview. An in-depth interview normally takes between forty-five minutes and two hours, and should take place in a small and comfortable setting. You should conduct yourself sensitively, not trying to cover too many topics, and not dominating the situation. No more than two in-depth interviews should be attempted in one day and notes should be written up and recordings checked as soon as possible after the interview. An interview normally begins and ends with informal chat.

You may want to record and transcribe interviews. I argue that it is better to record if possible but it is not essential (as are none of the prescriptions above – ethnography should take a flexible and reflexive approach to all data collection). However, taking notes in an interview that is not recorded requires skill and effort. Finally, there are ways you can check the validity of what people are telling you, but depending on your philosophical position you may be as interested in the role and construction of stories and myths.

Further reading

As with chapter 4, practical issues are best considered through practice and reading reports of other researchers' practice. There are several references throughout this chapter you can follow up and a considerable amount of research has been done using qualitative interviews, from which you can learn. Rubin and Rubin (1995) have very good practical tips from design through to conducting and analysing interviews, and have very good advice about interview guides.

Technology for recording and transcribing interviews changes so fast a book cannot remain up to date but I have found journalists to be better than social scientists at being at the cutting edge with information about what is being developed and how it is used.

7   Visual data and other things

We noted in chapter 1 that Malinowski advised not simply the collection of observations and words but also the collection of other forms of data. There may be any number of things that we would want to collect that would enable us better to understand the group of people we are coming to know. For Malinowski this included collecting and making your own statistical summaries, collecting artefacts, taking photographs, making lists, documenting habits, drawing maps and much more besides. It was argued that in some ways this reflected his positivism-informed need to collect evidence and facts, but in contemporary ethnography the collection of things other than words and observations need not be a positivist exercise. You may want to make use of or collect memos, photographs, advertisements, gossip, diaries, letters. The point of this chapter is to make you think about what else might be out there that is worthy of including as 'data'. I will start by thinking about visual data and then briefly consider other forms of data, before exploring two very specific approaches to the analysis of 'texts': semiotic and content analysis.

Visual data

Given that ethnography is an observation-based method of studying society it is interesting to note the relative underuse of visual images even today. Maybe we can explain this with reference to the historical prevalence of the use of words and texts as both evidence and the medium of description and explanation. We simply do not always know what to do with images and other things: they seem to be more complicated and troublesome than words. Yet, as Ken Plummer (2001a: 66) has noted, it does seem strange that something that a social scientist would consider something of a dream – 'life as it is lived accurately recorded as it happens, and constantly available for playback and analysis' – should have been so systematically overlooked. And even if you are not remotely seduced by natural science's ability to produce evidence, surely you would want to make use of such powerful tools for interpreting and understanding social experience as letters, diaries, film and photographs. However, a field of visual ethnography is emerging, albeit as a diverse specialism rather than being incorporated within mainstream ethnography (Ball and Smith 2001), and though it is still unusual to see articles or even books using pictures there is growing awareness that the visual is an important area. There are now several useful books that introduce the topic within sociology, anthropology and cultural studies, and at least three journals that feature the visual as a topic: *Visual Anthropology*, *Qualitative Sociology* and *Visual Studies*, of which the latter has now been running since the 1980s. Other journals, such as *Ethnography*, are happy to use visual images as part of research 'writing'. There is also an International Visual Sociology Association, and a Society for Visual Anthropology. However, some disciplines have embraced the visual more readily than others; it is becoming commonplace for anthropology conferences to have films showing, for example, and the University of Manchester now offers a PhD with Visual Media or an MA in Visual Anthropology, at the Granada Centre for Visual Anthropology. Much less seems to be happening in sociology and other disciplines.

Of course, there remain lingering problems for visual ethnography: publishers often resist the inclusion of images in texts as they cost more to produce and reproduce than words; and there are numerous legal, ethical and economic issues with taking photographs and film. They cannot be anonymised so easily as you can do with words, you have to get permissions to reproduce images published elsewhere, and publication of images can be refused.

Some people do not like to be photographed. I wanted to use pictures of older North European migrants in Spain, in order to support an argument that many stereotypes of old age are undermined in this context, but so far I have found it difficult to take photographs without people appearing uncomfortable. Sometimes participants will tell you what to take pictures of. These problems raise all sorts of interesting research questions about why participants might refuse, what they advise, and what you might use instead, but using images remains a challenge (Emmison and Smith 2000).

Visual data can cause difficulties for retaining anonymity

Claire (see chapter 8) conducted research among fishing families and other islanders she had grown up with. When it came to telling descriptive stories about life for fisher folk and their families she was able to retain anonymity for respondents by switching people's stories around a little – telling one person's story combined with another, for example. She would have liked to have used photographs to help tell her stories, but as she explained, how could she switch people's images around to obtain the ring of truth but retain anonymity?

When researchers first started to think about visual data it was usual to distinguish between images produced as part of the research 'writing' and images produced by the social actors being studied. According to a call for papers for a conference on visual media in 1999, the first were to be encouraged because 'communicating research findings by using visual media can vastly expand and strengthen the rhetoric of sociological expression' and the second were seen to be useful because 'images encode data about values, norms and practices that are often inaccessible to other forms of collecting and reporting information'. Now, this distinction is becoming blurred while some researchers construct images with the research participants as a research method, and others produce the finished presentation with the research participants themselves in a joined effort. However, I will attempt to explore the three uses separately:

- images as 'writing'
- 'found' images
- creative use of images.

Images as 'writing'

The tradition for taking photographs to support one's ethnographic data and presenting them with the written text as visual 'evidence' of being there dates back at least as far as Malinowski, who took and made extensive use of photographs as documentary evidence, as an aid to his scientific approach, providing a unique visual record of Trobriand life (Ball and Smith 2001, Wright 1994). While the early anthropologists were able to use photographs as a short cut to giving the readers a feel for the exotic, strange and distant cultures they studied (Emmison and Smith 2000), sociologists have traditionally used fewer photographs. Nels Anderson's *The Hobo* (1961 [1923]) and Frederick Thrasher's *The Gang* (1963 [1926]) are notable exceptions, but sociological ethnographers, who were preoccupied with obtaining the respondent's point of view rather than the ethnographer's, also tended to do ethnography closer to home than anthropologists, and thus were arguably less likely to take the opportunity to exoticise their 'natives'.

Though still not used widely, the tradition of using images to convey a message has continued through to the present day. Some people are using images of tourist areas, for example in the sociology of development, to demonstrate what is being developed, where and how. Plummer (2001a) mentions two interesting modern studies: Don Kulick's (1999) study of transvestites and transsexuals, in which, he says, photographs enrich the text – you can see what injecting silicon into the buttocks does to them! And Jerry Jacobs' *Sun City* (1974), an ethnographic description of a retirement community, where photographs are used to illustrate cleanliness and desolation. Even as I describe these to you I feel the frustration of not being able to show you the pictures. The point is that in these cases *the images are being used to make an argument* (even when they are used overtly as illustration). And the argument can be made very forcefully using visual media. I will always remember attending a seminar in which the presenter was describing the effects of building a new sports stadium in a run-down part of a large city. Locals were told that the development would be good for the local economy and therefore beneficial to them in terms of jobs, incoming visitors and boosts to trade. The presenter (whose name I have sadly forgotten) showed pictures of a great wooden fence that had been constructed around the stadium building site and which effectively cut off the nearby houses, causing people to walk miles to the shops. One picture which stays in my mind was of an elderly woman carrying bags of shopping, bent double with the effort, and the fence looming up behind her. It was a very effective use of visual imagery.

Pictures and film have therefore been used to *support* written data, to make the argument more forcefully or more profoundly. One example that is usually cited is *Balinese Character*, by Gregory Bateson and Margaret Mead (1942). But here, instead of the photographs supporting the written text, the photographs are the main medium of communication while the text has the support role. Between 1936 and 1939 Mead and Bateson worked among the Balinese, Bateson taking over 25,000 photographs while Mead took notes and asked questions. The book then displays 759 of the photographs with supporting text. Their argument is that pictures can convey more of Balinese ethos and character than words could do alone (Ball and Smith 2001). The photographs, which were taken randomly and spontaneously of natural events, show how the Balinese 'as living persons, moving, standing, eating, sleeping, dancing, and going into trance embody that abstraction which . . . we technically call culture' (Bateson and Mead 1942: xii, cited in Emmison and Smith 2000: 31). In other words, culture is not something that exists in words and texts; it exists in lives, in bodies and actions, and photographs are better than words for conveying this. The photographs are sometimes quite shocking, showing among other things images of ritual self-wounding and a dog eating a child's faeces. I cannot help wondering what would happen if we showed such pictures of contemporary subjects on our doorsteps.

But, the use of photography and film has not always been as spontaneous or as faithful to reality as that of Bateson. Indeed Ball and Smith (2001) argue that, from A. C. Haddon's 'The Torres Straits' exhibition of 1898 onwards, it has been quite commonplace for ethnographers to film and photograph staged events. So, visual media have been used to convey messages and make arguments, from Malinowski's scientific collection of facts and data to contemporary uses of photographs to tell stories about life in prison. But we need not stop there. Quantitative researchers have always used visual images to convey messages, in the form of bar charts, pie charts, tables and graphs, and there is no reason why ethnographers cannot use similar and more techniques in their presentation and writing.

'Found' images

A further possible use of visual media in ethnographic research is in the analysis and interpretation of visual data produced by the research participants. Posters that have been produced, advertisements, drawings, diagrams, indeed anything the participants make or present can be considered data and can aid in your attempts to make sense of their worlds. Worth (1980) calls these 'found' data to distinguish data that you find in the field from data you construct. In these cases you are likely to be asking questions such as: how has this image been constructed? What is being 'said' here? The term *photoanalysis* refers to the way you as a researcher might begin to analyse photographs and other visual material by asking yourself a series of questions about them, such as 'what is your immediate impression, what is happening, who is in the photograph, what about the background?' (Plummer 2001a: 65). This perhaps moves us away from ethnography to some extent and towards a more cultural studies, content analysis or semiotic approach (discussed below). However, I have used such techniques within ethnography, in order to explore the participant's view of the world as expressed implicitly through things produced. Contentiously, this may lead you to challenge or question what participants have told you at other times, and may lead you to think again about what you have been told, and maybe to reflect on and begin to analyse more deeply what you think is happening. But I do not believe that the ethnographer's view is always the same as the participant's, and nor need it be, otherwise why not let the participant tell his or her own story (and each participant a different one)? Social research, for me, has to be more than that. You do find you begin to interpret the many things you see and hear and try to explain them from your own perspective and drawing on your own view of the world. Visual media, therefore, can enable you to challenge what the research participants are telling you, and can direct your research in further or new directions.

Visual media can make an important contribution to ethnographic analysis: Mary's ethnography in a doctor's surgery

Mary was doing ethnographic research in a doctor's surgery in an attempt to understand attitudes towards and feelings about childhood asthma. Doctors and nurses had portrayed very positive attitudes and had described the many facilities and responses they have to the condition. Mary searched the surgery notice boards for leaflets and eventually found a few tucked behind other leaflets, not at all well displayed and rather dog-eared. However, rather than merely assuming the practitioners were lying, she raised this with them and they were actually very intrigued. It turned out that notice boards and displays were cared for by reception staff, who were usually too busy to spend much time on them. Mary was able to conclude that though the practitioners were generally very pro-active in helping people with asthma, they had not thought of the visual aspects of the waiting room as important in interaction between the patient and the practice.

How images are analysed or interpreted will depend on an ethnographer's theoretical, methodological and philosophical agenda. It is not my job to tell you how to analyse but merely to explore possibilities. We may want to search for what is *really* going on, what is *really* being said, but we should also remember that images and their interpretations, and the ethnographer's interpretations, will always to some extent be context dependent. Visual images can be analysed in terms of their content – what they say, what they contain, how they appear – as well as their utility – how they are used, where they are displayed. But they can also be explored in terms of how people talk about them and use them to talk about other things. Sarah Pink (2001), for example, describes how the women in her study saw a particular image of a woman bullfighter as representative of local traditional femininity and used it to talk more generally about traditional images of women, whereas the woman herself does not see herself as a traditional woman, and the photograph was taken on a very non-typical day during *feria*.

Creative use of images

Anthropologists have taken photographs and collected other visual artefacts since the dawn of the discipline. Malinowski took lots of photographs and told his readers to collect data on as many facets of life as possible. However, a goal of social science at the time was to emulate the natural sciences in its achievement of objective knowledge. Photographs were thus seen as useful in as much as they contributed to the truthful and verifiable representation of reality. But, by the end of the 1960s a debate had emerged about the value of visual images as objective, representative (of reality) and systematic. They were seen as too problematic to take seriously by many authors (Pink 2001). Some tried to respond to these criticisms with attempts to employ visual media in rigorous, scientific ways that control for the subjectivity of the researcher (Collier 1995, Mead 1995). Collier (1967) is a key text, representative of the insistence that ethnography observes and represents reality, rather than telling stories. The reflexive turn (discussed in chapter 9) in the 1980s began to challenge not only the use of the visual but the very idea that an ethnography can ever represent reality. Pink (2001) argues that Clifford's declaration that ethnographies are only ever partial views based on a series of exclusions, or at worst 'fictional representations' (stories the ethnographer decided to tell and constructs for a particular audience), helped create a favourable environment for the employment of the visual in ethnography. The debate between scientific realism and reflexive approaches that focussed on the construction of fictional representations continues today and sometimes takes place between the disciplines of sociology and anthropology (Pink 2001). Some anthropologists have argued that the visual demands an entire methodology of its own (MacDougall 1997) while some sociologists acknowledge the contribution of visual media to the discipline as a whole but in a support role (Prosser and Schwartz 1998). Chaplin (1994) goes further by suggesting that rather than 'reading' visual media or using them to record or illustrate, we should use them to create knowledge.

The two distinctions set out above are thus becoming increasingly difficult to sustain as researchers are using the visual in more and more creative ways. One such creative use is what has been called *photo elicitation* (Collier and Collier 1986). Here, rather than merely attempting to interpret images yourself as in photoanalysis, researchers work with research participants, asking them to talk and think about how images were made, and what they mean. One such use would be to take a family photograph album, and to sit with the family and get them to talk about the photographs, who is in them, where the event occurred, and also, perhaps, how the image was constructed, who was left out, why particular settings were chosen and so on. One of my students has used this approach very successfully to encourage discussion about the meaning and development of friendships through school and later in life. But as well as exploring existing images with participants, researchers can ask people to construct images such as film, drawings and maps with them. David, for example, was researching young people's social capital and decided to ask children to photograph and then talk about their neighbourhoods, their friends and their social groups. He later used spider's web diagrams to get young people to demonstrate and talk about their networks of social relationships.

Creative use of images and other data works especially well in combination with other methods. Samantha Punch (2003), in her research with children in poor farming communities in Bolivia, combined semi-structured interviews, informal interviews, participant observation, classroom-based tasks and interpretation of sources provided by the children including diaries, photographs and drawings.

Visual media can be used in creative ways within a project: Helen's ethnography in a business organisation

Helen was doing some research in a business organisation, exploring how people feel about the company they work for, and gradually became more and more aware that many workers spoke of a hierarchy whereas managers spoke as if there was not one. Managers would say things like 'we are all treated the same here, no one is more important than anyone else' and 'workers can go and speak to a line manager whenever they want, we are very informal. We have an open door policy.' Workers on the other hand were saying things like 'it's okay when you are a long way up the hierarchy' and 'there are so many layers here, so many people all above each other. Just look at the building.' This triggered Helen to look at the building and to get people to draw maps of it and people's place in it as well, so as to map the managerial structure of the organisation. It turned out that even managers, who described a flat organisation, mapped out a fairly rigid hierarchical structure that was mirrored in the design and layout of the building itself. The exercise led to some very interesting discussions with participants, and some valuable self-reflection on the part of participants.

Others have used images much more directly for research purposes. Some have used film to study interaction closely, for example, or have taken photographs in order closely to analyse visual aspects of situations later. Banish is a good example. He selected families from London and Chicago and interviewed them about their hopes and aspirations, comparing the two cities as well as the families themselves. But for each family he first took photographs as they wanted them taken and then based interviews around discussion of these. The photos are then displayed in the text alongside the interviews and observations. Thus they are being used to construct an argument as well as a methodology (see Plummer 2001a: 64).

This brings me on to film. For Ball and Smith (2001) ethnographic film is a subset of the documentary film, though it is difficult to determine how they differ. Ethnographic films have quite a long tradition, from ethnographers filming tribal peoples, especially engaged in rituals, through the documentary, to post-modern films that blur the boundary between researcher and researched. Philosophically they follow the same path as the photograph (and written ethnography). It is less likely we would find ourselves analysing films produced by social actors but we might use them as report, and we can also construct them with participants, or we might use them creatively and interactively. Ethnographic film-making has its Malinowski: Loizos (see Ball and Smith 2001: 310) argues for a realist, scientific, factual account captured on film, even while acknowledging that film can be used in very creative ways that less faithfully represent reality.

Of course, the development of video and now digital technologies for still and moving images has drastically altered the potential for the visual, and has critically challenged the idea that the camera never lies. You can cut people out, add them in, display images of people together who have never met, change eye colour, alter backgrounds, create montages and so on in endlessly creative ways. And of, course, so can your research participants. In the wider world of journalism, television and film-making, documentary and fiction have merged, and we have all learned to be critical of what we see. As a result, the visual is increasingly being used (or analysed) as a radical, critical tool (Plummer 2001a), and of course ethnographic film practice has been influenced by philosophical debates, and those influenced by post-modern and social constructionist philosophies have developed creative uses of modern technologies to support philosophical arguments.

Something called auto/ethnography emerged in the 1990s, the visual version of which involved participants using video and photograph to tell stories about their own lives. This is a version of what we think of as the video diary, which is becoming popular with television broadcasters (Russel 1998). For some ethnographers, the use of the visual is more emancipatory and powerful than the use of text. Ruth Holliday employed the use of video diaries in her study of the performative nature of identity. In a direct and overt engagement of her research participants in her study she asked 'queer subjects' to think about how their identities are constructed and displayed in everyday settings and to demonstrate this visually as well as through talk, using camcorders. The method captured both the visual and processual elements of self-representation more completely than purely aural data, she argues (Holliday 1999 and 2000). The visual element of the study served two important functions: empowerment of the respondents, who were able to construct their own presentation as well as confront Holliday's own interpretations (Holliday 2000); and emotional engagement on the part of the academic audience.

Three-dimensional data

So far we have concentrated on two-dimensional visual data: film, photographs, newspaper pictures, maps, drawings. In chapter 4 of their very useful book on this topic, Emmison and Smith encourage us to look at three-dimensional data, such as statues, artefacts, badges and other objects of material culture, and even at settings, arrangements, wear and tear, litter (what gets put out and how) and graffiti. 'Visual researchers, we suggest, have become fixated on the collection of images to the detriment of the wider concerns of a sociology of visual information' (Emmison and Smith 2000: 8). Such visual data, they argue, cannot be understood regardless of space and place. Then it might also be important to think about the built environment, the layout of buildings and so on. Some have looked at things like grooming and dress codes, or at spatial logic, for example of a dairy farm (Emmison and Smith 2000). Indeed, as Pink (2001) says, all experiences, interviews, observations and note-taking take place in settings with their own spatial arrangements, surrounding images and other visual media that cannot be 'taken home' yet frame our interpretations of events, actions and speech.

A note on other forms of data

As I have said above, an ethnographer does not restrict herself to collecting and/or analysing transcripts of interviews and/or field notes collected during participant observation. For an ethnographer, anything has the potential to be data, to tell us a little more about the world and the people we are trying to understand. Mason (1996: 71) lists a range of text-based documents that pre-exist ('found' data), including Acts of Parliament, minutes of meetings, and even shopping lists, and others that could be generated (or used creatively) as part of a research process, including written stories, diaries, and charts and lists that you compile on your own or with the research participants. Let's explore diaries, statistics and letters as just a few examples of the range of potential applications or uses of 'other' data. You may notice that the three uses of images as 'writing', 'found' images and creative uses of images can sometimes be distinguished. 'Other' data can be used to aid your presentation or your writing; existing or found data can be analysed in various ways; and data can be constructed in creative ways with research participants.

Diaries

An ethnographer, as well as writing field notes and reflecting on these in the form of some kind of intellectual diary, may want to keep a personal diary (chapter 4). Malinowski (1967) did this in order to separate facts from feelings, but you may use it for more than that. A diary, for example, can enable the reflexive approach encouraged by contemporary philosophical approaches to social science by making you think constantly about your own role in the research process, your own history and biography, decisions you make and how. A diary is a place where you can log the many things you thought did not seem relevant at the time of hearing about, seeing or thinking about them, yet may well turn out to be relevant at some later stage. A diary can enable you to empathise with a group as you reflect on your own apprehensions, ambiguities, surprises and joys. Similarly a diary can enable the iterative-inductive approach I recommend in this book, where research develops, unravels, and proceeds in a messy process of doing, thinking about, redesigning and constantly reflecting on research practice.

But there are more creative uses for a diary. You could ask research participants to keep one as a log of everyday experience (combined with a video if you like), encouraging them, as Holliday (1999) did, to be reflexive about their own lives. Or, you could use a diary to tell a story, as a form of writing up, or enable participants to do that, to construct their own argument, or tell their own stories. Oscar Lewis (1967) famously used diaries to describe the life in one day of each family he researched. You can do diary elicitation, by asking participants to discuss their own personal diaries with you; or diary analysis, where you would attempt to make some sense of existing diary materials. Or you could simply present existing diaries as records of people's subjectivities, with no interpretation on your part at all.

Statistics

Statistics are particularly interesting. There is no reason *per se* why ethnographers should not count things (Silverman 2001, Seale 1999); they can still be grounded in observational, ethnographic study so that phenomena are understood in context. You might want to collect and present your own for various reasons, to present summaries of participants, income distributions, age ranges and so on, or to summarise events, ownership of goods. You might use existing statistics to compare the distribution of attributes of your group of participants with a wider population. Or, more interestingly perhaps, you might want to know how particular groups have been classified or how ideas have been operationalised by those collecting statistics within your own population or group. Finally, you may think of more creative ways of collecting statistics with participants and jointly deciding on a story to tell.

Letters

Letters are more likely to be explored as 'found' data, I would imagine. I cannot think of any, nor have I come across any, examples of people using letters to make an argument or in creative ways with a research project. But by all means take that as a challenge if you like. Letters, of course, are very private things and as such are hard to come by, but they do have a prestigious history, beginning with the famous Polish Peasant (Thomas and Znaniecki 1927) and the Chicago School (see Plummer 2001a). In Hey's (1997) research on young girls' friendships she used notes that girls pass to each other in class as one form of data.

I hope this chapter inspires you to think about what could be done and how it can contribute to ethnography as described in chapter 1. I will now introduce some specific forms of analysis that have been associated with data that can be 'read' as text. Chapter 8 deals with ethnographic analysis more generically.

Texts, content analysis and semiotics

There has developed a tendency in some disciplines to view a wide range of phenomena, including especially documents, images, film and even interview transcripts, as 'text', which can then be subjected to various forms of analysis. Some people are employing these within ethnography (Manning 2001). Analysis of texts rests on two possible approaches: content analysis and semiotic analysis.

Content analysis has various definitions and applications. It is popular in cultural and media studies, communication studies, literary studies and political science, as well as to a lesser extent in sociology and anthropology. For many, content analysis is a quantitative exercise of systematically counting the incidence of certain words, phrases or images within pre-established categories, that appear in previously collected 'texts'. The stages (once the textual data have been obtained) include formulating a research question or hypothesis, sample selection, definition of categories, developing a protocol for coding, coding and analysing the results (see Bryman 2001: chapter 9 for a better introduction).

Content analysis has also been done qualitatively, with more emphasis on the interpretation of meanings of texts than on the quantification of codes and categories. Qualitative content analysis seems to include anything from exploring what certain objects mean for the research participants over and above the utilitarian (see for example Giulianotti 1997) to approaches that enable interpretation of texts while retaining the advantages of quantitative analyses (Mayring 2000). Altheide (1996) has coined the term ethnographic content analysis for content analysis that is more reflexive and iterative than traditional content analysis, but in which the process of extracting codes is often implicit. In Mayring's approach, on the other hand, the material is to be analysed systematically and divided into content analytical units following strict rules of procedure, which can be checked for inter-coder reliability. Content analysis is often used rather loosely to give credibility to the sorts of analysis I have described above, with reference to 'found' data.

Semiotics draws on the work of Ferdinand de Saussure (1974) and Roland Barthes (1972 and 1977) to analyse 'texts' in terms of the meanings they both denote and connote. The approach rests on the idea, from de Saussure, that meaning is derived not from a word itself but from its relationship to other words within systems of meaning. Semioticians develop these ideas to argue that anything that can be considered a sign (that is anything which can signify, or carry meaning, like a word, a photograph, or even an opera) can be analysed in terms of the system within which it gets its meaning. The science of signs (semiotics or semiology) is the way we understand a sign and systems of signs in terms of their interrelationships.

Barthes importantly distinguished between what signs denote and what signs connote. What signs *denote* are their first-order representations, or what we first see when we look at a photograph or badge for example. Signs also carry further meanings than the immediately apparent. In other words they have connotations, usually ideological. A picture of a woman holding a baby, can be seen as simply that, but can also be seen to *connote*, or to 'mean', that women are naturally nurturing. Things are therefore associated with meanings: cars with status, flags with national pride, hearts with love and also with health. But semiotics has to go deeper than content analysis in order to interpret how signs relate to each other to construct meanings. Barthes, for example, couples semiotics with a Marxist interpretation of ideology to demonstrate the relationship between systems of signs and systems of power and 'how certain ideologically loaded sign systems attempt to present particular views of the world as natural and therefore unchangeable' (Inglis and Hughson 2003: 136).

Semiotics has been used as a method in itself but has three applications in relation to ethnography: it has been used to explore the construction and connotations of ethnographic texts; it has used ethnography to provide material for semiotic analysis; and finally some semioticians see social actors as semioticians themselves, using signs to convey meaning intentionally or subconsciously for their own purposes (see Hebdige 1979). Manning (2001) suggests many ethnographers influenced by symbolic interactionism are 'loosely semiotic' in as much as they attempt to interpret the meanings of various signs and their role in the shaping of action. However, as Slater (1998) has noted, those working in the field of semiotics do seem to spend most of their time illustrating and supporting the theory rather than challenging it, and the resulting analyses do appear to be just one person's interpretation, the replicability of which remains obtuse. Analysis of course depends on the purposes for which you collected data and whether it was found, created or intended as 'writing'.

Summary

Visual and other forms of data are collected by ethnographers doing participant observation. Indeed, a whole field of visual ethnography is being developed, with books being written on the topic, journals devoted to or drawing on visual media, and conferences debating the use of the visual. Visual and other data are used in three ways. They are presented as 'writing' to support one's ethnographic data and to aid presentation of results. Data 'found' in the field, such as participants' own letters, diaries and photographs, are analysed alongside other means of learning about the group. And, increasingly, ethnographers are using visual and other media in creative and interactive ways with research participants in the joint analysis and production of ethnographic stories. There are some specific forms of analysis that are associated with the treatment of all forms of data as 'text': content analysis and semiotic analysis. This chapter has presented a brief outline of these for information, but the next chapter explores ethnographic analysis in depth.

Further reading

Pink (2001) has written the best book on visual ethnography I have seen but there are many others now on the market.

Plummer (2001a) provides the key text for documents, including diaries, life stories and visual data, and see Plummer (2001b) for their role in ethnography.

Qualitative content analysis is discussed in more depth by Altheide (1996), and Bryman (2001) has a longer introduction than I have provided here. Manning (2001) explores the interrelationship between ethnography and semiotics, and Slater (1998) offers an accessible introduction to semiotics more generally.

A discussion of statistics in ethnography raises issues about combining methods that I have not covered. For a good introduction see Bryman (1988) and Seale (1999: chapter 9).

Ruth Holliday's work (1999) is a good example of visual auto ethnography.

8 Ethnographic analysis: from writing down to writing up

Writing down and writing up

In this chapter we will discuss how to move from writing things *down* to writing things *up*. The division between writing down and writing up is somewhat artificial, as we shall see shortly, but for now let us think about what we mean by these terms. During fieldwork things are collected: we take notes of what people have said to us; we note down conversations we have overheard; we record (in writing, on tape, or even in photograph and video) certain events, stories, formulae; we collect news items or advertisements or anything of interest that tells us more about our topic; and we do interviews which we transcribe or write from notes (see chapter 4). This phase in many ways mirrors the data collection phase of survey research. It is the phase where information is gathered and stored (or written down). The writing up stage, in ethnographic research, is where we feel we have collected enough information and now we want to prepare it in such a way that it can be presented to others. In survey research, the data set is summarised by telling people how many respondents of certain ages did certain things or had certain attitudes, for example. In this way, a mass of information is summarised for other people to read. But a survey is also analysed in more depth than this. Researchers will look at a number of variables together and see how they correlate (doing multivariate analysis). In ethnographic research, things are not so very different. From the mass of data we have collected we want to summarise some points to tell a story about what we have heard and seen. But we often want to go a bit further than the descriptive, analysing the data we have collected, trying to make sense of how certain occurrences, phrases, phenomena (variables, if you like) go together. When we have done this we can begin to write things up in such a way that they are ready to present to others. So, although it is common to talk about writing up as being the stage that comes after the fieldwork, with the actual analysis being left somewhat obtuse (Fielding 2001), there is actually an important intervening stage: the analysis. Writing down (taking notes and collecting information) therefore leads to analysis (sorting and exploring the things written down and collected), which in turn leads to writing up (preparing what you have discovered in a way that can be presented to others).

However, the use of a model like that above lends the idea that fieldwork is like some other types of research that follow the scientific model of collecting data then analysing it, then preparing a report about your findings. In fact, while fieldwork has to follow this linear model to some extent, things are never that straightforward. Analysis is so tangled up with every stage of the research process that it is difficult to talk of an analysis phase. Indeed, if you do go out into the field and collect data with very little thought about what you might do with it all, you are going to have a very hard time when you come home and try to sort it out and write it up. This, actually, is not so very different from survey style research. No researcher designs a questionnaire or a survey without thought about the topic; as soon as questions are designed, then asked, there is some thought about what sorts of analyses we might make. If the questions were not asked in the survey or were not asked in a certain way, we cannot add them on at the end. For example, if we are doing a piece of health research about a new operation technique and it occurs to us that fear might be an important factor in recuperation, we cannot include this in the analysis if it was not asked in the questionnaire in the first place. So, a survey researcher has to think about the real world and what he or she knows about it, and has to predict what might be important issues in order to include them in the survey. In many cases he or she will draw on what she already knows (even, dare I say it, some fieldwork, though it might not have been recognised as such) or has learnt through experience in order to design the questionnaire. For survey researchers, analysis and what might get written up are in their minds at the early stages. They do not simply go out and collect data then see what they have got, and neither does a fieldworker. A fieldworker goes out with some questions in mind and starts to ask them of the setting. But in fieldwork a researcher can be much more flexible, and can widen the reach of the research, or narrow it, or even change direction to some extent, in the light of what he or she finds out and as theory is developed. Data collection, analysis and writing up (and of course the role of research design and theory) are much more inextricably linked in ethnographic research (Ezzy 2002). This is what in earlier chapters I have called the iterative-inductive approach. We therefore need a model that looks more like a spiral or helix, that demonstrates how analyses and writing up can lead back to more data collection and writing down. As Berg (2004) suggests, there is a tension between the theory-before-research model and the research-before-theory model, but this tension can be resolved if we think of research progressing not in a linear way but in a spiral, where you are moving forward from idea to theory to design to data collection to findings, analysis and back to theory, but where each two steps forward may involve one or two steps back.

The process is not circular: you do have to divide your time in a linear way to some extent. You cannot analyse until you have collected something, and you do have to stop collecting data and come home at some stage (some people would argue you need to come home in order to get some distance and begin more formal analysis). Though analyses go on as you collect data, and you are thinking about what you might present at the end as you go along, you nevertheless mostly collect data before writing it all up. To avoid driving myself and you crazy, I will summarise by repeating *the phases of writing down, analysis and writing up are distinct phases of the research process that are inextricably interlinked*. But for now we will look at them separately. Writing down and collection of data have been covered in previous chapters. In chapter 4 we learned all about note-taking in the field, and what sorts of information and data people can collect. In chapters 5 and 6 we thought about interviewing more specifically, and what sorts of data get written down or recorded and how. In chapter 7 we discussed visual and historical data. Let's now look at analysis and writing up.

Iterative-inductive analysis

I am often asked 'how do you analyse your data?' and I don't know how to answer. There is no statistical procedure, no progression from univariate to bivariate to multivariate analyses, but there is something shared by ethnographers, an implicit understanding of how data are analysed; or of how to get from writing down to writing up. In terms of labelled procedures that you can read about in books, ethnographic analysis comes closest to grounded theory, but ethnographic analysis is not always as prescriptive as the grounded theory approach, as discussed at the end of this chapter.

Analysis of your data, as I have said, is something that is ongoing. As you do a piece of ethnographic research, you start out with some questions abut the group or setting you are studying. As I discussed in chapter 2, this does not take the shape of a hypothesis as such, as this would be too restrictive and would depend on us knowing a lot about the subject to start with. (However, researchers returning to a setting they are familiar with to look at some topics more closely may well have questions that look like hypotheses in that they are quite specific and directed.) With a few research questions, an intellectual puzzle, or some foreshadowed problems, you are ready to enter the field. But if you know very little about your topic, you need to be prepared for some surprises. You might not even know who you need to talk to, or where you need to go to find out about your topic. You certainly might not know what questions to ask. It is a bit like using the internet to find out about something. As you learn a bit more you know which sites to use to find out even more. In some ways you restrict your search and in other ways you broaden it. Doing ethnographic research mirrors, in many ways, how we all learn about things in our daily lives. Becker (1970: 27) called this sequential analysis: 'important parts of the analysis being made while the researcher is still gathering his data'. We have two choices, Model 1 and Model 2.

Two models of how we all learn about things in daily life

Model 1. The doctor tells you you have got a certain ailment which you have never heard of before. You go out and read some books, and talk to some people, and search some web sites until you have gathered lots of information about this ailment. You end up with masses and masses of literature on the subject, and some notes (or memories) of what people have told you. You don't take it in as you go along, but you take it all home and then sort through it. At home you discover that a lot of what you have gathered is not relevant to your particular case. You look through the notes from conversations and note that there are a lot of contradictions in what people have said. Many of the web sites you discovered mention the name of your ailment but are on a different topic altogether. In the end, having sifted through it all, you have got a small amount of information that is useful and can help you understand your ailment a little, but you are also confused about the contradictions and sometimes you need to ask a person some more questions to clarify things, or search a bit further in the internet to find out something more specific, or you need to refer to a different book than one of the ones you have read mentions, but which wasn't on your list. You are left knowing some more about your ailment, but not very much. You have still got more questions than answers.

Model 2. The doctor tells you you have got a certain ailment which you have never heard of before. You decide to go out

continued on next page

and read some books, and talk to some people, and search some web sites until you have gathered lots of information about this ailment. The first few people you talk to seem to have conflicting information so you have to go back and ask them some more about their own condition. You then discover that the ailment and treatment vary according to other factors. You think a bit more about your own situation, your age and general health for example, and thus get a better picture of your own ailment. You explore some web sites, reading them as you go along. Some are of no use at all as they are not really on the topic you are interested in, others have links to web sites that turn out to be really useful. You have to read as you go along, discard some information and retain other bits, and you have to follow links. You look at some books. Some are too technical, others are too broad but from each one you learn a little more about your ailment. Gradually a picture is emerging for you. You keep searching until you find some books that are more useful and you take a lot of notes from those. By the time you have finished searching and gathering you are a lot more clear about your ailment and the ways it can be treated. Maybe you have some information you are not sure you can trust, but you have searched widely and not relied on one report. You go home with all your notes and photocopies and with your memory of conversations, and with a bit of effort you can sort it out into some sort of order that, if you wanted, you could keep for future reference or even show to others.

Ethnographic research more closely follows Model 2 than Model 1 as a way of learning. In ethnographic research you can go back and ask people again, and you can find the person you missed, or you can look for some more information and collect more data, because you don't gather blindly then bring it all home and see what you've got. *Analysis and data collection are interlinked.* You follow links, chasing up ideas and looking for other people and other facts that seem relevant to your topic. But all the time you have a subject, a general question in mind that you want to answer.

Of course, one thing that can happen when you do research in such a way is that your overall questions can seem completely irrelevant in a given setting, or the way you asked them can seem all wrong and you might find you have to change direction quite dramatically. This need not be seen as a bad thing. One of the beauties of ethnographic research is that as you learn you ask more questions and as you ask more questions you learn different things that send you off in different directions. The key is to be flexible. The beginnings of analysis, then, are those flashes of insight I mentioned in chapter 4, that will be written in your intellectual diary (or among your field notes). They are rarely systematic but 'come out of the interplay between a receptive and curious mind and a world explored over time and with diligence' (Rock 2001: 35). They also, sometimes, emerge from an interrelationship between you, your data and your research participants. Some researchers take back transcripts or informal analyses to their research participants and ask for their feedback. This does not apply only to participatory or action research (discussed in chapter 3), but is something all ethnographers can consider. James Scott (1985), for example, in his study of everyday peasant forms of resistance, let the villagers he researched among give feedback on his work and took their comments into account in developing his analyses.

In ethnographic research, analysis and data collection are inextricably interlinked: Caroline's and John's studies

Caroline wanted to look at women and homelessness. Her overall research question was 'how do young women experience homelessness?' Within that grand and rather vague question she had some more specific questions that included 'is being

continued on next page

homeless different for women than men, and in what ways?' and 'are women more vulnerable when homeless than men?' She carefully planned a piece of research that included spending some time in night shelters talking to staff and residents, and some time on the streets shadowing charity workers. She negotiated access very well, drawing on contacts she had made during a school project, and began her research. However, it soon became apparent to her that the real differences between men and women were when the women had children. Women with children do not appear as homeless in the same way as other people, in that they are quickly found temporary housing or are placed in bed and breakfast accommodation. Caroline decided that what she really needed to find out about was what it was like for these women – what she called the hidden homeless. So, she redesigned her study to ask questions about women with children and homelessness, and she had to renegotiate access in order to visit women in bed and breakfast and temporary accommodation. Interestingly, the fieldwork methods she had planned also had to change shape somewhat. In these new settings it was very difficult to try to do any participant observation, and her project came to rely more heavily on interviews than she had previously planned. Her findings were illuminating, nevertheless, and she was able to present a copy of her final report to the town council which had enabled her access to the women, as well as to the women who had participated.

John was interested in men and sexual abuse, and wanted to research male sexual abusers. Access to those who have not been identified proved to be impossible as no one readily admits to criminal behaviour, and he was therefore restricted to studying convicted male sexual abusers. This was very informative and he learnt a lot, but one thing he learnt of great importance was that men and sexual abuse seems to have something

continued on facing page

to do with male attitudes to sex more generally. As a result of this finding he widened his research to a study of men and attitudes to sex. He interviewed men from a range of backgrounds, studied pornographic literature and men's magazines, and talked to men in a very general way in a range of settings including the pub and football matches. In this way he learned more about male sexual abuse and its link to 'normal' heterosexuality than he would have, had he stuck rigidly to his original questions and methods.

James Peacock (1986) talks about this same phenomenon using the analogy of the camera. He says ethnography uses a harsh light and a soft focus. We shine a harsh light on a subject allowing us to see behind things, in corners and in shadows, and things we might have missed if we were not open to surprises and things that try to stay hidden. But we need a soft focus, so that we can leave the edges of our study vague to begin with and can change our focus to bring in aspects we might not have thought relevant. Iterative research with an emphasis more on induction than on deduction is also more empowering than purely deductive research since the participants always direct it to some extent. Participatory research can allow for participants' engagement with the research at all stages, from design through data collection to analysis and writing (Ezzy 2002).

However, to draw parallels with using the internet again, you do have to be careful not to allow yourself to be taken off in so many different directions you lose sight of what you want to know. Always you should have some sort of end product in sight, something to be working towards. And the only way to achieve this is by making and designing new research questions to guide you as you go along, rather than being vaguely pushed in many varied directions. Glaser and Strauss (1967) talk of iterative research design. By this they mean that you swing back and forth between research, data collection and analysis. It does not mean you have no research

questions or design, but it does mean that you have to keep looking again at your research questions and rethinking them and the
methods in light of findings. Whether or not you are taking a
grounded theory approach, ethnographic research tends to be
iterative.

I have spoken a great deal about how analysis is tangled up with
the data collection phase, with the presentation of descriptive data
and even the project design phase, but what do I mean by analysis?
Well, by this I mean *making some sense of it all*. This is intentionally
vague: making sense of it could mean summarising it, so that it is
manageable, presenting it under certain headings that link relevant
parts together, translating it so that others can understand it (sometimes what you have collected is in a foreign language or sometimes
it seems so strange to people from a different culture that it appears
as a foreign language). But, in a sense analysis is all these things. It is
summarising, sorting, translating and organising. It is moving from
a jumble of words and pictures to something less wordy, shorter
and more manageable, and easier for an outsider to understand.
It involves exploring deeply to see what is there that might not
be obvious, standing back to see what patterns emerge, thinking
and theorising to draw conclusions that can be generalised in
some way or other.

Sorting

So, how do you start? Well, as I have said over and over, you should
have started to make sense of it all as you went along, as you
collected data and thought about your research questions, and
decided who to ask what questions and where to do the next
piece of participant observation or interview. By the time you
reach what we call the analysis phase you should have some idea
of what it is you want to convey. Nevertheless, you have to do
something concrete with all the data you have collected. One of
the first stages of analysis is moving from a chronological order to
another kind of order. Field notes, interview transcripts and other
kinds of data have been collected chronologically, as you went

along, but it is unlikely that you will present them in this way. Analysis therefore involves some kind of sorting. You will sort your data into categories that suit yourself, and these can be thematic or descriptive or both. How you do this is up to you, and there is no formula available to help you (although, increasingly, researchers are trying to develop prescriptive techniques such as the Framework Approach of Ritchie and Lewis (2003)). Using a computer package can be a guide of sorts, as the facilities it has available can give you a clue about what you might want to do with your data, but first there are a few things to bear in mind.

- Keep good records that can be easily put into a computer or sorted in whatever way you choose. You will be amazed how often you regret not having collected a certain piece of information or noted down some crucial details. Bear the needs of analysis in mind as you collect your data.
- Analysing as you go along means collecting in a directed way to help you sort and contextualise. This can include audio and video tape, photographs and any other media you find useful to collect texts of myths, events, music, gossip or whatever else seemed important at the time.
- But remember that certain things will never have been recorded, and your memory remains a powerful research tool. As you watched an event take place, the smells, the sounds, the background noise, how you felt, how others told you they felt, the background whispers, the misunderstandings that came clear later. None of these may be recorded and yet any or all may prove to be illuminating at a later stage.
- You can sort your data by hand or by computer (using a software package for data analysis or merely a word processor); the procedures are similar. No piece of software removes the necessity for you to think carefully about what you are doing, and to keep your own ideas and familiarity with the data clearly in mind.
- Sorting involves chopping things up and assigning them to different categories or headings, but it is you who decides what belongs where, not any computer program. 'You make

assumptions about the phenomena you are cataloguing, about the categories they belong in, and in doing the sorting you open up some possibilities and close the door on others' (Mason 1996: 108).

- Nothing should be chopped up and divorced from its context. In other words, you should be able to assign a paragraph or event to a certain category without removing it from the rest of the field notes, interview transcripts and data that were collected simultaneously – the social context of speech and action (Hammersley and Atkinson 1995). New CAQDAS packages allow this.
- Be fully inclusive but not mutually exclusive. Your categories can overlap. Take a heading and add anything which might apply, allowing the same excerpt to go under other headings too. For example, one excerpt might belong under 'family' and 'sex' and 'stress'.
- Your categories will change during fieldwork and analysis – make sure your computer software, or whatever method you use, allows for this.

But above all, what is the purpose of sorting? Is it so that you can go over the data and see how often a certain thing occurred? If this is the case, you are playing a dangerous game. *You* collected the data and *you* decided how often to note down which things. Something might have happened numerous times but you didn't make a note of it, and something else might have happened a few times but each time you wrote at length about it. Does this make the latter more important? If you use a computer to help you count how many words are said on a certain topic or how many times something happened, all you will count are those things you thought relevant to note and to code with certain categories as you sorted the data. You are not necessarily identifying something important. Some people use computers and counting to try to make their research look more scientific, but I would argue that it is pseudo-scientific and even dishonest to think something is important if it occurs in field notes or sorting several times.

On the other hand, sorting makes us look at our data very, very closely and, as we do this we can see all sorts of patterns emerge (of course, once again, we should have been doing this all the time). We might notice, for example, that every time one topic is discussed the subject gets subtly changed by the respondent. This might only come out with close examination of transcripts and field notes. Sorting and categorising can also give you the chance to link together themes that previously seemed disparate.

Example of keeping analysis close to data collection

When I was doing research on British migration to Spain, I noticed that when two British people meet there they tend to kiss each other on both cheeks, as the Spanish traditionally do. This had never been written in my field notes because I hadn't thought it important until I realised I had seen it happen a lot. I started to watch more closely and note down similar things. I became aware that it is just the British migrants who do this and not the tourists, and that the migrants are more likely to do it when they are in the company of tourists. I then began to notice that in the company of tourists migrants would use the occasional Spanish word when talking to each other. This led me to thinking about the relationship between migrants and tourists, whereas until then I had focussed more on the relationship between British and Spanish people. I thus began, during fieldwork, a closer analysis of migrants and tourists and their behaviour and attitudes towards each other that I would not have been able to do once I had left the field. I started to sort through the notes and data I had collected, assigning things to a new heading of 'tourist/migrant relations', and discovered many new occurrences I had not noticed before.

Example of analysis while sorting data

Mark was doing a piece of research on young people and crime. He wanted to know how in certain youth cultures it seemed acceptable to take part in some minor criminal acts. He spent a long time with three groups, participating in shopping trips, spending the weekend and generally 'hanging about', and came to understand the youth cultures from their own perspective. When he began a thorough sorting of his data after fieldwork had finished he began to notice a pattern that he hadn't noticed during fieldwork. He noticed an important gender difference in talk about crime, criminal behaviour and attitudes to criminal acts. He was able to include some of this in his writing up, but as he had only noticed the pattern at the end of the fieldwork phase he was not able to explore it as much as he would have liked.

So, the trick is to sort as you go along, not leave it all till the end. Who you talk to, and the questions you ask, should always be directed by what you want to find out and what you are finding out. But a thorough re-sorting at the end before you begin the mammoth task of preparing your work for presentation to others is also to be recommended.

Computer software

A good way to think about the process of analysis is to work through a software program to see what it can do, since these have been designed with the analysis of qualitative data in mind. However, it is important to remember that computer programs are merely a way of helping you manage your data, in the same way you would previously have managed it by hand, using paper and scissors and lots of photocopies! Computers can help you sort your data but not analyse it. You are the one who does the analysis, you are the one who decides which paragraph or note belongs to which category, and you decided the categories you would use. You determine which chapters to write, and what to tell your audience, and you select the illustrations that you think are apt. If you let the computer do the work for you, you are in danger of forgetting that only some of what you saw and heard ever got recorded in your notes or in your visual or audio records. Your data are not real things; they are the best record you could collect of what you saw and heard, with relevance to the topic you were interested in. This does not mean that your data are invalid. This does not mean you cannot trust your data and that anyone else might have collected a whole lot of different material. It merely means that you are inextricably linked to your data at every stage of the process, so why try to clean yourself out of it at the analysis stage? In the end, the analysis of your data is a very messy process and there are no short cuts. 'There is no mechanistic substitute for those complex processes of reading and interpretation' (Hammersley and Atkinson 1995: 203).

Advantages of computer software are that it can speed up the sorting process, and can enable you to explore complex pathways that would be difficult to explore using cut and paste. It certainly provides a formal structure for storing the many forms of collected and created data as well as the ongoing analyses of these. But it can also make this more confusing, since often not all data can be stored in one program, and even those that can store multimedia cannot store your memory. Disadvantages are that it can cause you to distance yourself too much from your data as you allow the computer to make connections on your behalf. Some people use Computer Assisted Qualitative Data Analysis Software (CAQDAS) to bring ethnographic analysis closer to quantitative analysis, as they count instances of phrases or events, or even interpretations. There has been considerable debate as to the extent to which CAQDAS is associated with grounded theory, so that Coffey, Holbrook and Atkinson (1996) worry about the neglect of other approaches in the development and use of software. Fielding and Lee (1998) alternatively believe the assertion that there is a link between grounded theory and CAQDAS has been overdrawn. Their research with users has shown that CAQDAS users take many different approaches. CAQDAS not only supports code and retrieve types of analysis but also narrative, discourse and semiotic analyses.

Since reviews of software are immediately outdated I will merely offer some summary points and direct you to further reading and web sites. The web pages of the CAQDAS Networking Project (http://caqdas.soc.surry.ac.uk), which aims to provide practical support, training and information in the use of a range of software programs, are worth exploring. There are details about seminars and training courses and a regularly updated bibliography with links to several useful online articles. A particularly useful article is the one by Barry (1998), which compares two main programs: Atlas/ti and Nudist. There are over twenty CAQDAS packages available, but commonly used ones are QSR N6 (formerly Nudist), QSR NVivo, The Ethnograph, Atlas-ti, HyperRESEARCH and Qualrus. You might also visit www.scolari.co.uk, from where you can download demonstration versions and see screen shots of the programs published by Sage.

The initial aim of CAQDAS was to enable researchers to code and retrieve. That is, to mark text and assign codes to various segments, and to enable the researcher to retrieve all segments that share a particular code. The segments can be brought together while remaining in their initial context, and can have additional information, such as name, place and date of record, added to the coded section. Most programs also enable the attachment of memos and analytical notes to segments and passages. Several packages now include hypertext facilities which allow the construction of complex pathways and even the inclusion of graphics, video and sound (this also means secondary analysis can involve using some of the *context* of data collection such as field notes and photographs rather than just interview transcripts). It works like searching the internet, following a trace or path to different parts of the data, and is therefore more interactive and less linear than some approaches (Fielding and Lee 1995). Because of its speed and flexibility, hypertext has been shown to be useful in the early stages of analysis when researchers are browsing through various components of data (Fielding and Lee 1998). Coffey *et al.* (1996) note that hypertext software and hypermedia are particularly suitable for the diverse range of representational strategies (or writing techniques) that have been opened up by responses to the reflexive turn (see chapter 9).

Computer packages can assist analysis but not do it for you. In fact Kelle (1997) says CAQDAS programs could more correctly be called 'tools for data storage and retrieval' rather than for data analysis, and Ezzy (2002) argues that CAQDAS is just one tool to help you store, search and retrieve, to aid analysis, not *the* tool, and not *for* analysis. It is an aid, not a replacement for intelligent analysis, and need not replace other techniques you might use such as manual cutting and pasting, reading and rereading printed texts, and word processors and databases. A disadvantage worth noting is the time it can take to learn to use a package, and with the iterative-inductive ethnographic research I have described you cannot afford to wait until you have left the field to decide which computer package you will use to help you sort your data. However, Fielding (2001) says ethnographers need not fear that the ethnographic 'craft' will be undermined by the use of computers. Indeed since the analytic process in much ethnography has often been rather elusive CAQDAS can make it more transparent and more open. This does not mean that CAQDAS does not have its limits, and his chapter explores these, but it also has uses worth considering by ethnographers.

Databases or indexes

Another useful tool for storing, sorting and retrieving is a database. Once again, you would need to compile it as you go along rather than leaving it till the end of a fieldwork phase, and once again you could use a computer or cards and a box. It is up to you. These things are devices to help you with your research so there are no hard and fast rules. You use them to help you remember, store and sort, not to help you think or make sense of it all. I would recommend indexing separately – as you go along – anything which seems to lend itself to this method. These tools supplement notes and can help you to remember to log certain repetitive details. They cannot be used in the same way that questionnaire data can be used unless you have thought carefully about sampling procedures and representativeness, but they can certainly be useful tools for expressing how certain factors vary across the community or group.

Some information can be usefully compiled into a database

When I did fieldwork in Spain I began to realise that I knew a lot of information about a great number of people that I had never stored in one place. I started to compile a database of British migrants and ended up with information on over 300 individuals, about age groups, time spent in Spain, sex, whether they own their own property, health arrangements, family composition, and many other details. I began the database while I was in the field, so I was able to ask questions to fill in gaps in my knowledge as I went along. As time went on I became interested in the distinction between permanent and temporary migrants, and was able to use and add to my database to help me gather relevant information about separate groups (O'Reilly 2000a).

Note that identification of individuals may become a problem if you put these sorts of data on computer, or if you cannot remember who the pseudonyms you use apply to. This leads to problems of confidentiality, which we discussed in chapter 3. One memory aid is the use of photos in your index. This helps people get used to you taking photos, but has the problem of confidentiality again.

Description and analysis

Some people get hung up on doing complicated analyses of their data and forget to describe the obvious things that their reader will not know about. It is easy to become so familiar with your data that the urge to surprise your reader overtakes you and you forget to impart some crucial details. This is the case with survey research as well as with ethnographic research. One of the first things you should do as a survey researcher is look at the data set and describe some basic results (or present some univariate and bivariate analyses). You would perhaps say how many women and how many men you surveyed, for example, and if age was relevant you would show how age was distributed across the group. You might then look at a few simple things like how many people owned their own house, or how many were fit and healthy. With ethnographic research, we start by imparting some descriptive findings. We might want to give a history of the situation or the group and some background information, or what Scott (1985) refers to as some story telling. This is a crucial phase of the analysis of your data, that often does not reveal itself to you until you start to write things up.

Description and analysis are not entirely distinct

Frederick did ethnographic research with men who gave up work to care full-time for their children. He interviewed ten men and participated in their family lives, making breakfast, washing up, going on outings and even baby sitting. His findings were very interesting in that he suggested that men find it difficult to stay at home and care for the children because women help them so much that they feel inadequate. However, before he could explain this, his report (or written thesis) had to provide some description. So, he introduced each of the men to his reader by telling a little story of each one: how they came to the decision to stay at home and be full-time carer. Some were single parents and others had partners who worked full-time. Some lived in council housing, others in their own homes. These proved to be relevant factors to the later discussion and so proved to be crucial to the analysis. Some of the men were very tall and some were short, but since this was irrelevant to his overall argument, Frederick didn't discuss it. In this way we can see that what appears to be merely descriptive is actually part of the analysis.

Of course, description and analysis are always interlinked. In survey research, you choose which variables to present in univariate analysis and you decide which to cross-tabulate in bivariate analysis. It is not merely descriptive, but neither is it complicated analyses. It is always linked to your research questions and starts to answer the questions, but in some ways these are the data that jump out at you. In ethnographic research these descriptive data often take the form of what appear to be background data but which are in fact beginning to answer the questions you started with.

Descriptions enrich ethnographies, providing crucial background information

Claire's ethnography in a fishing village wanted to explore the effects of the European Common Fishing Policy on the community. She spent over a year talking to and spending time with people from all works of life, from decision-makers to housewives and children. She went on fishing trips, attended coffee mornings, and went to conferences on fishing policy, all in order to get a broad impression. Her final project report, her PhD thesis, will include several chapters outlining who lives in the community, how important fishing has been historically, what the Common Fishing Policy is and how it came about, and how the nature of fishing has changed in recent decades, including the effects of new technologies. She was getting very concerned at one point that she would never have space in her report to talk about her 'real' findings, as she had so much to say that was descriptive and background. But I pointed out to her that in order to make an overall argument, a lot of background information is important. These pieces of information are a crucial part of the findings.

The crucial thing to note here is that your written report, or whatever it is that you use to present your findings, will have an overall argument to make, and any descriptive material that helps to make that argument is important to include and any that is irrelevant can be excluded. But before excluding anything, ask why you wanted to include it in the first place. It might be more important than you realised.

We have been talking about the more descriptive part of the final presentation, and I have spoken as if this is distinct from, yet relevant to, more concrete analysis. However, some people present their findings in a very descriptive way as if they have done no analysis and as if the data speak for themselves – they don't! Whatever you choose to present has been chosen by you as something to present. For more on this see the next chapter.

Concepts

We have thought about sorting our data out into certain categories, we have thought about the uses and abuses of software packages, and we have thought about presenting some descriptive data. By now we can see some sort of presentation taking shape. Rather than a mass of data we have got some notes and other records sorted into categories that made sense as we went along; we have got a database or two of more specific information; and we have managed to report some of the more descriptive findings that tell people about the group we studied, its background and its character. To take analysis a stage further we might want to make some explanations about our findings,

Since our aim is often to describe in such a way that looks beyond the obvious, behind the surface, one important task in sorting and analysing our data is to find concepts which help us make sense of what is going on. Having sorted out the descriptive and background information, the next step is to read through your data looking for startling facts, for themes or patterns, or for inconsistencies which need explaining. Sometimes the analytical concepts will arise from the field – they will be in use by the participants themselves, that is to say they are their own concepts. For example, in my field-work in Spain there were four groups of migrants: those who live in Spain all year round, those who live there almost all year but escape the searing heat of the Spanish summer by returning to Britain for three or four months between June and September, those who migrate to Spain to escape the cold British winters, and those who move back and forth between Britain and Spain, apparently living in both places at once. This is how the migrants themselves spoke of the four groups, but I needed to use labels to abbreviate what were existing ideas, so I used the terms permanent residents, returning residents, seasonal visitors, and peripatetic migrants for the four groups (O'Reilly 2000a). I was not developing new concepts but was labelling, and thus making more apparent, some ideas that already existed in the minds and talk of the participants themselves.

Sometimes, however, you need to develop whole new concepts in order to describe something that you have seen emerge or that becomes apparent to you, but is not easy to describe. Concepts, like theories, are merely an easier way to think about a complex set of ideas. We use them to sort, abbreviate and explain. Rather than try to write up all your findings in one go, what you are trying to do is find some organising principles through which you can make sense of it all to yourself and then to others.

Concepts enable you to make sense of your data

Anna's (Åberg et al. 2004) research was about what quality of life means in the lives of men and women aged over 80 years (what she calls the oldest old). She used in-depth interviews of older people, their carers and people close to them, and participant observation in people's homes, in rehabilitation units and in care homes. When it came to writing up, Anna decided to produce a series of papers and articles rather than one single report. However, the first things she had to write were descriptive. She told of how she did the research, and what changes had been taking place in the health service that had led to the research; she described the different ways 'quality of life' is used by different groups, then she described her respondents a little. For Anna, there were core respondents, the older people,

continued on facing page

and other respondents, their carers and close ones. She found it necessary to include some description of each of these, though depending on what she was writing she included more or less of this. She found it had to be collected in one place in the first place before she could proceed to the next phase of analysis of findings. This is the phase where she really wanted to try to find some answers to her questions – what does quality of life mean for older people? One thing she had found as she had been doing her research and sorting through her notes and data was that people seemed to talk a lot about balancing expectations, on the one hand, against real possibilities, on the other. Older people often have physical reasons for not being able to do certain things, and so what might contribute to quality of life, for example visiting a friend, might be a physical impossibility. So, the older person, in order to achieve a balance in his or her life, might reduce expectations in order to meet them more realistically. For Anna, the concept of balance became a crucial organising concept in her work. She came to the conclusion that older people need a certain balance in order to achieve some life satisfaction, but said that if the balance is achieved by reducing expectations to a very low level, then what seems subjectively like 'quality of life' (in terms of balance) is achieved, objectively, on a low level of quality. People who expressed a high satisfaction with life, might actually be doing so because they had heavily reduced their hopes and expectations. This was a very good start, but she still had more things to sort out and describe. She began to find it necessary to distinguish between 'quality of life' as an objective measure and 'life satisfaction' as subjectively expressed by respondents. So, it was not merely concepts she was using; she was having to define clearly her own use and application of existing ideas. She went on to develop three new concepts: reorganisation, mental adaptation and mental activities. Using these concepts she was able to show that older people use

continued on next page

different strategies to help them cope with physical disabilities and achieve life satisfaction. Reorganisation involves reorganising your life physically to cope with new difficulties, for example using aids and equipment, or moving furniture and personal effects around to make life easier for you to move about. When re-organisation is not an option, mental adaptation involves convincing yourself that the thing you can't do is not that important, or in the words of respondents, 'taking life as it comes', 'don't expect too much'. They use *mental activities*, such as pastimes or thinking a lot about the past as a way to escape from present difficulties.

Anna used a series of existing and new concepts to help her organise and express her findings, and make sense of it all for her readers. We also learn from Anna that some of our sorting and writing is done for our own ends, not necessarily for a directly presentable piece of work. We might want to write a single, long piece of work that covers every aspect of our research we are interested in, much as a PhD thesis or project might do, but it might be for our own consumption; what we present to others might be only parts of the whole.

Theories

The relationship of theory to ethnographic research has been discussed in chapter 2. It is usual for theory to guide ethnographic research in more or less direct and apparent ways, but unusual for ethnography to be used to test theoretical suppositions. However, theories can come into their own in the analysis and writing up stages and begin to explain regularities and properties of the social world. A concept and a theory cannot easily be distinguished, since a theory is often built on one or more concepts, but theories vary in the extent to which they explain, or offer abstract propositions about, an entire society or limited aspects of social life (Brewer

2000). In ethnographic research we usually use theories when they help us understand the phenomena in question, and often need to adapt existing theories or adopt new theoretical ideas of our own to help us make sense of what is going on around us. A theory is only useful in as much as it helps us make sense of the world around us, so we apply theories to our data to see if they help us make sense of what we have heard and seen, using the bits that help, discarding those that do not, and in this way contributing to the ongoing development of theoretical ideas in social science.

It is often argued that ethnographic and other qualitative research suffers from the inability to be representative of a wider population. What is the use of close, one-off studies of tiny populations, asks this critique. It seems to me that the value of qualitative research comes in its being able to contribute to concepts and theories that are used more widely, and are therefore more generally applicable. This takes us back to the age-old debate between empiricists and theorists, where one side argues that we can only understand the social world through direct observation and the other side argues that direct observation is not enough at all (and sometimes of no value at all!). Most researchers have come to the conclusion that theories are only useful in as much as they help us explain the social world that we experience through our senses, and that as the world changes so must the theories, but at the same time empirical research is only useful if we can summarise a mass of disparate information using concepts and theories that help us make sense of what we see and hear. In this way, ethnographic research is not representative in the way that findings can be generalised statistically to a wider population from which a representative sample has been drawn. But, it can be representative in as much as the things we learn from it can have meaning for other situations, either through macro theory, that attempts to explain broad patterns, or micro theory that focusses on small-scale explanations relevant to certain settings and leaves the wider implications implicit.

Grounded theory

Ethnographers needing more apparently stringent or at least apparent guidelines will benefit from reading about the grounded theory approach. I will introduce it here, but this book does not attempt to reproduce that work. Barney Glaser and Anselm Strauss wrote their famous book, *The Discovery of Grounded Theory*, in 1967. Since then grounded theory, as an approach to qualitative research and analysis, has become famous and this single text is often cited (with or without the person doing the citing knowing much about grounded theory) as evidence of a careful, rigorous and systematic approach to one's work. However, Glaser and Strauss themselves came from quite different research traditions and their work has subsequently followed different paths, with Strauss developing his ideas later in collaboration with Juliet Corbin. For Strauss and Corbin, grounded theory is based on a methodology: 'a way of thinking about and studying social reality' that does see theory as being grounded in data without a simplistic adoption of inductive reasoning. Their methodology, they suggest, is not the only way of looking at the world but it is one way, and an insightful and valuable way. Some key features of this methodology follow.

- There is an interplay between researchers and the data, where the researcher is not afraid to draw on his/her own experiences when analysing, because 'these become the foundations for making comparisons and discovering properties and dimensions' (Strauss and Corbin 1998: 5).
- The theories that are produced are seen as modifiable, qualifiable, and open in part to negotiation, but, because these theories are grounded in data, researchers are confident about their validity.
- It is helpful if the researcher is flexible and creative, and open to criticism and debate. Grounded theory works well in team work.
- The research is essentially inductive: theoretical ideas have value but researchers are sceptical of them until they are grounded in data.

• Most grounded theory researchers hope their work has relevance for other academic and non-academic audiences (so research and intellectual endeavour are not divorced from people's daily lives).

This methodology has a lot in common with what I have described in this book as the ethnographic approach and is quite similar to how Willis and Trondman (2000) have described ethnography (see chapter 1). The techniques that the grounded theory approach offers are merely methods for putting this methodology into practice. The goal being not just to describe but to 'create new and theoretically expressed understandings' (Strauss and Corbin 1998: 8).

Many authors describing grounded theory focus on the techniques, but since grounded theory is not simply a set of techniques I will not concentrate much here on explicating the 'how to'. Anyone wanting to learn techniques can read the relevant texts for themselves (especially Strauss and Corbin 1998). I believe if one approaches research in an informed way, having considered methodology in the light of philosophical approaches as well as practical issues, then the actual decisions to be made along the way can be made in a reflexive and thoughtful manner. Indeed Strauss and Corbin are not at all prescriptive about methods, saying that people *rightly* use some of the techniques they describe and not others, mixing them with techniques of their own for a range of applications. They say, as I have said, that there may be some use of statistics, but qualitative research is essentially non-mathematical and interpretive. But for these authors interpretive does not stand in contrast to scientific. Indeed grounded theory is more objective and therefore scientific because it enables the research participants to set the agenda or to have a voice independently of the researcher's. They also say, as I have defined ethnography in chapter 1, 'a researcher does not begin with a preconceived theory in mind (unless his or her purpose is to elaborate and extend existing theory)' (Strauss and Corbin 1998: 12). Analysis for these authors is both science and art. The key goal is to *interpret qualitative data in order to discover concepts and relationships which are then organised into a theoretical explanatory scheme.*

I will introduce a few of the concepts on which grounded theory is based and this will use some of the language of grounded theory. Grounded theory consists of *asking questions* of our data and *making theoretical comparisons* to help us gain a better understanding of them. This work is to be done in creative ways through *micro-analysis*: careful scrutiny of the data, line by line. There are specific techniques for close analysis that acknowledge how our selves and our biases influence our thinking but that try to break through these. *Waving the red flag*, for example, involves watching for phrases such as 'never', 'always' and 'one mustn't' or 'can't' and rather than accepting them at face value asking under what conditions they apply in order to open them up for further inquiry. *Open coding* is a process though which *concepts* (which are tools to help us organise data) are identified. Concepts are framed in terms of their *properties* and *dimensions*. Properties delineate a concept; dimensions specify its range of properties. *Axial coding* relates coded categories to each other and to sub-categories along their properties and dimensions, and is the means through which researchers link process to structure, or the things that happen with their conditions. Finally, the analytic story or theory which emerges to explain phenomena becomes much sharper in the writing or presentation of it.

The difficulties I continue to have with grounded theory include the fact that phrases like 'researchers enjoy what can be done with . . . data once they are collected' (Strauss and Corbin 1998: 5) imply a separation between collection and analysis, whereas later the authors insist that 'concepts and design must be allowed to emerge from the data', implying the iterative approach I advocate in this book. Indeed I would describe their approach as iterative and would suggest that the emphasis on induction belies their actual methodological insistence on being both deductive and inductive. Ezzy (2002) reminds us, however, that qualitative researchers' early insistence that their work is inductive was a response to the hegemony of the deductive approach, and that most research actually draws on both inductive and deductive reasoning.

A further problem that is not well addressed is how theories become linked together in this approach. There is an implication that every piece of research generates new theory, which does not seem very helpful on a general level. However, there is some small acknowledgement that some research might actually be to test theory.

Finally, the real difficulty is in actually applying some of the techniques, such as micro-analysis, in practice to a large mass of data including field notes, interview transcripts, images and 'found' documents. Nevertheless, what Strauss and Corbin are attempting is to find a way to describe and control iterative-inductive research that is essentially messy and uncomfortable and in the end they agree is actually a matter of both art and science.

Summary

This chapter looked at how to begin to analyse your data, or how to move from writing things down to writing them up. We looked briefly at what sorts of data we have collected and what we might do with it. Then we thought a great deal about analysis in ethnographic research. We remembered that analysis is iterative and ongoing, not a separate stage that can start after data collection has finished. We thought about how to sort our data using computer software or databases, and how we might categorise what we have collected. We discovered that much of our material will be presented in quite a descriptive way, prior to moving on to a more complicated analysis and explanation. We thought about the use of concepts in helping us make sense of all we have collected and considered the role of theory. Finally, we were introduced to the grounded theory approach of Strauss and Corbin and noted its faithfulness to iterative-inductive research.

Further reading

For an excellent overview of CAQDAS see Ezzy (2002), which is not a review of programs since this would be quickly outdated but discusses the strengths and weaknesses of computer-assisted analysis generally as well as its implications for grounded theory and an iterative-inductive approach. Fielding and Lee (1998) give very broad-ranging reports on research with users, and see Fielding (2001) for a review of the role of computer applications in ethnography.

Various more formal forms of qualitative data analysis are being developed and their relationship to ethnography explored. You might want to see: Charmaz and Mitchell (2001) on grounded theory in ethnography; Cortazzi (2001) on narrative analysis in ethnography; Manning (2001) on semiotics, semantics and ethnography; Pollner and Emerson (2001) on ethnomethodology and ethnography (all in Atkinson *et al.* 2001); and, for an example of one form of discourse analysis, Hutchins and Klausen (2002); and, for an example of an attempt to build a bridge between conversation analysis and ethnography, Griffiths (1998).

On grounded theory specifically see Strauss and Corbin (1997 and 1998) and of course Glaser and Strauss (1967).

Brewer (2000: chapter 5) is useful for the uses or applications of ethnography, including applied research.

9 Writing, reflexivity and autobiography

Writing up and presentation

Having analysed your data the next step (if we can use that word when we have already acknowledged that the process is more of a spiral than steps, see chapter 8) is to think about how to prepare what you have found in a way that can be presented to other audiences. In other words we need to think about writing up. First I want to point out that what gets called 'writing up' is not usually a matter of writing up everything you have learned from the field; it is much more a matter of moving from what you think you know, or understand, to what you are going to communicate. Everything that is written is written *for* someone (even if that someone is yourself), and what is normally meant by writing up is turning what you have written in notes, memos, transcripts and so on into something that will be presented to another audience. Of course, you may write for different audiences, for example a report for your supervisor, an article for a journal on one particular topic, a thesis that attempts to deal with several issues in one place (Agar 1986). I am not going to assume here (as many methods texts do) that you have done your research, have discovered something and now want to write it all up, as if there is only one thing you will write from one project. For each piece of writing that you prepare from a project, you should think carefully about who you are writing for and what it is you are trying to produce. As you have been analysing, you have been writing.

The whole discussion, in the previous chapter, of description, sorting, developing concepts and thinking about theory assumed you were writing it down or preparing it for presentation. However, there is some kind of distinction between analysis and writing up. There comes a time when you have sorted and taken notes long enough and it is time you got something written in a more formal, organised way; and I believe that we have a responsibility as researchers to produce things that others will read, to disseminate our findings. That is not to say that as you write more formally you won't go back and start sorting and thinking again – you undoubtedly will. But at some stage more of your effort has to go into writing up than analysis, just as at some stage you have to stop trying to collect more data and think about what you are going to do with it all. The spiral has a beginning and an end.

The first point I would like to make then about ethnographic writing is that, just as in survey research you do not present an entire database and correlations of every variable with every other, you should not try to communicate everything from your ethnography. You are ready to write when you have looked at all your data and thought about all you know, and have decided on a story to tell, a thesis to present, or an argument to make (Berg 2004). If you have not reached this point, you should go back to the beginning and ask yourself what you wanted to know. What was your intellectual puzzle or topic or set of guiding questions? What were your foreshadowed problems (Malinowski 1922)? Did you begin by stating you would test a theory, develop a theory, challenge stereotypes, explain themes, aid understanding? You are not ready to write up if you have not thought about your data and how to make sense of it all in the light of your initial problems.

Try to bear these few points in mind as you prepare your written work.

- Start by writing up the things you are sure about.
- A title (even just a working one) helps the writing move along. It means you have decided what you are writing about!
- Decide, where possible and at each stage, when you are describing and when you are explaining.

- Don't try to organise before you know what you want to say: remember, it is not so important *how* you organise the final text as *what it contains overall.*
- Remember you have a reason to write. You are producing something for someone, not presenting everything you have found.
- *Enjoy it* – write it for pleasure if possible. Some people get started by pretending they are writing for a friend.

It can be very daunting to sit down and start to write something, but thankfully with the use of computers and the wonderful ability to cut and paste, delete and rewrite endlessly and painlessly, we can build up a written piece methodically, in tiny stages, starting with the things we are sure about and want to communicate effectively, or doing what Becker (1986) calls *freewriting* – writing in a free style, for yourself, without stopping to check references, spelling and grammar (Wolcott 2001). A title, or even a passage or two summarising what you are saying, can really help. You will be surprised how many times people try to write something when they don't really know what they are writing about. If you can summarise what you want to say in a few words, or sentences, it will help keep you focussed as you write. As you go along, try to establish what it is you are doing. I know these are difficult to distinguish exactly, but you should try to separate description from explanation, if only to keep you sane as you write. You will often, as I said in the previous chapter, begin analysis with some description – of your setting, your group, the individuals – and some background information, and then move on to look at some of the themes more closely, using concepts and theories to help you organise and make sense of it all. However, sometimes the actual act of writing can help you decide what you want to say, so don't keep putting it off until you are completely organised. Think and write about what you want to communicate and *organise* it all afterwards if it suits you to do it that way (it is certainly how this book got written!). Don't forget that most effective writing goes through a substantial number of revisions (Berg 2004, Walker 1987). Many first-time writers are unaware of how many times a piece of work will need to be revised from the first to the final draft. Try to keep your audience in mind as you write. Keep asking yourself: who is this for? What will the readers already know about the subject? What will interest them? And finally, try to make sure you enjoy it as you go along. If you find it all too painful it can make rather painful reading. I find one solution for writer's block is simply to move all books and papers away from my desk and write from the heart. It may be messy and need lots of rewriting, but at least for a while you will get something on paper and will allow space for your creativity to come through.

There is a standard format for presentation which single articles and even books tend to adhere to, as shown below. You don't have to stick to this if the convention does not fit what you have to say, but too much flexibility in the structure as well as style can be a daunting thing and you may benefit from realising how standardised many academic works actually are (Berg 2004, Gilbert 1993). The best advice I can give you is to read, read, read. Only by reading other authors' books, articles, reports and theses can you learn about formats, styles and techniques, and decide which approach suits you best.

A standard format for presentation

Introduction. This is often written in rough and then polished up later. Most people will tell you the introduction is the last thing they actually write, but I think it makes sense to draft it out early on. The introduction introduces themes, tells the reader what to expect, and locates your topic in some scholarly tradition, be it theories, a substantive field or conceptual issues. This is the place to say something about where you fit theoretically, your intellectual puzzle, and how your work fits in to an overall scheme, and perhaps to discuss concepts you are going to analyse or contribute to later.

continued on facing page

Literature review (see chapter 4). This could be in the introduction or in a separate chapter. It should be both substantive and theoretical/conceptual. Literature reviews that are contextually focussed can be very interesting. Rather than lists of what you have read on the British police or Asian minorities, for example, you could show what you have read about identity politics, the informal economy, the concept of a career, or the concept of community as these relate to your topic, and then move on to more specific reviews of substantive studies. Keep the literature review to a length appropriate to what you are writing (Wolcott 2001).

The setting and background. Again, this can be part of the introduction or a separate chapter/section. Here you can set the scene by describing the history of the situation you are interested in and the relevant policies or debates that led to your interest in the subject, and it can be a space for saying more about the particular group or people you studied – how typical or untypical they are, for example. It is also the place to explain details that the reader may not understand or know about, for example in Claire's case what the Common Fishing Policy is.

The methodology and methods. It is always important to have some description of how you found out what you did, so that people can know how to value your work, and can know what might be missing or what factors might have a bearing on your findings (see Hammersley 1998).

Findings. Finally, of course, the key thing to include is what you found out, or what you have decided to communicate. There are numerous approaches for presentation and organisation, as we shall see. It is a good idea to find a book or paper that you think suits what you want to do and use it as a model – there

continued on next page

is little to be gained from reinventing the wheel. You might want to separate your findings into descriptive and more analytical, as outlined in the discussion of analysis above, or you might want to intertwine these as you tell your story.

The conclusion. The conclusion should take the reader back to the beginning and to what you set out to do. It is also a good place to highlight emerging insights.

The reflexive turn

You may not want to follow the convention; I offer it to demonstrate that there is a convention from which you may veer if you wish. But whatever you choose to do should be done consciously and thoughtfully. During the 1980s, armed with ideas from textual criticism, cultural theory and literary theory, researchers (especially anthropologists) began to look critically at how and what ethnographers write. That is to say, informed to some extent by philosophical ideas about the social construction of everything we once thought of as 'real' (see chapter 2), they began to explore the production of ethnographic texts. While pursuing such an exemplary task they also began to explore the wider contexts in which ethnographic texts had been produced: contexts in which the power relationship between the researcher and the researched was unequal in favour of the researcher; the context of institutional and disciplinary constraints (and paradigms). This included what became known as the colonial critique, which began with Talal Asad's (1973) edited volume *Anthropology and the Colonial Encounter.* Key protagonists in this adventure were those in Clifford and Marcus' (1986) edited volume, whose 'focus on text making and rhetoric serves to highlight the constructed, artificial nature of cultural accounts' (Clifford 1986: 2), and later Marcus and Fischer (1986) and Clifford (1988) amongst others. Of course, feminist writers had been challenging the authority of ethnographic texts since the 1970s, arguing that 'the view from nowhere was always in fact a view from somewhere' (Spencer 2001: 444). The culmination of these trends was that writing was suddenly seen as central to what ethnographers do, and for a while it seemed that nothing was sacred, nothing to be saved from the critical eye of reflexivity.

For some, the outcome was a crisis in representation. In line with what Rob Stones (1996) calls defeatist post-modernism, some concluded that no voice was of any more value than any other and no ethnography any more trustworthy (Denzin 1992, Spencer 1989). Others have moved beyond the critical moment to try to reclaim some authority for the academic ethnographer, while retaining what was beneficial, intelligent and insightful from the reflexive turn; that is, an awareness that ethnographies are constructed by human beings who make choices about what to research, interpret what they see and hear, decide what to write and how, and that they do all this in the context of their own personal biographies and often ensconced in scientific and disciplinary environments (Hammersley 1998, Seale 1999, Spencer 2001). Ethnographers have since attempted to confront the challenges of the reflexive turn and the colonial encounter by locating their ethnographies historically, spatially and structurally in relations of power, time, global political and technological developments, and by including unbounded, fragmented and mobile communities (Humphrey 1993, Macdonald 2001). Where this all leaves us is with the requirement to think critically about writing itself and the context of research and writing. Reflexivity, or the reflexive turn, has three implications we should take on board. Reflexivity involves:

- thinking about what we read (and an awareness that ethnography is constructed)
- thinking about what we write and how
- acknowledging we are part of the world we study.

Thinking about what we read

One of the best ways to learn about ethnography is to read ethnographies, and to explore how they are conducted, on what sorts of topics, with what sorts of conclusions, and in what sorts of styles. One thing that critics in the reflexive turn noted was that many ethnographers traditionally had a tendency to write as if their account was the one true account, the one true voice of authority, thereby effectively silencing all other voices (Hammersley and Atkinson 1995). They wrote with confidence and with an expectation that their readers would trust what they were saying. But on what was this trust to be based? One way this can be achieved is by telling the reader all about what was done and how; in other words by explaining one's methodological approach and describing one's methods in full detail. But as I discuss below, this was (and is) not happening as often or as fully as one might expect. Those who explored the construction of ethnographic texts noticed that authors were using techniques such as verisimilitude, demonstrating being there, and writing in the ethnographic present. I will explore these for contemporary as well as traditional ethnographies.

Verisimilitude

An attempt is often made in ethnography at verisimilitude (the appearance of truth). Though it is quite widely accepted now that our understanding of the social world will always involve some amount of interpretation, and though many authors have come to acknowledge that ethnographers do not simply write up all there is to know about a topic or group, instead selecting which bits to report and which not, there is still a tendency to write with unquestioned authority. What makes ethnographers believable is often the way they write, rather than being convincing via a methodology section that they have a right to make the claims they make or that they can support the findings. Nor are they believed because they pack texts with facts, details, contexts, data (like scientists do, and as Malinowski attempted to do), because they don't. What you will notice as you read ethnographies is that findings are often presented as if they are facts not as interpretations. Most people do not use phrases such as 'it seemed to me that', 'I think maybe' or 'perhaps we can interpret this as an instance of'. They are much more likely to use phrases such as 'To Azande the question of guilt does not present itself as it would to us' (Evans-Pritchard 1976:

57), or 'A Manus child's family is very different from the picture of American life' (Mead 1975 [1930]: 51). Take marriage, for example: the new husband 'has every reason to hate his shy, embarrassed wife, who shrinks with loathing from his rough, unschooled embrace and has never a good word to say to him' (Mead 1975: 66).

In a more recent study authority and verisimilitude are achieved through the presentation of facts and figures. In their study of drug use and the effects of police tactics, Maher and Dixon (2002) make a conscious choice to use a style that looks more like statistical studies because of the audience they wish to address, and because they hope to effect change. The article is heavily peppered with quotes from research participants, presented as evidence for indubitable findings. The quantitative nature of findings is also implicit. For example:

> Both observations and interviews suggest that users who inject in public settings . . . are increasingly at risk of being interrupted by police either during preparation or actual administration. The most obvious consequence of this increased risk of being 'busted' is that some users are reluctant to carry injecting equipment. This means that, when they go to inject, they are less likely to have clean equipment.
>
> (Maher and Dixon 2002: 46)

And later

> The overt police presence has also exacerbated the incidence of high-risk injecting episodes in the area. Users who inject in public or semi-public settings are anxious to 'get on' and 'get out'. This can mean using any syringe that is available: either borrowing one or picking one up off the ground.
>
> (Maher and Dixon 2002: 48)

Being there

Ethnographic writing often seems to draw authority simply from the fact of the author 'being there' – as if that is enough in itself.

There is an implicit suggestion that as long as the author convinces the reader that he or she was definitely there, that is enough to convince of the authority to tell the story. Geertz argues that almost all ethnographers somehow manage to get themselves into their text: there are very few 'anonymous murmurs' (1988: 17). One technique is to hint at being there by giving a preamble, often descriptive, about the setting, about their feelings of strangeness on arriving; another is simply to write an occasional piece of text in the first person. Raymond Firth's *We, the Tikopia* is a classic work. It opens with an introduction from Malinowski, celebrating the book as an example of social *science*, and one from Firth, which stresses the need for 'lengthy, personal contact with the people one studies'. Then it begins with a style that seems to be directly continuous with travel writing (Pratt 1986):

> In the cool of the early morning, just before sunrise, the bow of the *Southern Cross* headed towards the eastern horizon, on which a tiny dark blue outline was faintly visible. Slowly it grew into a rugged mountain mass standing up sheer from the ocean; then as we approached within a few miles it revealed around its base a narrow ring of low, flat land, thick with vegetation. The sullen grey day with its lowering clouds strengthened my grim impression of a solitary peak, wild and stormy, upthrust in a waste of waters.
>
> (Firth 1957: 1)

He was there, there is no doubt about that, and his preamble takes the reader there with him. This was written in 1936. In 1987 Anthony Cohen's *Whalsay* was published, a study of a Shetland Island community. He opens:

> 11 April, 1973, a day of quirky, eccentric weather, typical of a Shetland winter. When I boarded the MV Earl of Shetland, in Lerwick, as first light was breaking, a moderate wind was blowing from the west, and continued in this benign manner during our ninety-minute passage. An invigorating morning . . . Waiting on the Symbister Pier for the boat were the

postman, Peter, there to collect the mail; Tammy, the Steamer's agent; Angus, with tractor and trailer, ready to haul milk and groceries up to the Co-op . . . I walked along the pier, full of the trepidation and self consciousness which always dominate the anthropologist as he intrudes upon the 'field'.

(Cohen 1987: 1)

He is making it very clear that this is all personal experience. He was there. Firth describes his approach, his experiences, first impressions and so on, but not really his methodology. Cohen has no methods chapter, but he is there in the pages: I went on board; we attended the meeting of the crofters. But, as Crapanzano argues (1986), the emphasis on being there did not mean these authors accepting they may have an effect; it was as if they were both there and not there, familiar and distant. Cohen is there in the pages but not when it comes to any analyses; then he disappears, so to speak. Firth uses phrases such as 'I was told that' and 'I heard no remarks about', but not so much that he is acknowledging his role in the construction of the story. The accounts remain solidly realist, with the author eliminated from the analysis (Macdonald 2001).

A more up-to-date example of being there can be found in Burawoy and Verdery (1999). This edited collection reports on lots of separate ethnographies of Russia, but none mentions research methods until in the Afterword Burawoy (1999: 301) says, 'All of us have spent many years in the countries we study . . . We are regional specialists who have made the study of the Soviet and post-Soviet World a lifetime engagement.' So, they were definitely there!

The ethnographic present

A further technique some authors use is what has been called 'the ethnographic present', treating the community as if it is frozen in time, neglecting history, processes and social change. A piece of ethnographic work is often written in the present tense, and once written stays in the present tense, regardless of the passing of time. This carries much more authority than the past tense would evoke.

For a classic example, an abridged version of Evans-Pritchard's famous work *Witchcraft, Oracles and Magic among the Azande* appeared in 1976, but was the result of fieldwork conducted in the 1920s (Gillies in Evans-Pritchard 1976: vii). The book title does not make this clear. Nor is the book written in the past tense, as if to acknowledge the passing of time. In her introduction, Eva Gillies noted the contradiction of using the present tense to describe a world long vanished in a homeland which now crossed several African states. Evans-Pritchard (1976: 1) says, for example, 'Azande believe that some people are witches', and later, 'Death is due to witchcraft and must be avenged . . . Today if a man kills a person by witchcraft the crime is his sole responsibility and his kin are not associated with his guilt' (Evans-Pritchard 1976: 5). A reader cannot be sure whether things have changed so much that this is not still the case, but the ethnographic present portrays fixed, immutable time. Similarly, Anthony Cohen, whose research was conducted in the 1970s and reported in the 1980s, writes:

> Life in Whalsay is always perceived as a struggle against formidable odds: the weather, remoteness, authority, cost, the perversity of local disagreements, petty jealousies, other people's incompetence, shortage of time. No one struggles harder than Magnie. Sometimes known as 'Powster' after the croft on which he was born, Magnie is the physical stereotype of the Whalsayman: powerfully built, with broad shoulders, his strength is prodigious as is his capacity for relentlessly hard work.
>
> (Cohen 1987: 38)

The present tense lends authority. Imagine these phrases in the past tense. But for all we know Magnie may not still be alive, never mind still powerfully built with broad shoulders and prodigious strength. This is not to say that ethnographers should necessarily write in the past tense, but merely to awaken your senses to some of the techniques for convincing a reader of the authority of the text. Many ethnographers are using the same techniques now, but some find ways to acknowledge also the tentative, provisional nature of their interpretation of events (e.g., Humphrey 1993).

Post-modern texts

The post-modernist response to the reflexive turn has been to accept and celebrate the complex, ambiguous, messy nature of the social world and ethnographic research, and self-consciously to abandon attempts to provide neat, ordered narrative accounts written in an authoritative voice (Hammersley and Atkinson 1995). Post-modernist and feminist critiques of modernist ethnography have thus led to experimental pieces employing a variety of literary and textual devices, some more avant-garde (and impossible to read) than others. Some have used the technique of 'author-saturated' texts, such as Elis (1995), who is both narrator and pro-tagonist in her story about chronic illness and the loss of a loved one. Carol Rambo Ronai (1995) provides what she calls a layered account of her 'retrospective participant observation'. Paget (1995) and Richardson (1994) combine art, literature and research; and others attempt collaborative texts that are proud to be honestly messy and fragmented (Brewer 2000).

Crucially, a post-modern ethnography evokes rather than repre-sents. It 'emerges through the reflexivity of text–author–reader and privileges no member of this trinity' (Tyler 1986: 153), and is frag-mentary because it is conscious of the fragmentary nature of the post-modern world. It might take any form, Tyler suggests, but never be completely realised. In other words, all attempts at writing the post-modern text are doomed to failure (or imperfection) because you can only transcend consensus by being imperfect!

Thinking about how and what we write

As I have said above, I do not mean to suggest that ethnographers should abandon any attempt to write with authority, or to write in the accepted style of their genre. Hammersley and Atkinson (1995) rightly warn against experimentation for the sake of it, and even Marcus (1994), one of the early protagonists of the writing as construction camp, has more recently argued that post-modern responses have gone too far. Brewer (1994) offers guidelines for how ethnographic writing can still be systematic and rigorous. What I would argue is that you should think about how you are writing, draw on the philosophy of social science to think about what you want to argue and with how much conviction, then select a style consciously. When we write we are constructing something and there are various ways that what is produced could have been constructed (Richardson 1998). We use rhetorical devices, as I have shown, and so should perhaps think some more about these and use them consciously and overtly. We should ask ourselves some questions before and as we write. Why not have a methods chapter? Would it undermine the authority of the work? Should it be a separate section or chapter or directly linked to the work and threaded through it? Should we write in the past or present tense? Should we write in the authoritative voice? Hammersley (1993 and 1998) believes, for example, that we can be authoritative as long as our authority is fallibilistic and limited. Above all we should remember the following.

- Chapters do not appear by themselves. We decide on them.
- Subheadings are not natural phenomena. They are imposed on the data.
- Many things could be written; many interpretations, in many forms, with many different focuses.
- We select what we will write and how.
- We have a reader in mind.

The same is true of survey research, of course. Analyses are made with a point in mind. Writing up of results is linked to initial questions; variables are selected, discarded, recoded in ways to suit one's purposes as well as one's theoretical framework. Some would say the whole process is often more art than science (Strauss and Corbin 1998)! Even the concepts we operationalise within a survey, or employ to make sense of the data we have collected, use imagery and analogies, for example the concept of social strata borrows from geology, and Darwin's concept of natural selection is a metaphor, drawn from unnatural selection, or selective breeding (Hammersley and Atkinson 1995).

Analyses of how we write led to a fear that we can retain no validity and that we should therefore scrap everything, and to what some have called a crisis in ethnography. Some like to think that in writing we present facts, and analysing how this is constructed actually undermines the scientific enterprise, as if 'exposing how the thing is done is to suggest that, like the lady sawed in half, it isn't done at all' (Geertz 1988: 2). These fears have led some to call textual analysis and reflexivity just so much navel gazing, narcissism, self-adoration (Babcock 1980, Okely 1992). Ernest Gellner (1988, cited in Okely 1992) said, of Geertz's book, that it should be locked away from students unless they were mature enough to cope with it. The truth is though, our relationship to our research and to the researched has changed, especially in the context of the critique of colonialism. The disciplines have been influenced by ideas in the philosophy of science (discussed in chapter 2) and it is no longer possible to pretend we are not part of the world we study. Clifford argues that all ethnography is inherently partial, and though this idea may be resisted by those who fear the collapse of clear standards of verification, if we accept it 'a rigorous sense of partiality can be a source of representational tact' (Clifford 1986: 7, and see Price 1983 for what Clifford calls 'an example of self-conscious, serious partiality'). Of course, such partiality involves also noting who our research is for. Even impartial access is not always guaranteed: Evans-Pritchard (1976), for example, was paid by the colonial administration, and Judith Okely (1983) who studied traveller-gypsies was given access by local council officers who were thinking about introducing sedentarisation.

What can we do? To help you construct your descriptions and arguments, *read*. Follow Irving Goffman's (1961) lead and draw on diverse written sources for inspiration in style as well as for locating sensitising concepts (Becker 1998, Hammersley and Atkinson 1995). Read fiction as well as academic texts and think consciously about the style you choose. Compare your work with travel literature, journalism, and academic works from different disciplines, to help you settle on a suitable approach. You thought carefully about your research puzzle (chapter 2); now think about writing. Think about who you are writing for, what is your intention, and what you want to convey. We may not want to accept the post-modern response, but we can still think about writing style, for example. As Laurel Richardson (1998) has said, many published ethnographies are boring, and you may want to use simile and metaphor to some extent (indeed it is impossible not to), but check overuse and cultural specificity. For example, what is a blue-eyed ethnographer? I remember once reading an article that talked about this, but I did not know what it meant. Compare books which write without much metaphor and simile, but which are boring, with those which are colourful but perhaps less convincing in terms of what we think of as science. *Wheeling and Dealing* by Adler (1985) has a methods chapter, writes in the past tense, and transports the reader into the culture by drawing on the vernacular.

> One group of three smugglers, who usually brought across 30 kilos of cocaine every four to six weeks (when they were working), ran a fairly simple operation. A pilot was hired for the run. This group didn't have a plane so they either tried to find a pilot who owned his own aircraft or rented a plane . . . A copilot was also hired to fly shotgun for security reasons . . . This latter individual's job was handling money, helping with the drug purchase, and carrying a weapon to prevent rip-offs.
> (Adler 1985: 179)

It is an interesting technique, but there are several words in the passage that readers might not understand, such as the 'run', flying 'shotgun' and 'rip-offs'. Compare that with Gervais and Jovchelovitch (1998), 'The health beliefs of the Chinese community in England'. This is a report based on ethnographic research about beliefs, opinions and superstitions, but is expressed in a factual scientific way (which is of course another rhetorical device). Do you think this is how the interviewees put it?

> Traditional Chinese medicine holds that good living habits are important in preventing disease and maintaining health because

they help the organism to keep an internal balance . . . Such notions form the substantive core of the representations found in our study. The binary oppositions between yin/yang, hot/cold, wet/dry, are at the core of a conceptual system used to explain the nature of health and causes of illness . . . Health is conceived as the harmonious balance of contradictory forces . . . Thus Chinese health beliefs are deeply entrenched in a world view.

(Gervais and Jovchelovitch 1998: 1)

Finally, you might also think about the order in which you write. Why should we assume that the social world is best represented in a series of chapters? Hammersley and Atkinson (1995: 250) argue 'the transformation of "the field" into "the text" is partly achieved by means of the narrative construction of everyday life'. Imposing a narrative is therefore again a device we use to order the mess of material to make it tell a story, but the ordering or narrative may be imposing sequence where you might not want it. You may want to leave some sense of the disordered nature of reality in your writing. Adler (1985: 9) worried about imposing a structure that does not necessarily exist on to reality, about 'trying to make too much rational sense out of this irrational world'. However, whatever you decide about writing, your responsibility is to those you studied. Studies can be rich, evocative, colourful, a pleasure to read, but should perhaps retain authoritative status as a piece of scholarly research if this is what you have told your respondents (and supervisors, colleagues, funding agencies). I cannot go and write a piece of fiction, and maybe earn much more from it than I do from academic books, when I promised my interviewees I was attempting to portray them more faithfully than the media had to date. It would be exploitative as well as deceitful. Similarly, we cannot become so radical in our writing that we forget that there was a social world out there that we studied, and social actors who allowed us into their lives to do so. Too much focus on the text as a construction disembodies the account from the fieldwork, whereas this book has shown how writing is inextricably bound up with data collection. If rhetorical deconstruction is to be consistent with (subtle) realist approaches to ethnography (Hammersley 1993), we need to think about style without neglecting scientific adequacy, and without losing all links between signifier and signified.

Acknowledging you are part of the world you study

Social researchers are part of the world they study, not some sort of objective, detached research tool. Even your *choice of topic* is influenced by your own personal biography, by funding bodies (who are themselves influenced by internal and national politics), your academic institution, your academic and personal biography. Who you gain access to and the type of access you gain are affected by your age, gender, class, personality and nationality. Your *interpretations* are affected by all of the above, plus your foreshadowed problems, your theoretical orientation, your academic training. So, you are not just experiencing and observing phenomena in their natural setting, you are interpreting, analysing, seeking, sorting, sifting, and even affecting outcomes by your own presence. Reflexivity means being aware of all these issues, but it does not mean abandoning your work because of them. We could conclude there is nothing real, just interpretation; there is no truth, all is relative. (And some people do!) But there is no need. We just need to be aware of the above limitations (and sometimes advantages – like your age, personality, contacts!) and to be honest about them, while trying to be systematic in our approach to every aspect of our work. We can produce valuable accounts of the social world which take into account and even take advantage of who we are and how we experience that world ourselves. We can allow our research practice to be informed by interpretivism as well as realism, by reflexivity as well as rigour.

Malinowski's diary (1967) notably demonstrated his constant bouts of irritation and his frustrations with the 'natives' he studied, at one particularly low point retorting: 'As for ethnology: I see the life of the natives as utterly devoid of interest or importance, something as remote from me as the life of a dog' (1967: 167). Faced with such a challenge to the authorial voice of the subjective observer, ethnographers began arguing that the reflexive turn should make us think more about the *practice* of ethnography (Ellis and Bochner 1996) as well as the ethnographer's own role in it, and a sub-genre of ethnographic writing emerged: the self-reflexive field-work account (Clifford 1986: 14). Some were written as or in the style of fictional accounts (Barley 1983, Gardner 1991) while others explored fieldwork practice in the light of the ethnographers' auto-biographies (Okely and Calloway 1992, Watson 1993). In a special edition of *Sociology* on autobiography, Cotterill and Letherby (1993), for example, offered autobiographical accounts of their own academic development and their experiences of feminist ethnography. As far back as 1973, Pocock (cited in Okely 1992) had advised a reflexive re-examination of anthropologists' texts in the light of their own biographies, and Clifford Geertz' *Works and Lives* (1988) attempted just this for some of the classical authors, including Bronislaw Malinowski and Ruth Benedict. For Cohen (1994) it is not enough merely to acknowledge that the self intrudes upon ethnography. We need to view the 'intrusive self' as a resource, one that constrains the temptation to generalise and simplify other people's lives. Which takes us right back to chapter 1 and Willis and Trondman's (2000) solicitation that ethnography respects the irreducibility of human experience.

But autobiography can be more of the same if we are not careful; more exoticising, fictionalising, sensationalising, and constructing the 'other' on which we can gaze with wonder. What is needed is to be able to locate yourself in your study honestly and openly, in an admission that observations are filtered through your own experience, rather than you being the detached voice of authority. This does not mean the text becomes one about you. It means confronting your relationship with others; it means conveying the context and your place in it. This all causes us to subvert the idea of the observer as a detached, impersonal research tool, but rather than undermining the scientific enterprise in fact it means we are being increasingly rigorous, increasingly sceptical, and avoids com-placency and blind faith. There are different ways of achieving this and currently ethnographers are still exploring writing styles and techniques. Diane Wilson (Wilson and Csordas 2003), for example, manages to locate herself in her story, and acknowledge that she is a believer in Navajo healing ceremonies, while using language more familiar to research in the positivist tradition. She explains her 'irrational belief' thus: 'I assume, based on my own experience and observation, and on the data of others, that Navajo ceremonies have non-random effects' (2003: 293).

Enabling researchers to be creative in their writing styles is to be encouraged (Hammersley and Atkinson 1995) but we still need to know how people did what they did. That is to say, we should include a section or chapter on methods (Hammersley 1998). Many anthropology books do not even have a methodology section, and where they do this is often distinct from the rest of the book, and can be very brief. Some simply offer a paragraph or two stating that the person did fieldwork. This is because anthropologists share a common understanding about what fieldwork is, but in sociology and other disciplines it is not so clear what is meant by ethnography or ethnographic methods. I would argue that, in any case, the reader is offered as full a description as possible of where the ethnography was done and how, with what misgivings, what mistakes, what expectations and disappointments, what revelations and what pleasures as might enable the reader not only to enjoy but to evaluate the written product. For an excellent example of how a full and reflexive account of the field research and subsequent report writing can serve to illuminate rather than undermine the process, see the fourth edition of William Foote Whyte's *Street Corner Society* (1993).

The value of ethnography

I would like to finish with a note or two about the evaluation of ethnographic research. Two key texts I would recommend are by Hammersley (1998) and Seale (1999). Hammersley's text, which is ostensibly about how ethnographic texts can be read, understood and evaluated, debates a range of controversial issues around the relevance, replicability, validity and scientific status of ethnography. Seale's book is for qualitative researchers generally, not just ethnographers, but provides valuable avenues for exploring similar issues.

Representativeness

Students of survey-style research are routinely taught that their work should be representative, reliable and valid (May 2001), and as a result researchers often look to ensure that qualitative research meets the same criteria. For research to be representative it should have value and relevance for the wider population from which the sample is drawn. This is to say, since we cannot interview or survey everyone in an entire population we take a sample, but we should ensure this sample is representative of the wider population in important ways so that conclusions drawn about the sample can also be inferred to the population as a whole. Qualitative researchers often respond with the argument that they are attempting to understand a few cases in depth rather than represent an entire population. What is gained in depth, it is argued, compensates for the lack of breadth. Indeed, ethnographic research often studies an entire group without thought as to whether or where the group represents anything wider. However, Seale (1999) argues that, rather than be so dismissive of the wider relevance of findings from qualitative research, maybe it would be worthwhile to think about whether we can *generalise* in some way, at least to similar groups in similar settings. Another way to think about this is in terms of inferences. Maybe what we discover can have *inferences* for another group, or maybe we can *transfer* what we have learnt to another group. Seale suggests that if we know enough about situations in the first place (both the one we are studying and the one we might want to make inferences for) then that enables us to decide whether they are similar enough, in relevant ways, for us to be able to transfer findings from one setting to another. Another way ethnographic research might have wider relevance is through the role of theory. This was discussed in chapter 8. The theories that ethnographic research produce and/or refine are stories about connections between things that may have relevance beyond the ethnographic situation in which they were produced, but, of course, remain open to revision and refinement in the light of new empirical data.

Validity

Validity is about whether the research is measuring what it intended to measure, or, alternatively, whether it is plausible or credible, and there is enough evidence to support the argument (Hammersley 1998). I would argue that ethnographic research is better at dealing with problems of validity than survey research because it involves direct and sustained contact with human agents, who can tell us when we are misunderstanding, misrepresenting, or simply 'barking up the wrong tree'. It is iterative-inductive, and involves constantly moving backwards from our research questions to the data, and back to refine our questions or line of enquiry in light of what we discover. Ethnographic research respects the irreducibility of human experience, and acknowledges the complex, messy nature of human lives and understandings. But there are other ways we ensure validity. We can first of all ask whether what we argue has 'face validity'. That is to say, on the face of it does this make sense? If not, then we should look more closely and try to understand why. Perhaps we have not done our work thoroughly enough. But perhaps, on the other hand, what we are learning really does challenge what we thought was common sense. Hammersley (1998) argues that validity is also ensured when we are committed to our work, and to doing it thoughtfully and carefully; when we confront our prejudices and deal with them in order to avoid bias; and when we present the wider community with enough information to enable them to judge for themselves and to challenge our findings. Seale (1999) makes a similar point when he says we should employ the criterion of fallibility; that is to say that we should acknowledge that our findings are only true for as long as we have not found evidence to the contrary, and that evidence should be actively sought.

Reliability

Reliability in survey research is about being able to ensure that if another person came along and did the same study they would have the same findings. It is linked to the idea of standardisation discussed in chapter 5. But, as we discovered there, as well as at length in the discussion above, ethnographic research has to acknowledge the role of the researcher in the research, to be reflexive about the interaction that takes place in the field, and where possible to theorise the relationship. We can produce valuable accounts of the social world which take into account and even take advantage of who we are and how we experience that world ourselves. Calls for replicability rely on naïve realist assumptions that there is a single external reality that can be known irrespective of how we come to know it. The social constructionist response would be that everyone has his or her own account of the world and there is no way of judging between them. The ways ethnographies are responding to post-post-modernism are varied and forms are still emerging; subtle realist (or more self-aware realist) accounts of research can be seen emerging across a range of disciplines and journals. Hammersley and Seale, for examples, have attempted subtle realist responses by suggesting practical ways we can ensure some degree of replicability, while acknowledging that complete replicability is unrealistic and even undesirable.

Summary

This chapter has considered the role of writing in ethnography and advises readers to think about writing as they thought about other aspects of the research process. When writing up ethnographic research there is a standard format, or convention, one can follow, but convention should not be followed for its own sake. Since the reflexive turn of the 1980s the production of ethnographic texts has come under careful scrutiny. Ethnographers must now think critically and reflexively about writing and about the contexts of research and writing. We explored how ethnographers have used rhetorical devices to establish authority in their writing and the post-modern response in the creation of experimental pieces. Post-positivist and subtle realist ethnographers are responding to post-modernism by thinking reflexively and consciously about writing styles, about the role of the ethnographer in the construction of texts, and about the responsibilities ethnographers have to their research participants, and are attempting to retain systematic rigour in all phases of the research process. This chapter concluded with an exploration of the subtle realist defence of ethnography and its scientific status post-post-modernism.

Further reading

For an excellent aid to writing, full of advice, tips and examples, see Harry Wolcott's (2001) *Writing Up Qualitative Research*.

For detailed, reflexive accounts of fieldwork practice and the role of selfhood, personal relationships and autobiography in ethnography, see Okely and Calloway (1992) and Watson (1993). You might enjoy Powdermaker's *Stranger and Friend* (1966), which integrated biography with a discussion of methods. She talks about her methods in a biographical way in the context of four projects and argues: 'The anthropologist is a human instrument studying other human beings . . . it is an illusion for him to think he can remove his personality from his work and become a faceless robot.'

See May (2001: chapter 2) for a useful summary of the role of theory in social research.

Hammersley (1998) and Seale (1999) are the best accounts to date of how ethnography can be evaluated. Brewer's (2000) book also presents itself as defending ethnography against its post-modern critics and demonstrates that it is still possible to make truth-like statements from ethnographic research. He also discusses the future for ethnography after the reflexive turn and in the context of globalisation.

Bibliography

Åberg, A. C., Sidenvall, B., Hepworth, M., O'Reilly, K. and Lithell, H. 'Continuity of the self in later life: perceptions of informal caregivers', *Qualitative Health Research* 14(6): 792–815(24).

Adler, P. A. (1985) *Wheeling and Dealing: An Ethnography of an Upper-Level Drug Dealing and Smuggling Community*, New York: Columbia University Press.

Agar, M. H. (1986) *Speaking of Ethnography*, Beverley Hills, CA: Sage.

Alasuutari, P. (1995) *Researching Culture: Qualitative Method and Cultural Studies*, London: Sage.

Altheide, D. L. (1996) *Qualitative Media Analysis*, Thousand Oaks, CA: Sage.

Anderson, N. (1961 [1923]) *The Hobo*, Chicago: University of Chicago Press.

Asad, T. (ed.) (1973) *Anthropology and the Colonial Encounter*, London: Ithaca Press.

Atkinson, P. (1990) *The Ethnographic Imagination: Textual Constructions of Reality*, London: Routledge.

—— (1992) *Understanding Ethnographic Texts*, London: Sage.

Atkinson, P., Coffey, A., Delamont, S., Lofland, J. and Lofland, L. (eds) (2001) *Handbook of Ethnography*, London: Sage.

Babcock, B. (1980) 'Reflexivity: definitions and discriminations', *Semiotica* 30(1/2): 1–14.

Ball, M. and Smith, G. (2001) 'Technologies of realism? Ethnographic uses of photography and film', in P. Atkinson, A. Coffey, S. Delamont, J. Lofland and L. Lofland (eds) *Handbook of Ethnography*, London: Sage.

Banton, M. (1977) *The Idea of Race*, London: Tavistock.

Barley, N. (1983) *The Innocent Anthropologist: Notes from a Mud Hut*, London: Penguin.

Barry, C. A. (1998) 'Choosing qualitative data analysis software: Atlas/ti and Nudist compared', *Sociological Research Online* 3 (3).

Barthes, R. (1972) *Mythologies*, London: Jonathan Cape.

—— (1977) *Elements of Semiology*, New York: Hill and Wang.

Bateson, G. and Mead, M. (1942) *Balinese Character*, vol. II, New York: New York Academy of Science.

Becker, H. (1970) *Sociological Work: Method and Substance*, Chicago: Aldine.

—— (1986) *Writing for Social Scientists: How to Start and Finish Your Thesis, Book or Article*, Chicago: University of Chicago Press.

—— (1998) *Tricks of the Trade: How to Think about Your Research While You're Doing It*, Chicago: University of Chicago Press.

Benton, T. (1977) *The Philosophical Foundations of the Three Sociologies*, London: Routledge and Kegan Paul.

Benton, T. and Craib, I. (2001) *Philosophy of Social Science: The Philosophical Foundations of Social Thought*, Basingstoke: Palgrave.

Berg, B. L. (2004) *Qualitative Research Methods for the Social Sciences*, 5th edn, Boston: Pearson.

Berger, P. and Luckmann, T. (1967) *The Social Construction of Reality*, London: Allen Lane.

Bhaskar, R. (1997 [1975]) *A Realist Theory of Science*, London: Verso.

Blaikie, N. (1993) *Approaches to Social Enquiry*, Cambridge: Polity Press.

Bloor, M. (1985) 'Observations of abortive illness behaviour', *Urban Life* 14: 300–16.

—— (2001) 'The ethnography of health and medicine', in P. Atkinson, A. Coffey, S. Delamont, J. Lofland and L. Lofland (eds) *Handbook of Ethnography*, London: Sage.

Blumer, H. (1969) *Symbolic Interactionism*, Englewood Cliffs, NJ: Prentice Hall.

Brewer, J. (1994) 'The ethnographic critique of ethnography: sectarianism in the RUC', *Sociology* 28: 231–44.

—— (2000) *Ethnography*, Buckingham: Open University Press.

Bryman, A. (1988) *Quantity and Quality in Social Research*, London: Unwin Hyman.

—— (2001) *Social Research Methods*, Oxford: Oxford University Press.

Bulmer, M. (1982) 'The merits and demerits of covert participant observation', in M. Bulmer (ed.) *Social Research Ethics*, London: Macmillan.

—— (1984) *The Chicago School of Sociology*, Chicago: University of Chicago Press.

Burawoy, M. (1999) 'Afterword', in M. Burawoy and K. Verdery (eds) *Uncertain Transition: Ethnographies of Change in a Post Socialist World*, Oxford: Rowman and Littlefield Inc.

Burawoy, M. and Verdery, K. (eds) (1999) *Uncertain Transition: Ethnographies of Change in the Post Socialist World*, Oxford: Rowman and Littlefield Inc.

Burgess, R. G. (1984) *In the Field: An Introduction to Field Research*, London: Allen & Unwin.

Cassidy, R. (2002) 'The social practice of racehorse breeding', *Society and Animals* 10: 155–70.

Chalmers, A. F. (1999) *What Is This Thing Called Science?*, 3rd edn, Buckingham: Open University Press.

Chaplin, E. (1994) *Sociology and Visual Representations*, London: Routledge.

Charmaz, K. and Mitchell, R. G. (2001) 'Grounded theory in ethnography', in P. Atkinson, A. Coffey, S. Delamont, J. Lofland and L. Lofland (eds) *Handbook of Ethnography*, London: Sage.

Cicourel, A. V. (1964) *Method and Measurement in Sociology*, New York: The Free Press.

Clifford, J. (1986) 'Introduction: partial truths', in J. Clifford and G. Marcus (eds) *Writing Culture: The Poetics and Politics of Ethnography*, Berkeley: University of California Press.

—— (1988) *The Predicament of Culture*, Cambridge, MA: Harvard University Press.

Clifford, J. and Marcus, G. E. (1986) *Writing Culture: The Poetics and Politics of Ethnography*, Berkeley: University of California Press.

Coffey, A., Holbrook, B. and Atkinson, P. (1996) 'Qualitative data analysis: technologies and representations', *Sociological Research Online* 1 (1).

Cohen, A. P. (1987) *Whalsay: Symbol, Segment and Boundary in a Shetland Island Community*, Manchester: Manchester University Press.

—— (1994) *Self Consciousness: An Alternative Anthropology of Identity*, London: Routledge.

Collier, J. (1967) *Visual Anthropology: Photography as Research Method*, Albuquerque: University of New Mexico Press.

—— (1995) 'Photography and visual anthropology', in P. Hockings (ed.) *Principles of Visual Anthropology*, Berlin and New York: Mouton de Gruyter.

Collier, J. and Collier, M. (1986) *Visual Anthropology: Photography as a Research Method*, 2nd edn, Albuquerque: University of New Mexico Press.

Cortazzi, M. (2001) 'Narrative analysis in ethnography', in P. Atkinson, A. Coffey, S. Delamont, J. Lofland and L. Lofland (eds) *Handbook of Ethnography*, London: Sage.

Corti, L., Foster, J. and Thompson, P. (1995) 'Archiving qualitative research data', *Social Research Update* 10.

Cotterill, P. and Letherby, G. (1993) 'Weaving stories: personal auto/biographies in feminist research', *Sociology* 27(1): 67–80.

Crapanzano, V. (1986) 'Hermes' dilemma: the masking of subversion in ethnographic description', in J. Clifford and G. Marcus (eds) *Writing Culture: The Poetics and Politics of Ethnography*, Berkeley: University of California Press.

de Koning, K. and Martin, M. (1996) 'Participatory research in health: setting the context', in K. de Koning and M. Martin (eds) *Participatory Research in Health*, London: Zed Books.

de Saussure, F. (1974) *Course in General Linguistics*, London: Fontana.

Deegan, M. J. (2001) 'The Chicago School of Ethnography', in P. Atkinson, A. Coffey, S. Delamont, J. Lofland and L. Lofland (eds) *Handbook of Ethnography*, London: Sage.

Denzin, N. (1992) 'Whose Cornerville is it anyway?', *Journal of Contemporary Ethnography* 21: 120–32.

Denzin, N. K. and Lincoln, Y. S. (eds) (1994) *Handbook of Qualitative Research*, Thousand Oaks CA: Sage.

Ditton, J. (1977) *Part-Time Crime: An Ethnography of Fiddling and Pilferage*, London: Macmillan.

Dodier, N. and Camus, A. (1998) 'Openness and specialisation: dealing with patients in a hospital emergency service', *Sociology of Health and Illness* 20(4): 413–44.

Douglas, J. D. (1976) *Investigative Social Research: Individual and Team Field Research*, London: Sage.

Elis, C. (1995) *Final Negotiations: A Story of Love, Loss and Chronic Illness*, Philadelphia: Temple University Press.

Ellen, R. F. (ed.) (1984) *Ethnographic Research: A Guide to General Conduct*, London: Academic Press.

Ellis, C. and Bochner, A. P. (eds) (1996) *Composing Ethnography: Alternative Forms of Qualitative Writing*, Walnut Creek, CA: AltaMira.

Emerson, R. M., Fretz, R. I. and Shaw, L. L. (1995) *Writing Ethnographic Fieldnotes*, Chicago: University of Chicago Press.

—— (2001) 'Participant observation and fieldnotes', in P. Atkinson, A. Coffey, S. Delamont, J. Lofland and L. Lofland (eds) *Handbook of Ethnography*, London: Sage.

Emmison, M. and Smith, P. (2000) *Researching the Visual*, London: Sage.

Eriksen, K. T. (1967) 'A comment on disguised observation in sociology', *Social Problems* 14: 366–73.

Eriksen, T. H. (1995) *Small Places, Large Issues: An Introduction to Social and Cultural Anthropology*, London: Pluto Press.

Estroff, S. (1981) *Making It Crazy: An Ethnography of Psychiatric Clients in an American Community*, Berkeley: University of California Press.

Evans-Pritchard, E. E. (1976) *Witchcraft, Oracles and Magic among the Azande*, Oxford: Clarendon Press.

Ezzy, D. (2002) *Qualitative Analysis: Practice and Innovation*, London: Routledge.

Feyerabend, P. K. (1981) *Problems of Empiricism: Philosophical Papers*, vol II, Cambridge: Cambridge University Press.

Fielding, N. (1981) *The National Front*, London: Routledge and Kegan Paul.

—— (2001) 'Computers in qualitative research', in P. Atkinson, A. Coffey, S. Delamont, J. Lofland and L. Lofland (eds) *Handbook of Ethnography*, London: Sage.

Fielding, N. and Lee, R. (1995) 'The hypertext facility in qualitative analysis software', *ESRC Archive Bulletin*.

—— (1998) *Computer Assisted Qualitative Research*, London: Sage.

Firth, R. (1957) *We, the Tikopia: A Sociological Study of Kinship in Primitive Polynesia*, London: George, Allen and Unwin.

Flick, U. (2002) *An Introduction to Qualitative Research*, 2nd edn, London: Sage.

Fraser, R. (1979) *Blood of Spain: The Experience of Civil War 1936–39*, Harmondsworth: Penguin.

Gadamer, H. G. (1989) *Truth and Method*, London: Sheed and Ward.

Gardner, K. (1991) *Songs at the River's Edge: Stories from a Bangladeshi Village*, London: Virago Press.

Garfinkel, H. (1967) *Studies in Ethnomethodology*, Englewood Cliffs, NJ: Prentice Hall.

Geertz, C. (1973) *The Interpretation of Cultures*, New York: Fontana.

—— 1988 *Works and Lives: The Anthropologist as Author*, Oxford: Polity Press.

Gellner, E. (1988) 'Conscious confusion: review of works and lives by C. Geertz', *Times Higher Educational Supplement*, London.

Gerould, D. (1992) 'Chronology. Stanislaw Ignacy Witkiewicz and Bronislaw Malinowski', in D. Gerould (ed.) *The Witkiewicz Reader*, Evanston, IL: Northwestern University Press.

Gervais, M. C. and Jovchelovitch, S. (1998) 'The health beliefs of the Chinese community in England: a qualitative research study', London: Health Education Authority.

Gibbs, A. (1997) 'Focus groups', *Social Research Update* 19: 1–7.

Gilbert, N. (1993) *Researching Social Life*, London: Sage.

Giulianotti, R. (1997) 'Enlightening the North: Aberdeen fanzines and local football identity', in G. Armstrong and R. Giulianotti (eds) *Entering the Field: New Perspectives on World Football*, Oxford: Berg.

Glaser, B. G. and Strauss, A. L. (1967) *The Discovery of Grounded Theory: Strategies for Qualitative Research*, Hawthorne, NY: Aldine de Gruyter.

Goffman, I. (1961) *Asylums: Essays on the Social Situation of Mental Patients and Other Inmates*, New York: Doubleday.

Gold, R. L. (1958) 'Roles in sociological fieldwork', *Social Forces* 36: 217–23.

Goward, N. (1984) 'Personal interaction and adjustment', in R. F. Ellen (ed.) *Ethnographic Research: A Guide to General Conduct*, London: Academic Press.

Griffiths, L. (1998) 'Humour as resistance to professional dominance in community mental health teams', *Sociology of Health and Illness* 20(6): 874–95.

Grinyer, A. (2002) 'The anonymity of research participants: assumptions, ethics and practicalities', *Social Research Update* 36.

Hammersley, M. (1993) 'The rhetorical turn in ethnography', *Social Science Information* 32: 23–37.

—— (1998) *Reading Ethnographic Research*, 2nd edn, London: Longman.

Hammersley, M. and Atkinson, P. (1995) *Ethnography: Principles in Practice*, 2nd edn, London: Routledge.

Harding, S. (1986) *The Science Question in Feminism*, Milton Keynes: Open University Press.

Harrison, B. and Lyon, E. S. (1993) 'A note on ethical issues in the use of autobiography in sociological research', *Sociology* 27(1): 101–9.

Heaton, J. (1998) 'Secondary analysis of qualitative data', *Social Research Update* 22.

Hebdige, D. (1979) *Subculture: The Meaning of Style*, London: Methuen.

Hey, V. (1997) *The Company She Keeps: An Ethnography of Girls' Friendships*, Buckingham: Open University Press.

Heyl, B. S. (2001) 'Ethnographic interviewing', in P. Atkinson, A. Coffey, S. Delamont, J. Lofland and L. Lofland (eds) *Handbook of Ethnography*, London: Sage.

Hicks, D. (1984) 'Getting into the field and establishing routines', in R. Ellen (ed.) *Ethnographic Research: A Guide to General Conduct*, London: Academic Press.

Hobbs, D. (2001) 'Ethnography and the study of deviance', in P. Atkinson, A. Coffey, S. Delamont, J. Lofland and L. Lofland (eds) *Handbook of Ethnography*, London: Sage.

Holliday, R. (1999) 'The comfort of identity', *Sexualities* 2(4): 475–91.

—— (2000) 'We've been framed: visualising methodology', *The Sociological Review* 48(4): 503–21.

Holy, L. (1984) 'Participant observation and the interpretative paradigm', in R. Ellen (ed.) *Ethnographic Research: A Guide to General Conduct*, London: Academic Press.

Humphrey, R. (1993) 'Life stories and social careers: ageing and social life in an ex-mining town', *Sociology* 27(1): 166–78.

Humphreys, L. (1970) *Tea-Room Trade*, Chicago: Aldine.

Hutchins, E. and Klausen, T. (2002) 'Distributed cognition in an airline cockpit', in S. Taylor (ed.) *Ethnographic Research: A Reader*, London: Sage.

Inglis, D. and Hughson, J. (2003) *Confronting Culture*, Cambridge: Polity.

Jackson, A. (1987) *Anthropology at Home*, London: Tavistock.

Jackson, J. E. (1990) '"I am a fieldnote": fieldnotes as a symbol of professional identity', in R. Sanjek (ed.) *Fieldnotes: The Making of Anthropology*, Ithaca, NY: Cornell University Press.

Jacobs, J. (1974) *Sun City: An Ethnographic Study of a Retirement Community*, New York: Holt, Rinehart and Winston.

Johnson, J. (1990) *Selecting Ethnographic Informants*, London: Sage.

Junker, B. (1960) *Field Work*, Chicago: University of Chicago Press.

Kelle, U. (1997) 'Theory building in qualitative research and computer programs for the management of textual data', *Sociological Research Online* 2 (2).

Kelly, L. (1988) *Surviving Sexual Violence*, Cambridge: Polity Press.

Kemp, J. H. and Ellen, R. (1984) 'Informal interviewing', in R. F. Ellen (ed.) *Ethnographic Research: A Guide to General Conduct*, London: Academic Press.

Kleinman, A. (1997) *Writing at the Margin: Discourse between Anthropology and Medicine*, Berkeley: University of California Press.

Krueger, R. A. (1994) *Focus Groups: A Practical Guide for Applied Research*, 2nd edn, London: Sage.

Kuhn, T. (1970) *The Structure of Scientific Revolutions*, Chicago: University of Chicago Press.

Kulick, D. (1999) *Travesti: Sex, Gender and Culture among Brazilian Trans-gendered Prostitutes*, Chicago: University of Chicago Press.

Kuper, A. (1997) *Anthropology and Anthropologists: The British School 1920–1970*, Harmondsworth: Penguin.

Lassman, P. (1974) 'Phenomenological perspectives in sociology', in J. Rex (ed.) *Approaches to Sociology*, London: Routledge and Kegan Paul.

Lewis, O. (1951) *Life in a Mexican Village: Tepoztlan Restudied*, Urbana: University of Illinois Press.

—— (1967) *Five Families: Anthology of Poverty*, New York: New Ameican. Library.

Lofland, J. and Lofland, L. H. (1995) *Analyzing Social Settings: A Guide to Qualitative Observation and Analysis*, 3rd edn, Belmont CA: Wadsworth.

Macdonald, S. (2001) 'British social anthropology', in P. Atkinson, A. Coffey, S. Delamont, J. Lofland and L. Lofland (eds) *Handbook of Ethnography*, London: Sage.

MacDougall, D. (1997) 'The visual in anthropology', in M. Banks and H. Morphy (eds) *Rethinking Visual Anthropology*, London: New Haven Press.

McRobbie, A. (1982) 'The politics of feminist research: between talk, text and action', *Feminist Review* 12: 46–57.

Madriz, E. (2000) 'Focus groups in feminist research', in N. K. Denzin and Y. S. Lincoln (eds) *Handbook of Qualitative Research*, 2nd edn, London: Sage

Maher, L. and Dixon, D. (2002) 'Policing and public health: law enforcement and harm minimization in a street-level drug market', in S. Taylor (ed.) *Ethnographic Research: A Reader*, London: Sage.

Malinowski, B. (1922) *Argonauts of the Western Pacific: An Account of Native Enterprise and Adventure in the Archipelagoes of Melanesian New Guinea*, New York: Dutton.

—— (1926) *Crime and Custom in Savage Society*, London: Kegan Paul, Trench, Trubner.

—— (1932) *The Sexual Life of Savages in North Western Melanesia*, London: Routledge.

—— (1935) *Coral Gardens and Their Magic*, London: Allen and Unwin.

—— (1960) *Sex and Repression in Savage Society*, London: Routledge.

—— (1967) *A Diary in the Strict Sense of the Term*, London: Athlone.

Manning, P. K. (2001) 'Semiotics, semantics and ethnography', in P. Atkinson, A. Coffey, S. Delamont, J. Lofland and L. Lofland (eds) *Handbook of Ethnography*, London: Sage.

Marcus, G. E. (1994) 'What comes (just) after the "post"? The case of ethnography', in N. K. Denzin and Y. S. Lincoln (eds) *Handbook of Qualitative Research*, Thousand Oaks, CA: Sage.

Marcus, G. E. and Fischer, M. (1986) *Anthropology as Cultural Critique*, Chicago: University of Chicago Press.

Maso, I. (2001) 'Phenomenology and ethnography', in P. Atkinson, A. Coffey, S. Delamont, J. Lofland and L. Lofland (eds) *Handbook of Ethnography*, London: Sage.

Mason, J. (1996) *Qualitative Researching*, London: Sage.

Mauthner, N., Parry, O. and Backett-Milburn, K. (1998) 'The data are out there, or are they? Implications for archiving and revisiting qualitative data', *Sociology* 32(4): 733–45.

May, T. (2001) *Social Research: Issues, Methods and Process*, 3rd edn, Maidenhead: Open University Press.

Mayring, P. (2000) 'Qualitative Content Analysis', *Forum for Qualitative Research* 1(2).

Mead, M. (1975 [1930]) *Growing Up in New Guinea*, New York: Morrow Quill Paperbacks.

—— (1995) 'Visual anthropology in a discipline of words', in P. Hockings (ed.) *Principles of Visual Anthropology*, Berlin and New York: Mouton de Gruyter.

Messerschmidt, D. A. (1981) *Anthropologists at Home in North America: Methods and Issues in the Study of One's Own Society*, Cambridge: Cambridge University Press.

Middleton, J. (1970) *The Study of the Lugbara: Expectation and Paradox in Anthropological Research*, New York: Holt, Rinehart and Winston.

Miles, M. B. and Huberman, A. M. (1994) *Qualitative Data Analysis: An Expanded Sourcebook*, 2nd edn, London: Sage.

Moore, S. (2000) 'Research, reality and "hanging around"', *Sociology Review* 10(3): 8–13.

Morgan, D. (1988) *Focus Groups as Qualitative Research*, London: Sage.

Morrow, V. and Richards, M. (1996) 'The ethics of social research with children: an overview', *Children and Society*, 10: 90–105.

Nader, L. (1970) 'From anguish to exultation', in P. Golde (ed.) *Women in the Field*, Chicago: Aldine.

O'Connell Davidson, J. and Layder, D. (1994) *Methods, Sex and Madness*, London: Routledge.

Okely, J. (1983) *The Traveller-Gypsies*, Cambridge: Cambridge University Press.

—— (1992) 'Anthropology and autobiography. Participatory experience and embodied knowledge', in J. Okely and H. Calloway (eds) *Anthropology and Autobiography*, London: Routledge.

Okely, J. and Calloway, H. (eds) (1992) *Anthropology and Autobiography*, London: Routledge.

Oommen, T. K. (1997) *Citizenship, Nationality and Ethnicity*, Cambridge: Polity Press.

O'Reilly, K. (2000a) *The British on the Costa del Sol: Transnational Identities and Local Communities*, London: Routledge.

—— (2000b) 'Trading intimacy for liberty: British women on the Costa del Sol', in F. Anthias and G. Lazaridis (eds) *Gender and Migration in Southern Europe,* Oxford: Berg.

—— (2001) 'Blackpool in the sun: images of the British on the Costa del Sol', in R. King and N. Woods (eds) *Media and Migration*, London: Routledge.

Paget, M. (1995) 'Performing the text', in J. Van Maanen (ed.) *Representation in Ethnography*, London: Sage.

Paperman, P. (2003) 'Surveillance underground. The uniform as an interaction device', *Ethnography* 4(3): 397–419.

Parry, O. and Mauthner, N. (2004) 'Whose data are they anyway? Practical, legal and ethical issues in archiving qualitative research', *Sociology* 38(1): 139–52.

Peacock, J. (1986) *The Anthropological Lens: Harsh Light, Soft Focus*, Cambridge: Cambridge University Press.

Pink, S. (2001) *Doing Visual Ethnography: Images, Media and Representation in Research*, London: Sage.

Plummer, K. (2001a) *Documents of Life 2*, 2nd edn, London: Sage.

—— (2001b) 'The call of life stories in ethnographic research', in P. Atkinson, A. Coffey, S. Delamont, J. Lofland and L. Lofland (eds) *Handbook of Ethnography*, London: Sage.

Pocock, D. (1973) 'The idea of a personal anthropology', Paper presented to the Dicennial Conference of the ASA, Oxford.

Pollner, M. and Emerson, R. M. (2001) 'Ethnomethodology and ethnography', in P. Atkinson, A. Coffey, S. Delamont, J. Lofland and L. Lofland (eds) *Handbook of Ethnography*, London: Sage.

Popper, K. (1968) *The Logic of Scientific Discovery*, London: Hutchinson.

Powdermaker, H. (1966) *Stranger and Friend: The Way of an Anthropologist*, New York: Norton.

Pratt, M. L. (1986) 'Fieldwork in common places', in J. Clifford and G. Marcus (eds) *Writing Culture: The Poetics and Politics of Ethnography*, Berkeley: University of California Press.

Price, R. (1983) *First-Time: The Historical Vision of an Afro-American People*, Baltimore: Johns Hopkins University Press.

Prosser, J. and Schwartz, D. (1998) 'Photographs within the sociological research process', in J. Prosser (ed.) *Image-based Research: A Sourcebook for Qualitative Researchers*, London: Falmer Press.

Prout, A. (1986) '"Wet children" and "little actresses": a primary school's hidden curriculum of the sick role', *Sociology of Health and Illness* 8: 113–36.

Punch, M. (1986) *Politics and Ethics of Fieldwork*, London: Sage.

—— (1994) 'Politics and ethics in qualitative research', in N. Denzin and Y. S. Lincoln (eds) *Handbook of Qualitative Research*, London: Sage.

Punch, S. (2003) 'Childhoods in the majority world: miniature adults or tribal children?', *Sociology* 37(2): 277–95.

Reed-Danahay, D. (2001) 'Autobiography, intimacy and ethnography', in P. Atkinson, A. Coffey, S. Delamont, J. Lofland and L. Lofland (eds) *Handbook of Ethnography*, London: Sage.

Ribbens, J. (1989) 'Interviewing: an unnatural situation', *Women's Studies International Forum* 12: 579–592.

Richardson, L. (1994) 'Nine poems: marriage and the family', *Journal of Contemporary Ethnography* 23: 3–14.

—— (1998) 'Writing: a method of inquiry', in N. Denzin and Y. S. Lincoln (eds) *Collecting and Interpreting Qualitative Materials*, London: Sage.

Ritchie, J. and Lewis, J. (2003) (eds) *Qualitative Research Practice: A Guide for Social Science Students and Researchers*, London: Sage.

Rock, P. (2001) 'Symbolic interactionism and ethnography', in P. Atkinson, A. Coffey, S. Delamont, J. Lofland and L. Lofland (eds) *Handbook of Ethnography*, London: Sage.

Ronai, C. R. (1995) 'Multiple reflections of child sex abuse. An argument for a layered account', *Journal of Contemporary Ethnography* 23(4): 395–425.

Rose, D. and Sullivan, O. (1996) *Introducing Data Analysis for Social Scientists*, Buckingham: Open University Press.

Rosenhan, D. L. (1973) 'On being sane in insane places', *Science* 179: 250–8.

Rosie, A. (1993) '"He's a Liar, I'm Afraid": Truth and Lies in a Narrative Account', *Sociology* 27(1): 144–52.

Rubin, H. J. and Rubin, I. S. (1995) *Qualitative Interviewing: The Art of Hearing Data*, London: Sage.

Rudestam, K. E. and Newton, R. R. (1992) *Surviving Your Dissertation: A Comprehensive Guide to Content and Process*, London: Sage.

Russel, T. (1998) 'Autoethnography: journeys of the self', www.haussite. net/haus.0/SCRIPT/txt2001/01/russel.html.

Samuel, R. and Thompson, P. (eds) (1990) *The Myths We Live By*, London: Routledge.

Savage, J. (2000) 'Ethnography and health care', *British Medical Journal* 321: 1400–2.

Schatzman, L. and Strauss, A. (1973) *Field Research: Strategies for a Natural Sociology*, Englewood Cliffs, NJ: Prentice Hall.

Schutz, A. (1971) 'The stranger: an essay in social psychology', in A. Broderson (ed.) *Alfred Schutz: Collected Papers II: Studies in Social Theory*, The Hague: Martinus Nijhoff.

—— (1972) *The Phenomenology of the Social World*, London: Heinemann.

Scott, J. C. (1985) *Weapons of the Weak: Everyday Forms of Peasant Resistance*, New Haven: Yale University Press.

Seale, C. (ed.) (1998) *Researching Society and Culture*, London: Sage.

—— (1999) *The Quality of Qualitative Research*, London: Sage.

Shipman, M. (1988) *The Limitations of Social Research*, London and New York: Longman.

Silverman, D. (2000) *Doing Qualitative Research: A Practical Handbook*, London: Sage.

—— (2001) *Interpreting Qualitative Data: Methods for Analysing Talk, Text and Interaction*, 2nd edn, London: Sage.

Skeggs, B. (2001) 'Feminist ethnography', in P. Atkinson, A. Coffey, S. Delamont, J. Lofland and L. Lofland (eds) *Handbook of Ethnography*, London: Sage.

Slater, D. (1998) 'Analysing cultural objects: content analysis and semiotics', in C. Seale (ed.) *Researching Society and Culture*, London: Sage.

Spencer, J. (1989) 'Anthropology as a kind of writing', *Man* 24(1): 145–64.

—— (2001) 'Ethnography after postmodernism', in P. Atkinson, A. Coffey, S. Delamont, J. Lofland and L. Lofland (eds) *Handbook of Ethnography*, London: Sage.

Spradley, J. P. (1979) *The Ethnographic Interview*, London: Holt Rinehart and Winston.

Stanley, L. (1993) 'On auto/biography in sociology', *Sociology* 27(1): 41–52.

Stanley, L. and Wise, S. (1983) *Breaking Out: Feminist Consciousness and Feminist Research*, London: Routledge and Kegan Paul.

Stones, R. (1996) *Sociological Reasoning. Towards a Past-modern Sociology*, London: Macmillan.

Strauss, A. and Corbin, J. (eds) (1997) *Grounded Theory in Practice*, London: Sage.

—— (1998) *Basics of Qualitative Research*, 2nd edn, London: Sage.

Taylor, S. (ed.) (2002) *Ethnographic Research: A Reader*, London: Sage.

The, A. M., Hak, T., Koëter, G. and Wal, G. v. d. (2000) 'Collusion in doctor–patient communication about imminent death: an ethnographic study', *British Medical Journal* 321: 1376–81.

Thomas, W. I. and Znaniecki, F. (1927) *The Polish Peasant in Europe and America*, New York: Dover.

Thompson, P. (1988) *The Voice of the Past*, 2nd edn, Oxford: Oxford University Press.

Thrasher, F. (1963 [1926]) *The Gang: A Study of 1,313 Gangs in Chicago*, Chicago: University of Chicago Press.

Tonkin, E. (1984) 'Language learning', in R. F. Ellen (ed.) *Ethnographic Research: A Guide to General Conduct*, London: Academic Press.

Tyler, S. A. (1986) 'Post-modern ethnography: from document of the occult to occult document', in J. Clifford and G. Marcus (eds) *Writing Culture: The Poetics and Politics of Ethnography*, Berkeley: University of California Press.

Urry, J. (1984) 'A history of field methods', in R. F. Ellen (ed.) *Ethnographic Research: A Guide to General Conduct*, London: Academic Press.

Van Maanen, J. (1988) *Tales of the Field: On Writing Ethnography*, Chicago: University of Chicago Press.

Walker, M. (1987) *Writing Research Papers*, 2nd edn, New York: Norton.

Warwick, D. P. (1982) 'Tearoom trade: means and ends in social research', in M. Bulmer (ed.) *Social Research Ethics: An Examination of the Merits of Covert Participant Observation*, London: Macmillan.

Watson, C. W. (ed.) (1993) *Being There: Fieldwork in Anthropology*, London: Pluto Press.

Wellin, C. and Fine, G. A. (2001) 'Ethnography as work: career socialization', in P. Atkinson, A. Coffey, S. Delamont, J. Lofland and L. Lofland (eds) *Handbook of Ethnography*, London: Sage.

Whyte, W. F. (1951) 'Observational field-work methods', in M. Jahoda, M. Deutsch and S. W. Cook (eds) *Research Methods in Social Relations*, vol. II, New York: Dryden Press.

—— (1981) *Street Corner Society: The Social Structure of an Italian Slum*, 3rd edn, Chicago: University of Chicago Press.

—— (1993) *Street Corner Society: The Social Structure of an Italian Slum*, 4th edn, Chicago: University of Chicago Press.

Willis, P. (2000) *The Ethnographic Imagination*, Cambridge: Polity.

Willis, P. and Trondman, M. (2000) 'Manifesto for ethnography', *Ethnography* 1(1): 5–16.

Wilson, D. and Csordas, T. J. (2003) '"Now you get your answer . . ." Healing talk and experience in the Navajo Lightning Way', *Ethnography* 4(3): 289–332.

Winch, P. (1958) *The Idea of a Social Science*, London: Routledge and Kegan Paul.

Wolcott, H. F. (2001) *Writing up Qualitative Research*, 2nd edn, Thousand Oaks CA: Sage.

Worth, S. (1980) 'Margaret Mead and the shift from "visual anthropology" to the "anthropology of visual communication"', *Studies in Visual Communication* 6(1): 15–22.

Wright, T. (ed.) (1994) *The Anthropologist as Artist: Malinowski's Trobriand Photographs*, Studies in Development and Cultural Change 19, Saarbrücken: Nijmegen.

Index

eBooks – at www.eBookstore.tandf.co.uk

A library at your fingertips!

eBooks are electronic versions of printed books. You can
store them on your PC/laptop or browse them online.

They have advantages for anyone needing rapid access
to a wide variety of published, copyright information.

eBooks can help your research by enabling you to
bookmark chapters, annotate text and use instant searches
to find specific words or phrases. Several eBook files would
fit on even a small laptop or PDA.

NEW: Save money by eSubscribing: cheap, online access
to any eBook for as long as you need it.

Annual subscription packages

We now offer special low-cost bulk subscriptions to
packages of eBooks in certain subject areas. These are
available to libraries or to individuals.

For more information please contact
webmaster.ebooks@tandf.co.uk

We're continually developing the eBook concept, so
keep up to date by visiting the website.

www.eBookstore.tandf.co.uk